D0931148

The Evolution
of an
American Town:
Newtown,
New York,
1642 – 1775

MAP 1

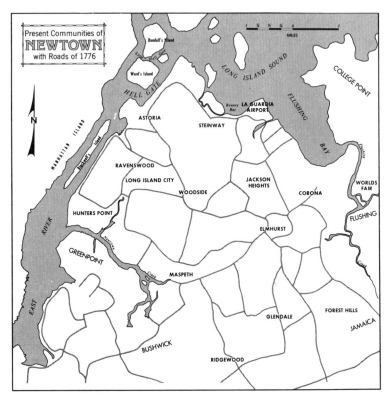

SOURCE: Adapted from *Town Minutes*, I, xx; Peter J. Guthorn, *British Maps of the American Revolution* (N.J., 1972), p. 52. Map drawn by Spencer Ulrey.

The Evolution
of an
American Town:
Newtown,
New York,
1642 – 1775

JESSICA KROSS

TEMPLE UNIVERSITY PRESS
PHILADELPHIA

Temple University Press, Philadelphia 19122
© 1983 by Temple University. All rights reserved
Published 1983
Printed in the United States of America

Library of Congress Cataloging in Publication Data

Kross, Jessica.
The evolution of an American town.

Includes index.
1. Newtown (Queens County, N.Y.)—History.   2. New
York (N.Y.)—History—Colonial period, ca. 1600–1775.
3. City and town life—New York (State)—History—
18th century—Case studies.   I. Title.
F128.68.N48K76   1983   974.7'243   82-10420
ISBN 0-87722-277-0

Dedicated to my parents
Ethel Novack and Jay Alan Kross

CONTENTS

TABLES

FIGURES

MAPS

INTRODUCTION

On a bright August day in 1776 British troops, hoping to forestall American independence, moved through fields of wheat and apple orchards to the farming village of Newtown, which lay six miles from what is now New York City. One hundred and twelve years earlier to the month an English fleet had sailed into New York harbor and taken New Amsterdam, and indeed all of New Netherlands, from the Dutch. In that period, Newtown emerged as a distinctive community, a touchstone for understanding the New York colonial experience and an illuminating contrast to New England colonial life.

The literature on colonial America is full of town studies, but almost all of these look at New England. The New England town is most obvious physically, with its central well-tended green, its white-spired meeting house, and its carefully preserved dozen or so colonial houses that speak to us immediately of a world gone by. As Kenneth Lockridge notes, "The New England Town is one of the myths out of which Americans' conception of their history has been constructed, along with such others as The Liberty Bell, George Washington, and The Frontier."[1]

New York also has its own unique persona. It is best summarized in the title of one of the more recent and better studies of the colony, *A Factious People*. Not for New York the quiet, perhaps even dull, life of archetypical New England. New Yorkers were on the move. Hungry for land, power, and profit, they symbolized another, less romantic, aspect of the American spirit—acquisitiveness, heterogeneity, and instability. Milton Klein, the dean of New York historians, sees New York, not New England, as home of that new man, the American. And this was literally true, since Hector St. John Crèvecoeur lived in Orange County, New York. According to

Klein, "New York represented, in germinal form, the very nation that had come into existence by the late nineteenth century."[2]

But are New England and New York so far apart? Is it possible, as Jack Greene suggests, that perceptions of difference arise partially from looking only at one place and not both together? If New England is not quite as monolithic as the older literature suggests, and if New York is more stable, if both places underwent similar experiences that evoked the same responses, then perhaps the two are closer and partake of an "Americanness" that includes stability and change.[3]

Students of New England have already illustrated local life in the colonial period, but students of New York have written few studies of any local institutions. Patricia Bonomi's "Local Government in Colonial New York: A Base for Republicanism," looks at Kingston. Langdon Wright's "In Search of Peace and Harmony: New York Communities in the Seventeenth Century" and assorted very specialized articles in *The Journal of Long Island History* are about all that is available. Most of the literature focuses on New York politics. As Douglas Greenberg says in a recent article on Middle Colony historiography, "Politics have held special interest to students of the Middle Colonies because for most of the colonial period, mid-Atlantic political life assumes the aspect of a mystery novel: we know what happened, but we have only clues to who did it and why." Historians have only recently shifted their attention to local studies, "a majority of which remain unpublished." There are no recent monographs on a New York colonial community. Newtown is the first of these modern studies.[4]

This study has as its primary and explicit goal an analysis of the changes that one New York community underwent from its founding in 1642 to the American Revolution. These changes all proceed in a single direction from the undifferentiated to the specific, from simpler forms to more complicated ones, and from fewer options to more choices. This process occurred in the political, the economic, and the social sphere. No part of life was immune.

Newtown's political structure became both more highly specialized and more bureaucratized. Under the Dutch, a constable and three magistrates combined administrative, legislative, and judicial functions. By 1691 town officers were implementing laws passed by the General Assembly, not by the town, and they no longer sat as a civil court. Their responsibility was almost purely administrative. The number of officers increased, and by 1775, the town yearly elected a constable, assessors, collectors, a supervisor, fence viewers, trustees, highway surveyors, appraisers of intestate estates, and highway overseers. The broad range of duties once handled by a few had narrowed and were performed by many.

Towns became mainly administrative units because other governmental agencies took up former town concerns. Dutch provincial government had only two levels: the town and the province. The English established an intermediate level called first a shire and then a county. Shire government organized a large geographic area into ridings. Both shire and riding were judicial rather than administrative units. In 1683 the English forsook the shire and ridings in favor of smaller counties. Counties exercised both administrative and judicial functions but divided those duties into separate institutions. After 1686 a county board of supervisors, composed of one supervisor elected yearly from each town, taxed the county and took care of other responsibilities such as jails, vermin bounties, coroners' fees, vagrants and vagabonds, and the salaries of Queens County's two representatives to the General Assembly, which began meeting in 1691. The Court of Sessions and Common Pleas, composed of judges appointed by the governor, tried civil and criminal cases.

Government became more complicated as the years passed. It had more officials at each level and the number of levels increased. The implication of this growth for townsmen was governmental flexibility, not bureaucratic burden. Local development took place in harmony with county and provincial development, not in competition with it. Newtowners believed that government was their servant and they its master. When this order threatened to reverse they took action.

Greater governmental specialization went hand-in-hand with growing economic diversity. Newtown was always part of the larger economic life that New York City permitted. The city took in townsmen's produce and in return offered imported goods and specialized services. From the very beginning, some people within Newtown combined farming with entrepreneurial ventures. Most were farmers who might also have a side skill that they exercised when the need arose.

As townsmen suffered the inevitable pressures of population on a limited land supply, they exercised a broader range of economic choices. These included farming on a smaller scale, mixing farming with crafts, augmenting crafts with garden produce, selling goods or services, hiring out as landless laborers, or leaving Newtown. As the eighteenth century moved on some townsmen clearly changed their perception of themselves from "yeomen" to artisans. Those calling themselves cordwainers, weavers, and blacksmiths also left behind small plots, agricultural implements, and larders bearing wheat, corn, and barley. Newtown also attracted specialists. By the 1760s the town had at least four schoolteachers, a secondary-level academy, an innkeeper, and a merchant.

Townsmen not only produced more and different items, they also consumed a wider variety of goods. Wills suggest that seventeenth-century wealth meant newer or more of the basic pots, pans, plows, scythes, and clothing that everyone else had. By the first quarter of the eighteenth century the better off had different goods, not just more of the same. Silks, silver buttons, and gold jewelry graced townsmen's persons. One even owned a riding chair. And even middling villagers came to enjoy cinnamon, sugar, tea, and chocolate. The most telling example of townsmen's integration into the great Atlantic mercantile empire were Newtown's black slaves. By 1700 they outnumbered servants, and in 1790 they formed about 20 percent of Newtown's total population. They were an "exotic" commodity to which townsmen apparently had easy access.

African slaves formed part of the town's diverse population. Other residents, with the exception of a few Indians, were white. The first settlers of what would become Newtown were a core of Englishmen, who came from various New England settlements, surrounded by a polyglot sprinkling of individuals given land grants by the Dutch. The 1686 patent made all of these settlers town inhabitants. In addition to different ethnic backgrounds these townsmen practiced different Protestant religions. The non-English were overwhelmingly Dutch Reformed and they stayed that way. The earliest English settlers were "Independents." This seems to have meant that they practiced a congregational form of church organization with presbyterian theological leanings. In 1715 the Newtown church joined the Philadelphia Presbytery. A few seventeenth-century townsmen were Quakers. And after 1700 some townsmen joined the Protestant Episcopal Church. By 1775, townsmen could choose from among all four denominations. These congregations formed religious communities within Newtown but also wedded townsmen to coreligionists in other towns.

Newtown's increasingly wider range of political, economic, and social choices were founded upon attitudes and values that united townsmen with each other, with other New Yorkers, and with other British colonial Americans. These values included liberty, the sanctity of private property, the legitimacy of profit, family, and harmony.

The Englishmen who came to America brought with them certain assumptions about the roles of governors and the governed. Ultimately, government rested upon the consent of the governed. That consent was earned by a government that protected life, limb, and property. Liberty and property were indivisible, as townsmen made clear in their 1653 petition accusing the Dutch government of violating the former by endangering the latter. Both law and custom would sanctify property. In the eighteenth century, law would neglect moral transgressions such as fornication but prosecute bastardy when the state might have to pay for the child.

The right to the fruits of labor is but one step removed from the right to the fruits of investment. Townsmen believed in profit. The wills and inventories clearly show economic diversification, which came to include money-lending. Bonds and mortgages became commonplace. By the 1760s the colony itself lent money through a provincial loan office.

Townsmen usually held mortgages from one another that were within their ethnic group. The Dutch tended to borrow from fellow Dutchmen. However, Newtowners rarely mortgaged land to family members. Instead, the town and probate records show that parents gave land to offspring or sold it to them at less-than-market prices. As land became harder to acquire, larger land grants and whole farms went to relatives. They never reached the open market.

Families understood and accepted responsibility for their own members. Parents cared for their children and when those children reached adulthood they cared for their elderly parents. In the eighteenth century the courts ruled that this responsibility extended down to grandchildren. Men's wills made special provisions for the future comfort of their widows. Parents and grandparents showed their concern for children with physical or mental disabilities.

Townsmen's family cycle of birth, growth, and death took place in a remarkably peaceful setting. Newtown, like most colonial towns, had no police force or vigilante association to keep peace. Yet order was the norm, violence the exception. Assault was rare, murder almost unheard of. The courts punished slander and defamation. They also directed hostilities into non-threatening channels. In the seventeenth century the town court was both forum and arena. Most townsmen rarely appeared there, some performed regularly. Governmental reforms in 1691 phased out the public local court and replaced it with the more private justice of the peace. This change marked the end of an older-fashioned communal judgment.

The substitution of private chastisement for public humiliation was just one of the steps that shifted emphasis from community to individual values and that marked the growth of Newtown. And it happened elsewhere in colonial America. Pointing out this shared experience is the secondary and implicit goal of this study of Newtown. Colonial New England scholars have looked only at New England, and colonial New York scholars have looked only at New York. Each has claimed his or her area unique. Newtown raises questions about such claims.

The task of showing change in Newtown required making some organizational and stylistic decisions. This study is organized into four chronological segments: 1642–1664, the Dutch years; 1665–1691, the period of English conquest and reorganization; 1692–1723, the years when town land was available; and 1724–1775, the years of adaptation to land scarcity and imperial pressure. Within each segment there are two or three chapters that discuss the political, economic, social, religious, and legal structures within each time frame.

Every historian makes decisions about the forms of citation and the quotation of archaic materials. Citations here are entered with full title where they first appear in each chapter. Those materials cited frequently and some journals are abbreviated. These are listed in full in the list of abbreviations. All spelling has been modernized although sentence structure has been left intact. Dates before the adoption of the Gregorian calendar in 1752 are Old Style but the year has been given as if it began on January 1st.

In the course of this study I have received the help of many people and institutions. The original research was partially financed by a Rackham Graduate Student Research Scholarship and two Edward S. Beck Fund Scholarships, both from the University of Michigan. Computer assistance, typing, xeroxing, and the preparation of maps were provided through two University of South Carolina Research and Productive Scholarship grants. Dr. John G. Sproat, Chairman of the Department of History of the University of South Carolina, was most generous in giving me summer release time, secretarial help, small grants, and unflagging support. The Social and Behavioral Science Laboratory provided computer facilities and counselling. J. Spencer Ulrey of the Department of Geography made the maps used here.

While space precludes naming all who assisted me in gathering information, I must mention the staffs of the Historical Documents Collection at the Paul Klapper Library, the New York Historical Society, the New York Public Library, the Long Island Historical Society, the Museum of the City of New York, the Long Island Room of the Queensboro Public Library, and the Haviland Records Room of the New York Yearly Meeting. The rectors of the Dutch Reformed churches of Jamaica and Newtown and the St. James Episcopal Church in Newtown were also most kind.

David T. Konig, Charles Lesser, Jean W. Mustain, Carl E. Prince, Darrett B. Rutman, John Shy, C. James Taylor, and two exceptionally generous readers for Temple University Press read a draft of this manuscript. Their diligence and expertise have saved me from many errors large and small. And finally, I must give thanks to David R. Chesnutt, who read various incarnations of the monograph with gentle patience, good humor, and a keen eye. Anyone who has ever undertaken a book-length study knows how important it is to have such a friend.

PART ONE

1642 – 1664:

Newtown under Dutch Sovereignty

CHAPTER 1

The Founding of the Town

English colonial settlers came to America with plans for the future and with ideas and skills from their pasts. Some of their hopes were modified by the natural and cultural environments which they found here; however, much of what they already knew proved useful and formative. The environment, within important limits, was malleable. To a larger extent than they had any reason to expect, they created a world which closely resembled the one they had left behind.

By 1642, the year that Governor William Kieft granted Reverend Francis Doughty and his associates the charter to found a town, both theory and practical experience provided settlers with guidelines for selecting settlement sites. These, at least for the northern colonies, were fairly standard. First, as Richard Hakluyt had pointed out as early as 1578, a town must be accessible, preferably "on the seaside so (if it may be) you may have your own navy within bay, river or lake." Second, it should have cleared land, not primordial forest. Third, it needed natural fresh or salt meadows for livestock, as well as good soils, clays or other building materials, plentiful sweet water, and a "temperate" climate. Finally, it should contain useful animals and plants, especially timber. Francis Doughty's choice of what would become Newtown shows that he knew his lessons well.[1]

The need for easy water transportation to both local and overseas political and market centers implied that the earliest settlements would be either coastal or on major rivers. Bruce Daniels found this pattern true for Connecticut and it probably was also the case in Massachusetts and Rhode Island. In the Chesapeake, river transportation was crucial to the formation of plantations and settlements. And in New Amsterdam, the Dutch settled on the tip of Manhattan Island, up the Hudson River at Albany, and on Staten and Long Islands.[2]

Newtown fit into this spatial pattern located as it was on the northern shore of western Long Island. To the north lay the East River, Hell Gate, and the northeastern tip of Manhattan Island. To the west flowed Newtown Creek, a tidal inlet, which gradually narrowed down like a vein into capillaries. These small streams, called "kills" by the Dutch, marked the line between Newtown and Bushwick, which was founded a few years later in 1661. Past the hills to the south sat the town of Jamaica, incorporated in 1656. To the east lay Flushing Bay and the village of Flushing, chartered in 1645. Newtown was the first of the English villages on western Long Island, and, being first, townsmen chose what must have appeared to them as the most desirable location (see Map 2).[3]

The earliest town settlers of 1642 placed their houses at the English Kills on an abandoned Maspeate Indian site. In this choice they again were following standard practice. Indian agricultural and settlement patterns required a large number of relatively small bands which moved every few years. The clearings left behind were denuded of large trees and could be worked immediately. Later, townsmen moved to the east along Horsebrook Creek. Evidence of Indian settlement here is lacking, but it was unusual for the settlers not to take advantage of an old Indian site or a natural clearing.[4]

Finally, Newtown offered both the fresh and salt meadows that attracted all agricultural settlers. The Dutch and English Kills to the west, the head of Flushing Creek to the east, and various meadows and swamps noted in Map 2 promised pasturage. These grasses were, in fact, unable to meet the colonists' expectations, being the only flora in the eastern woodlands biologically inferior to their European counterparts. No less an observer than Captain John Smith pointed

MAP 2

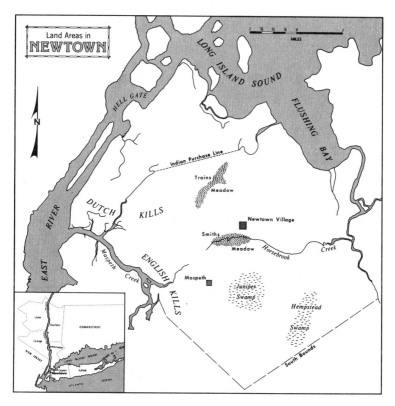

SOURCE: Compiled by author. Map drawn by J. Spencer Ulrey.

out this problem which would be partially solved by the mid-seventeenth century through the introduction of English grasses that rapidly spread by themselves at the expense of the native forms.[5]

Newtown's location and favorable meadows drew people who also appreciated the area's other assets. Soils and topography had taken their essential features from the last ice age. The Wisconsin Glacier's terminal moraine formed the South Hills just within Newtown's south boundary. The spits and necks were glacial and held the towns's most fertile soils. As Bruce Daniels noted for Connecticut, the earliest settlers were aware of these soil values. It was no accident that Newtown's prominent early families, the Halletts, the Lawrences, the Fishs, Thomas Wandall, and the Alsops settled upon what soil maps show to be the town's better lands. Along the East River, to the west of Hell Gate, glacial soils known as Galveston clay allowed William Hallett to turn out brick by the thousands. Most of the rest of Newtown was Miami stony loam, an all-purpose soil which can support grass, grain, orchard, and garden crops. In the mid-nineteenth century, when Newtown's agriculture was as intensive as contemporary technology could make it, townsmen could use only 63 percent of town land. During the colonial period this percentage would have been even lower. And yet, the town was well endowed by contemporary standards. When Yale's Dr. Timothy Dwight toured Long Island in 1804, he mentioned that Newtown had "good soil, and a surface in many places not unpleasant."[6]

The rolling terrain of Newtown contained many small year-round streams, and the high water table which fed them also provided townsmen with ponds, wells, swamps, and numerous fresh-water springs. Precipitation averaged forty-five inches annually and fell throughout the year. Drought was rarely a problem and neither was a harsh climate. Protected by the ocean, Long Island had a growing season between 173 and 220 days, the longest in New York. Extreme weather was

MAP 3

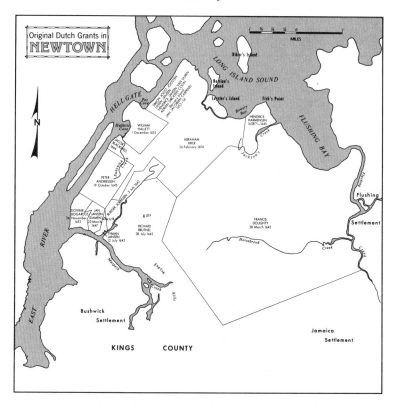

Original Dutch Grants in
NEWTOWN

LONG ISLAND SOUND

HELL GATE

FLUSHING BAY

Riker's Island

Berrian's Island

Lawster's Island

Fish's Point

Pot Cove

Bowery Bay

JACOB JACOB COOPER
LOURENS DIRCK VAN DUYN
LOURENS DIRCK VAN DUYN
ADAM BRUCKELS COON
JAN RICHER CARRELS

Hallett's Cove

WILLIAM HALLETT
1 December 1652

ABRAHAM RYKER
26 February 1654

HENDRICK HARMENSEN
1638(?)—1645

Creek

Jackson's

PLACOB BLACKWELL
1664

Sweerds Creek

PETER ANDRIESSEN
19 October 1645

ROGER JOSELIN 3 July 1643

Flushing

Flushing Creek

N

EAST RIVER

GOVINE BOGARDUS
26 November 1652

JAN JANSEN/ DAMEN
23 March 1647

Dutch Kills

Maspeth

TYMAN JANSEN
13 July 1643

RICHARD BRUTNEL
28 July 1643

Kills

FRANCIS DOUGHTY
28 March 1642

Settlement

Horsebrook

Creek

Creek

English Creek

Kills

Bushwick

Settlement

Jamaica
Settlement

KINGS   COUNTY

MILES

SOURCE: Adapted from *Town Minutes*, I, xviii. Map drawn by J. Spencer Ulrey.

unusual, even though winters could be cold, snow-filled, and long, and summers might develop humid heat waves. More often temperatures ranged between zero and ninety-five degrees, with a mean reading of fifty-one.[7]

In the seventeenth century, "climate" meant more than just weather. The Dutch were among the first to describe the climate of New York in terms of health as well as temperature and precipitation. New York was a healthy place to live, especially compared to English Virginia, where "the English die . . . very fast" if unseasoned, "that is . . . [un]accustomed to the land." John Miller, an English clergyman writing in 1695, found few favorable things to say about New York, but noted, "The air of this province is very good," and the wind blew frequently, thus keeping it clear. The "sweet air" so eagerly sought out and commented upon was air free from obnoxious odors, but clean-smelling air was not automatically healthy, though only the Swedish naturalist Peter Kalm raised this question. Newtown's swamps and salt marshes harbored mosquitoes, and colonists were probably subject to malaria.[8]

Other animals were less dangerous. Townsmen trapped wolves in wolf pits and both whites and Indians killed them for the bounties on their hides; however, Newtown felt sufficiently secure from wolves by 1692 to resent paying taxes for county-wide bounties. Smaller predators such as foxes, which preyed on poultry and therefore became a nuisance only after flocks were established, would also have prices on their heads. More important were deer, squirrels, and the great flocks of geese, ducks, and swans that stopped on their annual spring and fall migrations to feed in the marshes. Partridge and grouse nested in the fields.[9]

The island's three marine environments also gave townsmen's diets variety. Catching eels in the fresh-water ponds was especially popular and provided a pleasant and useful way to spend an afternoon with friends. Newtown Creek, the East River, and Flushing Bay are salt water. They contained cod, herring, and haddock. Finally, the tidal pools and salt marshes, where land and sea met, supported oysters, clams, crabs, and mussels. "Clamming frolics" were still another way to spend the day with company while adding to the family larder.[10]

Wild plants, like wild beasts, added diversity to local diets. As with fishing and clamming, the gathering of berries and nuts was a social affair. In the spring people searched out wild strawberries and grapes. In the autumn they found walnuts and chestnuts. The tobacco, corn, beans, and squash that the Indians planted, while domesticated, were foreign to the first settlers. Squash was an early favorite, "the ease with which it is cooked render[ing] it a favorite too with the young women."[11]

Newtown's natural potential was rich and varied. Its physical resources, however, were limited. Newtowners' decision to settle where they did, knowing these liabilities, strongly indicates the direction of their aspirations. They were primarily interested in agriculture, not maritime pursuits or commerce, and their agriculture would be mixed farming, not cattle raising. Commercial fishing was better undertaken on eastern Long Island, where harbors provided shelter. Commercial shellfishing was better suited to Jamaica's Great South Bay. Large pasturelands lay to the east on Hempstead Plain, but Newtown's meadows and marshes could only support smaller herds of cattle or sheep.

Perhaps ultimately more important to the town's future prosperity were Newtown's topographical peculiarities which made travel with bulky commodities to and from New York City difficult. First was the Hell Gate, a confined strait in the East River six miles from the city. Daniel Denton described it in 1670 as "a narrow passage, [through which] there runneth a violent stream both upon flood and ebb, and in the middle lieth some islands of rocks, which the current sets so violently upon, that it threatens present shipwreck; and upon the flood is a large whirlpool, which continually sends forth a hideous roaring."[12]

A second barrier to transportation was Newtown's shore

line. Rugged cliffs rose up to one hundred feet all along the
southern East River coast extending along the Long Island
Sound to Port Jefferson. Where these bluffs met the water
their bases were undermined by the tide causing periodic
landslides. This rock-strewn coast along much of Newtown's
shore and beyond was indented with a variety of coves, bays,
harbors, and inlets. Newtown had neither bay nor harbor,
thereby precluding development as a market center or central
town. Streams, including Maspeth Creek, which was actually
a tidal inlet, while useful in powering mills were impediments
to land travel since they required ferries or bridges to cross
them. Moreover, the fresh-water streams were too shallow to
serve as inland waterways.[13]

A third constraint upon travel were the South Hills on
Newtown's southern border. These hills, while not especially
high, marked the boundary between the more rolling rocky
soil north of the glacial moraine and the sandy outwash soil
south of it. While the soils north of the hills were more fertile,
the sandy plains south of the hills were easier to travel across.
The King's Highway would run south of the hills through Jamaica, not through Newtown, and Jamaica would be Queens
County's "central place," where markets, courts, and jails
were located. Townsmen would always be able to get to New
York City just six or seven miles away, but they would never
attract large-scale trade to Newtown. Entrepreneurs in town
made sure they acquired riverfront properties west of Hell
Gate's dangerous whirlpool. Thomas Wandall owned lands on
Maspeth Kills west of Hell Gate, and William Hallett worked
as a boatman and became one of those skilled at navigating the
current. His wharf on lands jutting into the East River was
also just to the west of the flood at Halletts Cove.

Newtown's physical environment affected the choices
which townsmen made. But so did the social environment in
which they found themselves embedded. The English colonists who came to western Long Island before 1665 settled under Dutch sovereignty, and both they and the Dutch were part

of a larger historical and political setting buffeted by forces over which they sometimes had little understanding, and less control. The story of New Netherlands has been told elsewhere. It will be noted here insofar as it affected Newtown.[14]

The Dutch were the first Europeans to settle the lands around Manhattan and western Long Island. This commercial effort was part of the much larger contest being waged by the Spanish, French, English, and Dutch for control of the finite wealth the world was thought to provide. New Netherlands quickly showed itself to offer little besides furs. In the grand scheme of things it was unimportant, a small cog in the wheels of the Dutch West India Company, but it was a possession nonetheless and one that was worth preserving.

Threats to Dutch control increased as Englishmen settled in New England along the borders with New Netherlands. This expansion of New England affected the Dutch in two ways. First, the English, especially in Connecticut, encroached upon Dutch territory. In 1635 they founded towns on the Connecticut River and interfered with the Dutch fur trade at Fort Hope. In 1639 they moved west again and established New Haven. They also cast their sights on Long Island, where Lyon Gardiner purchased Gardiner's Island off Long Island's eastern tip from the Indians. Second, through trade and expansion they undermined Dutch relations with the Indians. By 1639 the Dutch had to worry about both hostile New Englanders and hostile natives.[15]

Fear for the safety and profitability of New Netherlands led the Dutch West India Company into decisions which proved to have unexpected and unpleasant consequences. The best comparison is with the Virginia Company and Jamestown. In Virginia, as sociologist Sigmund Diamond noted, "one of the principal devices used by the Company to attract labor and to increase productivity was that of easing the terms on which land could be acquired. The effect of the reform was to create within the Company a new group of statuses differentiated from one another." These statuses, and the roles which they implied, existed outside the Company and in competition with it. When people's needs were better met beyond Company authority the Company lost its control over the population.[16]

The same thing happened to the Dutch West India Company. Profits depended upon a settled population, but few Dutchmen felt the need to leave their secure and prosperous homeland for an uncertain and economically unappealing wilderness. In order to attract people, the Company had to make concessions. In 1629, the Amsterdam Chamber promised its large stockholders rights to sizeable land grants provided that they settle fifty adults on the land within the first year. The landowners were called "patroons," a word new to the Dutch experience and modelled on the English "patron." The patroonships were supposedly agricultural ventures, and the Company specifically denied patroons access to the fur trade. Every one of them failed to bring its owners a profit, and only Rensselaerswyck survived even the 1630s.[17]

The failure of the patroonships meant that the Dutch West India Company needed other measures to attract settlers. In 1639 the Company conceded two important privileges. Colonists were allowed land, and they were given access to the fur trade. This more liberal policy brought two kinds of settlers into New Netherlands between 1639 and 1650: adventurous Dutchmen and restless New Englanders. Young independent Dutchmen, seeking their fortunes, stayed for varying lengths of time. These men, similar to the Virginia planters, became the "commonalty" which caused Governors Kieft and Stuyvesant so much trouble. They viewed the possibilities of their environment in much broader terms than did the Company, and, indeed, in ways similar to the English. The newcomers saw that building up a society complete with a range of economic choices and social and political statuses, as opposed to a trading post under company control, would be to their own benefit, and this they proceeded to do.[18]

Settlement patterns mirrored New Netherlands' society with all the peculiarities and problems that Dutch colonists created under the liberal reforms of 1639. First, Dutchmen chose to live on individial farmsteads rather than in incorporated villages. Of the 605 patents recorded between 1639 and 1664, only fourteen were granted to towns or settlements, and of these fourteen, only seven were granted to Dutchmen. Second, these farms were scattered since individual land owners chose places that could be farmed, namely areas already cleared of timber where the ground was broken. Indian sites were preferred, but Indian villages had been widely separated. There were 164 grants in New Amsterdam proper. Manhattan Island contained another 115, while Kings County held 59, Staten Island 1, the rest of Long Island 51, New Jersey 15, Delaware 30, and the Hudson Valley 122. Instead of towns, like New England, New Netherlands had isolated farms like the Chesapeake. The large number and widespread dispersal of homesteads made adequate defense impossible and broke down societal cohesion.[19]

Englishmen also moved to New Netherlands. These settlers had first gone to New England as part of the Great Migration, which began in 1630 and ended in 1640 with the outbreak of the English Civil War. Some, like Francis Doughty, left because of religious heterodoxy. As contemporary Thomas Lechford put it, "One master *Doughty*, a minister opposed the gathering of the Church there, alleging that according to the Covenant *Abraham*, all men's children that were of baptised parents and so *Abrahams* children, ought to be baptised; and spake so in public, which was held a disturbance." Others, like William Hallett, were fleeing the law. Hallett, accused of adultery with the cousin and sister-in-law of John Winthrop Jr., fled to the Dutch, where, through the offices of Winthrop, he and Elizabeth Fones Winthrop Feakes Hallett were granted asylum. Most, undoubtedly, came for more mundane reasons.[20]

There had always been a few English in New Amsterdam, just as there had always been individuals from a host of other countries. But many of the new English settlers came to found communities in cohesive little bands after splintering off from, or being driven out of, existing New England towns. They applied to the director general for permission to settle, and agreed to take an oath of fidelity to the Dutch. In return, these villages were granted charters giving them religious, judicial, and administrative powers. Indeed, perhaps as a lure to independent-minded Englishmen and as recognition that Englishmen, especially those in New England, were used to greater liberty than Netherlanders, the Dutch granted English towns greater autonomy than they would the soon-to-be-established Dutch towns. By 1647 five English villages, including Newtown, had been founded under the Dutch flag. The increasing numbers of both Dutch and English after 1639, and their aggressive competition for land and furs, helped bring on the Indian wars of the 1640s.[21]

Initial contacts with the Indians had been peaceful and profitable. The few Dutch traders and farmers had posed no threats to Indian territory. Such harmony was short-lived since neither Dutchmen nor Englishmen ever recognized the Indians as equals. As each side dealt with the other, misunderstandings based on cultural misperceptions smoldered.

The Dutch and the Indians fought two wars that affected Long Island settlement. Kieft's War (1643–1644) was actually a series of raids by Dutch and Indians in which each side suffered losses of life, crops, and homesites. The underlying causes were an ill-begotten collection of accumulated wrongs, grievances, and misunderstandings. European cattle grazed in Indian cornfields; the Dutch refused to supply local bands with guns and ammunition; and individual Dutchmen sold watered brandy to the Indians. Moreover, the Netherlanders failed to protect the Indians from other tribes. When eighty or ninety Indians armed with guns attacked the Westchester Wecquaesqueek, the Dutch not only idly stood by but afterward took the opportunity to attack the scattered, beaten Wec-

quaesqueek, killing men, women, and children. Border upris-
ings and retaliations followed this cowardly act.[22]

The Europeans also had their grievances. They felt Indians should fence corn fields and be punished for killing European cattle. Indian servants stole from their masters, and, finally, there was the murder of Claes Smits, a wheelwright
killed in retaliation for an unresolved murder twenty years
previous. Smits was killed by a Wecquaesqueek, and so it was
thought fitting to kill all the Wecquaesqueek in payment for
the murder of one Dutchman. Governor Kieft's world view
did not include Indian notions of justice, and he had no idea
that his actions against one tribe would provoke continued
hostilities in which eleven tribes joined. In August 1643, the
Indians burned some outlying farms. Later the Dutch mobi-
lized and joined with the English villages on western Long Island in a destructive display that aroused the previously neutral Long Island tribes. By September, at least seven bands
were on the warpath. Destruction was widespread from New
Rochelle, where Ann Hutchinson was murdered, to New Jersey and Long Island. Francis Doughty's Maspeth settlement
was one of the casualties. With their farmsteads in flames,
both English and Dutch settlers fled to Manhattan.[23]

Kieft's War affected both the colony as a whole and
the area that would be Newtown. On the broadest level, the
war provided a climate wherein the various weak threads of
New Netherlands' political and social structure could unravel.
More immediately, war provoked a leadership crisis in New
Netherlands which led to an uneasy and self-conscious alliance between the Dutch and English settlers against the
colony's administration.

Peter Stuyvesant, the last Dutch Governor, arrived in
New Netherlands in 1647. He brought with him a modified
plan of government that, among other things, reaffirmed the
right of towns to send advisory, although not binding, reports

to the provincial government and ordered further town and village founding. Neither these Company reforms nor Stuyvesant's own changes altered the fundamental problems of the colony, which stemmed from the incompatible motives held by the Dutch West India Company and the settlers. The English colonists bore English notions of representation and property which, like those in Virginia, based status and roles on their land holdings. They agitated for greater access to the political sphere and denied the Company control over land and furs. Moreover, Dutch and English colonists shared common perceptions of the environment and refused to allow the Company to limit their access to its promise. Both their grievances and their theory of government and of the social contract were clearly stated in a document drawn up in 1653 called the "Remonstrance."[24]

The Remonstrance, written "by the Deputies from the English villages . . . who, with Deputies from the Dutch villages, were . . . invited to advise on the writing of a letter to the Lords Mayors on the state of the country," articulated a set of beliefs about the responsibilities of both government and the governed. First, it acknowledged that both God and nature establish government "in the world for the maintenance and preservation of peace, and the good of mankind, not only agreeably to Nature's laws, but in accordance with the rules and precepts of God." Second, it reaffirmed that the colonists, being citizens of the Netherlands "and not a conquered or subjugated people," had the same rights as those in Europe being "settled here on a mutual covenant and contract entered into with the Lords Patroons, with the consent of the natives, . . . from whom we purchased the soil with our own money." It then went on to list six grievances.[25]

The first grievance showed fear of arbitrary government in which "one or more men should arrogate to themselves the exclusive power to dispose, at will, of the life and property of any individual . . . without the consent, knowledge or election of the whole Body, or its agents or representatives." The second noted that the Indians were dangerous, yet the government offered no protections. The third protested that officers were appointed without the nomination or consent of the people, contrary to the laws of the Netherlands. The fourth said that laws were issued solely by officers or magistrates without the consent of the people and that it was therefore impossible to know what the laws were. The fifth complained that the government had refused to issue patents to townships. And the sixth claimed that lands were given to a few individuals instead of to townships. This practice undermined the strength of the province.[26]

The Remonstrance must be seen in the context of English attitudes toward contracts, law, and private property. The Mayflower Compact, for instance, is an excellent example of a document created to bind men together and establish their fealty to law in a situation where their rights to both legal and customary protection were uncertain. It was also a social contract, as were town covenants. They bound people together through the written word, thereby sealing their civil responsibilities to one another.

New England's establishment of law paralleled its townsmen's early commitment to it. One of the grievances against John Winthrop's government was the lack of a legal code. Winthrop preferred to use discretionary power unfettered by a written body of law. Moreover, he realized that Massachusetts' regulations conflicted with the laws of England. The deputies disagreed and drew up what became known as the Body of Liberties. Composed of one hundred provisions, it provided for both trial by jury and freehold tenure of lands. The Remonstrance did not request a law code, as such, but protested against "the establishment of an arbitrary government among us" that would subvert the "customs, freedoms, grants and privileges of the Netherlands," and opposed the passage of laws that were never communicated to those who had to abide by them.[27]

New England also protected private property. In Plymouth, a colony originally underwritten by a joint stock company, settlers briefly held communal lands. That experiment, also launched in Virginia, quickly failed in both places. Colonists, regardless of their other motivations, wanted their own holdings. The Body of Liberties safeguarded these.

Jealous belief in the sanctity of private property soon pit townsmen against the state. A clear example, explicit in its implications, was the case brought against George Giddings of Ipswich, Massachusetts, in 1655. Giddings refused to pay his share for a minister's house and was prosecuted in front of Judge Samuel Symonds. Symonds ruled for Giddings claiming that any subject who has civil title to property cannot have it taken away from him "without his own free consent." In other words, no taxation without representation. Newtown felt the same way, and did so as part of its English heritage, brought over with the town's first settlers.[28]

The Remonstrance's first three grievances set out the conditions under which government can rule. Legitimate government represents the people through their own chosen delegates. It has an elected assembly (which the government of New Netherlands lacked), and this representative government oversees lower-level units that choose their own leaders. Its major responsibilities are to protect private property through granting patents, and life and limb by providing adequate defense. If government provides these essential services, then the people should obey it. If it does not, then that government has forfeited its right to rule. This argument surfaced more than once before its final flowering in the 1760s and 1770s.

The Dutch and the English settlers found it in their best interest to cooperate against the authorities in New Amsterdam. Unfortunately, the larger picture placed Englishmen against Dutchmen. Both sides threatened to mobilize the Indians, an important component of the social landscape, against the other.

The first Anglo-Dutch War (1652–1654), a conflict hav-

18

ing little to do with what was then an Imperial backwater, provided the catalyst for English identification and ethnic mistrust. In 1652, the Amsterdam Chamber warned Stuyvesant that both the New England colonists and his resident Englishmen could make trouble. They advised caution but also recommended he consider an alliance with the Indians against New England, *if* the New Englanders threatened New Netherlands. Using Indians, who were perceived as savage and vicious outsiders, escalated a conflict beyond the norms of civilized, hence predictable, warfare. A copy of this letter was intercepted and given to Governor Eaton of New Haven, who used it to fuel English settlers' fears of the Dutch.[29]

Anti-Dutch activities within the English towns on Long Island were neither internally well-coordinated nor orchestrated from the New England mainland. Instead, various individuals took it upon themselves to play on general anti-Dutch sentiment and fear of the Indians. For example, Captain John Underhill, hero of the 1637 Pequot War, shuttled back and forth between Long Island, Connecticut, and Rhode Island. In 1653, he called upon the English in New Netherlands to submit to the English Parliament.[30]

Underhill's example spurred others, and soon Englishmen, sporting commissions from Rhode Island, indulged in acts of piracy against Dutch shipping off Long Island. This general lawlessness, about which the Dutch could do nothing, led to the Remonstrance. Stuyvesant's hostility to the demands of the Remonstrance reinforced English dissatisfaction when rumors flew in 1654 recounting the massacre of Englishmen. When news came of an invasion from New England, some of the towns openly counselled recognition of the purported invaders and direct correspondence with Boston. The proposed fleet never came. Instead, on July 16, 1654, confirmation of a declaration of peace between the Netherlands and England arrived. For the moment ethnic hostilities subsided, only to be replaced by racial ones.[31]

After Kieft's War, relations with the Indians had been

uneasy. Old grievances remained and both sides felt the press of New England expansion. The Peach War, which erupted in the autumn of 1655, was triggered by five hundred Indians from various tribes who came to New Amsterdam while Stuyvesant and his army were off conquering New Sweden. Perhaps the Dutch panicked—at this point it is impossible to know who began the shooting. Before the three-day rampage was over, Staten Island and New Jersey saw fifty murdered, twenty-eight farms burned, nine to twelve thousand bushels of grain destroyed, and five hundred cattle lost. On Long Island, the Indians burned to the ground William Hallett's new plantation at Hell Gate. The Peach War was the last Indian resistance to bother western Long Island.[32]

The Halletts were not the only family removed from the shelter of a population center in 1655. Along the coast and strung out along the kills were isolated farmsteads. These settlers lived on what was called the "outbounds," outside both the jurisdiction and the protection of a town. Their choice to live far from others, given the dangers which they knew they faced, demonstrates an independence and an individualism sometimes at odds with common sense. This set of values, held by both Dutchmen and Englishmen, would remain, even when the outbounds became part of Newtown town.

The legacy of Kieft's War also had an impact on Newtown. The most immediate consequence of the war was the desertion of homesteads. Francis Doughty never returned to the Maspeth site even though he later claimed the land under his 1642 grant. Without settlers the patent was void; now nobody owned the land. In 1652, Englishmen reestablished a settlement within the old Doughty patent. The new settlers created their town in a new place. They moved east, closer to Flushing Creek and farther from the scattered Dutch settlers along Maspeth Creek. Again they chose a site near water, in this case Horsebrook Creek where John Coe set up his flour mill. The townsmen renamed their village Middleburgh and, requiring the sanctity of a legal document, asked Governor Stuyvesant for a patent confirming these rights.

Stuyvesant agreed to help the new village and those in the area of the charter were called upon to surrender their patents. Not all did so willingly, but potentially more troublesome was Newtown's lack of a patent, and for that Peter Stuyvesant was to blame. Perhaps due to the press of work or the anxieties of the unsettled 1650s, the Dutch governor never gave Middleburgh its charter, even though in the Remonstrance the town specifically asked for it noting that "great expense and trouble" had gone into settlement. Still greater cost and turmoil would follow as Newtown fought its neighbor Bushwick for over a century trying to recapture lands on the border between them.[33]

The continuing demand upon Peter Stuyvesant for a patent shows how deeply rooted in the settlers' cultural framework such a document was. In England, municipal corporations had traditionally protected towns from central authority and granted them varying measures of local autonomy. As David Konig notes, Massachusetts Bay settlers did not set up a commonwealth but an English borough corporation. Peter Stuyvesant continued to do nothing about a patent so the town took what would have been its next step anyway. In 1656, Middleburgh negotiated with the sachems and bought, for £55, the land shown in Map 3. This tract roughly corresponded to the 1642 patent and still excluded the Dutch and English farms outside its bounds. The town land was purchased outright, the Indians reserving for themselves hunting rights on the south side.[34]

Middleburgh, or Newtown, as it was now sometimes called, paid the Indians in two installments, the first in 1656 and the second ten years later. Money was raised from the inhabitants by subscription. The 1656 list, known as the Indian rate, contained fifty-five entries. The amount that people paid into the Indian purchase ranged from Robert Coe and Edward Jessup's eighty shillings, to James Way and John Hobby's two shillings. This initial inequality would be important later when the town divided its land. In 1664, Middleburgh bought a second small piece of land from the natives. This section lay to the south and must have been close to the Jamaica border. Only those who wished some share in this land were called upon to pay for it. In 1666, Newtown having extinguished Indian claims registered the Indian deed with Governor Richard Nicolls. He chose to use 1666 as the date for the town's founding, thereby reestablishing one of the oldest towns as one of the newest.[35]

Although Middleburgh had no Dutch charter, the Dutch recognized it as a town and allowed it to conduct its business under the provisions of the 1642 Doughty patent. That grant, the first given by the Dutch, created a generalized set of rights and duties. It also delegated what the Dutch felt to be important town functions:

> power of erecting of towns building of churches, with power of exercising the reformed Christian religion which they profess and also ecclesiastic discipline. With power of administering the highest middle and lowest justices as also for civil controversies not exceeding fifty guilders to determine & in criminals to condemn or mulct or fine not exceeding fifty guilders . . . and of putting the said sentence in execution, . . . as also with power to nominate certain of themselves a sufficient number and present them to the governor of the New Netherlands that from amongst them may be chosen to government both politic as also civil . . . for the which said privileges . . . [they] are bound and shall be bound so long as they shall be possessors of the said lands to acknowledge & said Lords for their High Lords and patrons and the tenth part of the [in]crease of the land tilled with the plow or mattack or any other

tools (only orchards gardens not exceeding a holland acre excepted) to be paid after ten years.

Under this liberal charter the adult male freeholders yearly
nominated candidates for the town government from which
the Dutch governor appointed the town's officers. Elegant in
its simplicity, and broad in its responsibilities, this government
exercised administrative, judicial, and legislative functions.
The ruling board, called magistrates, raised and collected
taxes and sat as a petty civil court hearing cases concerning
such matters as trespasses and debts. A town clerk kept the
town meeting minutes and registered land transactions, and a
constable carried out law enforcement.[36]
    Newtown's liberties, while granted under Dutch sov-
ereignty, and somewhat circumscribed by the lack of an elected representative assembly, seem very similar to those held
by Massachusetts and Connecticut towns. Recent students of
early Massachusetts disagree on how much freedom towns
had, but they did have the authority to create a church. Indeed, that was one of their charges. Moreover, the Town Act
of 1635 recognized that towns disposed of land, made local
rules, and enforced them through fines and elected officials.
Connecticut towns, modelled after Massachusetts towns, differed in some degree because they were once removed from
their English predecessors, and because they were more dependent on Connecticut's General Court for their powers.
The earliest towns preceded the founding of the colony in
1639, but in that year Connecticut passed laws creating and
limiting town government. Even though these towns apparently had less autonomy than Massachusetts ones, their functions included responsibility for a church, jurisdiction as an
original court, and election of officers to oversee the town.
Newtown's earliest settlement probably owed more to Connecticut than to Massachusetts, judging by the limited biographical information on the town founders.[37]

The Dutch granted townsmen charters that incorporated many of the features of English and New England towns, and not surprisingly, townsmen made choices well within the range of New England experience. Like some, but certainly not all, Massachusetts townsmen, Newtowners were very conservative in their elected list of magistrates (from which the Dutch governor chose) and the duties which they gave them. They elected the same people over and over. Only ten men filled the thirty-two magistrate slots between 1652 and 1662. The names are all English—Hazard, Coe, Gildersleeve, Betts, Jessup, Palmer, Fish. Dutchmen would be included later. Moreover, they let few implied powers adhere in these offices. This mistrust of too much discretionary power in a few hands was also true in some Massachusetts towns. When the town wanted something else done, it elected an ad hoc committee. In 1662, when the Dutch tithes fell due, Newtown appointed Edward Jessup, Francis Swaine, and Richard Betts to consult with Governor Stuyvesant. Likewise, when the town needed fence viewers in 1663, it chose Ralph Hunt, John Cocherin, Thomas Lawrence, and Francis Swaine.[38]

Town administration changed in 1663. Feeling themselves independent from the Dutch, Newtowners elected seven men

> to carry on their town. . . . [I]t is further ordered by the inhabitants that the above said seven men shall have power to act for this present year . . . in such affairs of the town as concerns its public good as building a meeting house [,] repairing the town house for the comfort of the minister or what eve[r] else shall concern the public good only the deposition of lands remains in the towns [sic] hands that is to newcomers.

The next year townsmen elected magistrates, a constable, and a clerk, as they had done before. They also selected five more men "chose for to order town affairs." But these all-purpose officers, called "townsmen," who resembled Connecticut's "townsmen" or Massachusett's "selectmen," were never mentioned again. In 1664 the English conquest brought new governmental forms to Newtown. Under the "Duke's Laws," which regulated local government, townsmen elected eight overseers. Later this number would be reduced to four. The chores of the men chosen to "order" town affairs would be done specifically by ad hoc committees.[39]

Most of the routine affairs of the village were administered in Middleburgh. At their town meetings the inhabitants voted to build and maintain a town house which, as an undifferentiated structure, would serve as meeting house, church, or school. In deference to the wilderness around them they volunteered to raise money for a wolf bounty. They tried to keep the village pleasant, voting in 1662 "that whosoever has cats or dogs or hogs lying dead in any place to offend their neighbors they must either bury them or throw them into the creek." And they tried to keep it upright, noting that a man who occasionally came into town should be removed, "him being a man of an evil report."[40]

In New Netherlands, England and New England, towns handled such day-to-day problems; however, the provincial government still exerted nominal authority over the towns, which it considered part of New Netherlands. This connection was an organic one, constrained everywhere by the very nature of the power available to central government. Thomas Jodziewicz calls this relationship "dual localism." Writing of seventeenth-century Connecticut, he says, "The individual town's main concern was its own local development be it economic, social, political or religious. At the same time, the General Court's concern was with the colony's provincial, local development." Langdon Wright, looking at colonial New York, says much the same thing. He characterizes the history of local government there as "an ill-defined and unstable balance between central authority and local automony."[41]

Townsmen readily acquiesced to provincial oversight when little was at stake. When Governor Stuyvesant called for a general fast and day of prayer in response to what seemed an increasing crime rate and immorality, Indian problems, and an outbreak of smallpox, Middleburgh was one of the villages in which the proclamation was read. The town's liquor dealers paid the same excise tax as did New Amsterdam. Townsmen passed laws consistent with those of the colony, and they utilized the Dutch court system, occasionally suing or being sued before the municipal court of New Amsterdam.[42]

For those questions beyond the town's competence or strength, townsmen willingly turned to the next level of authority which was the Dutch governor and his council. In 1660, the inhabitants voted Sheriff Elias Bayly out of office but he refused to step down. A number of townsmen then petitioned Governor Stuyvesant "to put him by and set another in his place." The next year, townsmen complained about Quakers. Stuyvesant, a staunch advocate of Reformed Protestantism, took swift action against what seemed to him and the majority of colonists a heretical and seditious sect.[43]

More interesting, and possibly more important, were disputes over the fine line between private property and public welfare. When Governor Stuyvesant called upon all those who had private grants within Middleburgh to surrender them, John Gray refused, and became hostile and abusive when confronted by the magistrates of Middleburgh. They charged him with disorderly and disrespectful behavior and he was arrested. His defense sounds very modern. He was protecting his property from the intrusion of the state, but his society subordinated his needs to the larger good. The record says:

> After the other side has now been shown and proved to the prisoner, to wit, that the land, claimed by him and which he has bought from others, had first been given and granted to the village in common on

26

the condition, that they would surrender the patents, they had received, and in the interest of the
community assert no claims of more right and title
in the lands, covered by the patents, than other inhabitants, if more people should come to the village
of Middleburgh and settle there . . . the prisoner
. . . regrets his actions and words in this regard and
submits with an humble prayer for grace.

Gray was forgiven. The court voided his sentence of whipping and banishment but fined him and ordered him "with un-
covered head and bent knees," traditional symbols of public
humiliation, to ask forgiveness from God, the government,
and the magistrates of Middleburgh. John Gray remained
in Newtown, married, had children, and died there around
1663.[44]

A second example of the conflict between private ownership and the public good involved lands the town reserved
for a minister. Newtown was originally founded by a clergyman, and the town, throughout its history, tried with varying
success to keep one. Part of a minister's salary was a yearly
stipend that varied from time to time, but ministers were also
given houses and lands on which they grew crops like any
other townsman. Middleburgh's first minister was Mr. John
Moore, who may have come with the 1652 settlers. In 1657
seven alarmed residents, foreseeing a dispute over the ownership of the minister's land, petitioned Stuyvesant to void the
town's gift of this property to Mr. Moore. They argued that in
giving him free title, "we are wronged and the town left destitute if Mr. Moore please to leave us or if he should die for we
know men are mortal then we are to seek both for a minister
and house to entertain him." Fears of mortality were well-
founded for later that year Moore died of a "pestilential disease" leaving the issue of his house unresolved. In 1661, Newtowners again petitioned Stuyvesant to let them give the
minister's house to a schoolmaster and to order the town to

begin to repair it, the building having gone to "rack and ruin" in a dispute between Moore's heirs and Middleburgh. Once again Stuyvesant made it clear that this structure was "built for the public use of the ministry, and by that means it may nor cannot be given and transported for a private heritage."[45]

Thomas Stevenson's troubles constitute one last example of a disagreement that went beyond the town. Stevenson, it was charged, had closed a road, appropriated a water pond, and extended his fence into the river thereby making it hard for cattle to pass from the woods. In addition, contrary to village usage, he fenced all his valley by one fence when it should have been divided, he retaining one-third and the other two held in common. The Dutch-appointed arbitrators heard both sides. Their ruling clearly and explicitly upheld the public interest, and yet it also allowed personal initiative when the public good was already served. Stevenson was ordered to reopen the old road, but he was allowed to keep his water hole since it filled by rain water and was not a creek or a spring. The arbitrators noted that his neighbors could also dig water holes as he did, and all would have enough. His fence would have to end at the shore since private property ended at the water. Stevenson's valley, which he claimed by prior patent, went the way of John Gray's lands. Previous patents were voided with the note that a "private farm or plantation never ought to be prejudicial to a village." He was allowed to keep one-half of the land, the other half being put into the town common to which he had rights like other inhabitants.[46]

The Dutch administration never evoked the loyalty that Connecticut's inhabitants felt for their province even though it allowed the towns self-government. Part of the problem was cultural. Newtowners were self-consciously and proudly Englishmen, with neither love for nor identification with the Dutch. Part of the problem was structural. Without a representative assembly tying the local unit to the province, townsmen felt alienated and isolated. Their needs were unmet and their voices unheard. This government, while able to settle minor disputes, could not protect the town from outside threats and, therefore, Englishmen would not accept it as a legitimate source of authority. If townsmen did not openly express their views of the limitations of Dutch power in words, they made it clear by their actions. When the tithes came due in July of 1662, townsmen met with the Dutch and agreed to pay "eighteen schepels, one half of wheat, the other of peas." But they never did. Instead, that same year, while the Dutch and Connecticut were again contesting boundaries, New England sent its emissaries to the English towns with letters declaring them subjects of Connecticut. In response, Middleburgh sent John Coe and Edward Jessup to Hartford. And yet, Middleburgh never accepted Connecticut's authority, either. As conditions deteriorated in 1664, the village declared itself subject, not to nearby Connecticut but to distant Charles II.[47]

In a fit of patriotism, recalling the glorious days of the Norman Conquest, Middleburgh changed its name to Hastings and joined with the other English towns in voting the English adventurer John Scott, president. Within a month, Scott was jailed in Connecticut and Hastings went its own way, an independent village under the English crown. Such independence was short-lived. August saw the English fleet under Richard Nicolls capture New Amsterdam without a shot fired. Hastings, a lively vital farming village of about 250 inhabitants formally changed its name to Newtown, a name which custom had earlier bestowed, and townsmen settled in as subjects to the king and the Duke of York.

CHAPTER 2

The Roots
of Social Structure

The early Newtowners spent their first years under Dutch authority, but Dutch rule rested lightly, leaving individuals and towns the freedom to evolve their own ways of life. What these townsmen fashioned was a New England-style agricultural village with geographic mobility and considerable contact with the outside. English models of town government, albeit in truncated form, shaped town business and the administration of law and justice. Old World values persisted and brought townsmen the comfort of dissenting Protestantism and social hierarchy.

The colonists in most of the new settlements were a restless lot. Their migration from Hampshire, Dorset, Norfolk, Sussex, or Essex in England to Massachusetts or Connecticut was their hardest journey, or at least their longest, but it was probably not their first. Peter Clark has written that in pre–Civil War England migration was "an almost universal phenomenon affecting the great mass of the national population." Most of this mobility was local, with people moving short distances within subregions. The less well-off went further, drifting from countryside to village, village to town, town to city, and then, as James Horn suggests, port city to America, the New World being just another step in the search for a decent livelihood. The single, mostly young males who landed in the Chesapeake fit the group that Clark calls "subsistence migrants." The families who emigrated to New England were more likely to be Clark's "betterment migrants," those who moved not merely to survive but to rise within the social and economic order.[1]

Given the cultural trend toward mobility in England, it would have been surprising to find everybody stationary in the New World. Newtown's settlers had all lived elsewhere in America before coming to the village. Among the original purchasers were the patentees of other towns who were looking for a place to settle as well as lands with which to speculate. Richard Gildersleeve, William Lawrence, and Robert Coe were founders of Hempstead; Robert Coe and Brian Newton were patentees of Jamaica; and William Lawrence was named in the Flushing patent. None of these men died in Newtown.[2]

Newtown's earliest list of settlers is the 1656 purchase list. Composed of fifty-five entries, of which fifty-one are recognizable names, the Indian rate serves as the base line for the town's founders. Of the fifty-one purchasers, thirty-one appear on at least one other tax list for a crude persistence rate of 61 percent. Of the twenty missing, five died before the next existing tax list of 1662. The refined persistence rate of the purchasers, at least until 1662, is 71 percent. These figures are well within the range of New England persistence rates. In Rowley, Massachusetts, the crude rate for 1643–1653 was 59 percent. The refined rate was 71 percent. In Dedham, between 1648 and 1660 the crude rate was 52 percent and the refined rate 63 percent.[3]

Population turnover made town life dynamic. As new people came they brought with them their own ways of organizing their personal lives and their social structures. New Netherlands had an obvious ethnic mix, but by no means a monopoly on cultural pluralism: the difference was in degree, not kind. David Grayson Allen clearly shows that English settlers brought pronounced regional differences to the New World. Allen lists the place of origin for the settlers of his five Massachusetts towns. Some, like Rowley, had an overwhelming majority from one place, in this case, Yorkshire. Hingham had two separate migrations, one from the West Country and

one from East Anglia, composed mainly of families from Norfolk. These two groups, with two different notions of church
organization fell, into a "sad unbrotherly contention." Still
more unruly, Newbury provides the best example of pluralis-
tic tensions: "In spite of their proximity [Wiltshire-Hampshire]
these men came from a variety of subregions and derived their
assumptions about law and social institutions, as well as about
methods of agriculture, from very different sources . . . . Unlike peaceful Rowley, or usually quiet Hingham, Newbury
was born in contention and was easily aroused throughout the
seventeenth century."[4]

Given that geographical diversity marked many Massachusetts Bay towns, there must also have been regional pluralism in the Connecticut and New York towns that eventually
filled with those who left the Bay colony. Unfortunately,
Newtown's settlers left few records. Of the fifty-one identifia-
ble names on the Indian rate, only eight can be traced, all of
these to the eastern counties from which most of the New England migration came. Four were from Hertfordshire, two
from Suffolk, one from Essex, and one from Norfolk.[5]

Why was society so mobile? Sometimes people were
forced to move, as were William Hallett for his immorality
and Francis Doughty for his unorthodox religious beliefs.
Sometimes they saw new places as safer or more economically
appealing. Abraham Frost first appeared on the December 4,
1666, tax rate. A few years previously he had petitioned the
General Court at Stamford, Connecticut, for relief claiming
he was in "a poor and mean way," possibly because his wife
and children had been kidnapped by the Indians, although
they were later returned. By 1666 Frost was, at least, a taxpayer, his assessment of 3s. 8d. putting him in the thirty-sixth
of fifty slots on the list. By 1678 he had not done much better
and was assessed for only ten acres, two cows, and a horse. He
was not listed on the 1683 tax list. Sometimes they just could
not get along with family or neighbors. In 1662, townsman
Francis Swaine wrote back to England: "Loving Brother and

Sister . . . fatherlaw Cornish is dead and my motherlaw is married again unto Danill Estelle that was Mr. Wosters servant of Salysberye, and we have much difference in respect to our division being both upon one farm: I think I shall remove shortly."[6]

Francis Swaine needed space away from his new father-in-law. This space was available because land was plentiful. Middleburgh's Indian purchase of 1656 comprised about 13,000 acres and an additional 3,000 acres lay on the outbounds. Middleburgh's 13,000 acres were held like stock in a corporation. Some of this stock was released immediately to the shareholders. Most shares, however, were kept in reserve. Outbound lands were privately held by individuals in large compact parcels, most of which had been given by the Dutch magistrates. Not everybody lived on their grant. Some of these outbound holdings were speculative and their owners lived in New Amsterdam; others were legacies or inheritances in trust. Often, these farms were rented out. In 1661 Marcus de Sousoy "hired land" of 108 acres from Anneken, widow of Dirk Smit. In 1662 Govert Loockermans rented out his farm in Maspeth. These privately owned plantations provided townsmen with an alternative source of land. They lay beyond town control and restricted Middleburgh's ability to monitor its population.[7]

While Newtown's outbound lands made it different from New England towns, that difference should not be exaggerated. Newtowners, like their New England counterparts, were conservative and preferred to divide land in known ways. David Grayson Allen has shown that Massachusetts towns had a variety of land grant procedures. By 1642, Rowley had granted townsmen an average of 23.1 acres per person. Watertown, on the other hand, had allotted an average of 124 acres per person. In Connecticut, as Linda Bissell notes, Windsor and Hartford gave out large grants. Clearly, there was no single "New England" way. Newtown's land distribution fits within the range that Allen delimits.[8]

Newtowners parcelled out first shares very cautiously. Those who were townsmen—who paid for the Indian purchase, or bought the shares of those who did, or were admitted to the corporation—acquired lots on which to build a house and farm. Others were given land as payment for services, like thatching the townhouse. According to the 1662 tax list, which levied five stivers, the equivalent of five English pennies, per acre, holdings ranged from ten to fifty acres. These small farmsteads made Newtown, like Andover, Massachusetts, remarkably egalitarian with respect to real estate. As in New England towns, those who owned shares also had a claim upon all other lands, meadows, swamps, and woods that the town owned. Those who owned parcels of land but no shares had no additional property rights.[9]

In 1663 the town decided to put more land in the hands of townsmen, using a way some of them had known in England. At a town meeting they decided to lay out two large common fields, one between the rear of their lots and Train's meadow (see Map 3) and the other on the south side of town "wherever most convenient." A common field was a large area of land completely surrounded by a fence. Each person owned a strip of land in the field that he worked, and each strip carried with it the obligation to keep up the common fence. Within the fence no barriers separated one man's strip from another's. Choice of strips was by lot.[10]

Common fields required cooperation and probably were suggested by those who had had some experience with them in England, but Middleburgh's experiment with an open-field system included a limited number of townsmen and lasted but a short time. It sounds like Allen's description of lands in Essex and Suffolk, England, and Watertown and Ipswich, Massachusetts. Those who owned land in them decided when to plow, when to seed, and when to harvest. They agreed upon what crops to plant and they usually shared tools and draft animals. Some men would balk at the restrictions that a common field system imposed upon their time and choice. And, more importantly, they placed greater value on compact private holdings, like their Dutch and English neighbors had, as some had known in New England and the Old World. These they would fashion into farms for themselves and their sons.[11]

Even before Newtowners laid out the common fields, they began consolidating their holdings by buying and selling land with one another. In 1664, as a means of protecting the south boundary from other towns' occupation, townsmen voted to give six acres to any inhabitant who would settle there. With the warning that no one could take in strangers without a town vote, and that all would be taxed by the town, townsmen broke up the compact village. To these settlers, as to those in Ipswich, Massachusetts, from whence at least a few townsmen had migrated, land was more important than proximity.[12]

The ideal of a nucleated town center that afforded both physical and moral protection has captured the imagination of those writing about New England. Indeed, the "New England town" is part of America's cultural mythology. Students have been caught between the past of their imaginations and the past that really existed. Some of the early geographers, like Edna Scofield, realized that the model was flawed, yet had trouble abandoning it. She noted that compact settlements were not an unconscious response to English precedents but a conscious response to the need for protection. However, she reported, as early as 1637 people began moving to more isolated farmsteads. Carville Earle, a more recent geographer whose specialty is the Chesapeake, sees towns as bastions against barbarism. Kenneth A. Lockridge's *A New England Town: The First Hundred Years* supports this theme, and David Konig agrees, stating that the impulse behind legal and governmental institutions of both town and county was man's depravity. More recent studies suggest that land holding and nucleation, like so much else, embraced a variety of patterns, not just one pattern. David Grayson Allen's work on Massachusetts is seminal, putting to rest the myth of the monolithic New England town.[13]

The skills that men brought with them left more distinct tracks in the records than men's origins. Townsmen needed land from which to create farms, but the evidence suggests that many also had additional talents. Thomas Reede was a carpenter, and James Lorison a mason. John Coe and Edward Jessup, the two men highest on the 1662 rate, were millers who owned mills at opposite ends of the town. T. H. Breen and Stephen Foster found that 273 migrants from Norfolk and Kent were predominantly artisans. Sumner Chilton Powell says that the Sudbury settlers were farmers in England. John J. Waters Jr. suggests that the West Country men who settled Hingham were agrarian while the East Anglians, the same group Breen and Foster studied, were artisans. Farmers could also have other unidentified skills.[14]

In 1662 the cooper Thomas Cornish died leaving property worth £138 of which lands were valued at £38. His estate, the only one with a surviving inventory from these years, shows he was a farmer, though he was listed as having a trade. His cattle were worth £52, or 38 percent, other animals (swine, horses, and bees) composed 12 percent, and crops (corn and tobacco) made up another 9 percent. The last other large item, bedding, was valued at 6 percent of the farm. Cornish's farm tools, his carts, plow, sickels, and scythes; his household goods, pots, pans, trays, forks, and fireplace equipment; his other furniture, one chair, one table, chests and boxes; his clothing plus his saddles, bridles and harness, together comprised 7 percent of his estate. His debts amounted to £36, which presumably his estate satisfied.[15]

Thomas Cornish's personal estate was worth about three times more than his real estate. This ratio, says Jackson Turner Main, suggests inexpensive and sufficient land. Main found that, in Connecticut between 1650 and 1669, inventories showed a high percentage of personal wealth, usually in cattle and grain. After 1669, when the economy showed a downturn, personal wealth declined. David Grayson Allen found that Massachusetts towns could have a variety of patterns. In Rowley, land comprised between one-third and one-half of men's estates, but in Hingham, where men saw land as a commodity, land was worth more. Obviously, attitude, as well as availability, guided men's activities.[16]

Thomas Cornish was a solid citizen having even the luxury of some pewter, but he must be placed within the context of Newtown's economic structure. Gloria L. Main's work shows that those leaving behind probate records were older and wealthier than the population at large. No birth date exists for Thomas Cornish, but in 1641 he married Mary Stone. If this marriage occurred when he was twenty-five, then he was around forty-six when he died in 1662. His son John, born in 1642, would have been twenty, old enough to add needed farm labor and so raise the value of the farm. His youngest son, Benjamin, was only ten years old and might have been more of a liability than an asset.[17]

The one tax list on which Cornish appeared is problematic because it is a voluntary wolf bounty rate and not a mandatory tax. Cornish paid twelve stivers, the same amount as twelve other men. Three men paid more and nineteen gave less, but some of the town's wealthiest inhabitants, like William Blomfield and Thomas Wandall, chose not to contribute at all. Of the twelve other men who paid twelve stivers, eleven appear on the 1662 tax list. Seven of the eleven are assessed for thirty to forty acres. In sum, it seems that Thomas Cornish at his death was a man in the prime of life, but one who probably had not yet reached the apex of his wealth potential. He was in the top half, but probably not the top tenth, of Newtown's tax-paying population.[18]

Thomas Cornish's inventory records what one man was worth in 1662, but it also shows something about the economy in which he functioned. The crops listed were his market crops of corn and tobacco. Along with beaver skins and wampum, tobacco served as currency, and his might have been grown elsewhere and given to him in trade. Bees provided another source of income, and he must have sold beef and pork since his cattle and swine made up so much of his property. In 1656, he could have taken them to the Saturday market in New Amsterdam, where "meat, pork, butter, cheese, turnips, carrots, and cabbage and other country produce" were sold.[19]

The prices that farmers like Cornish received may well have been low judging from the diet that inmates in the New Amsterdam jail enjoyed. The weekly ration for an adult jailed in New Amsterdam was three pounds of beef, one and one-half pounds of pork, and one eight-pound loaf of bread. He also received two cans of small, i.e. weak, beer per day in summer and one can in winter. This hearty diet suggests that foodstuffs were relatively plentiful.[20]

The goods and services that Thomas Cornish provided rarely brought him cash money. The colonial economy never had enough coin. Moreover, Newtown's economy, rooted in a small-scale face-to-face society, functioned on trust. Debits and credits were entered in ledgers at their value, backed by the goods and the good names of townsmen. When Goodwife Cornish needed flour, she went to the mill with a few pounds of butter. The wheat was valued at six shillings per bushel and the butter at six pence per pound. A running account showed who owed what to whom at any given time, as did receipts that changed hands. Those whose accounts showed money owed could use their credit to buy other things even though such a debit was not legal tender. If Thomas Cornish owed the miller thr⌐ shillings, the miller could buy cloth from a New Amsterdam merchant and pay with Cornish's debt, if the merchant were willing. The merchant then asked Cornish, not the miller, to pay him. Cooper Cornish would do so in pork or in pipe staves.[21]

Middleburgh's economic sphere included New Amsterdam. In 1656 the council instituted a weekly market for the convenience of both country and city residents. Middleburgh settlers reached this market either by foot to the Brooklyn Ferry or by boat. Their small canoes could easily navigate the East River's rocky shore. In 1658, New Amsterdam bakers carried their wheat to Middleburgh's mills, returning to the city with flour. Some entrepreneurs went farther. Thomas Wandall owned land and housing in New Amsterdam that he rented out, and both he and Jan De Kaper were at various times engaged in the Virginia tobacco trade. Other Middleburgh residents did business in the city or appeared before the municipal court at New Amsterdam for redress against city inhabitants who did business with them. Ellen Wall bought a full anker (ten gallons) of brandy from Antonio Van Alst in 1660 and carried it to Middleburgh. When Ritzert Airy failed to deliver the small boat that Thomas Wandall hired, Wandall hauled him before the municipal court and demanded damages for the cargo he had lost. The town also had contact with other villages as well as the metropolis, New Amsterdam, and peddlers and other itinerants selling odds and ends or liquor visited there. Newtown was never closed off from the larger world.[22]

Newtowners relied first on themselves, but they also realized that they needed to protect those unable to help themselves. Young children and widows were the most vulnerable. When Elizabeth Feakes eloped with William Hallett, the Connecticut General Court tried to protect the property rights of her children. In cases where both parents died the children were even more exposed. In 1654, Joanna Wheeler, a widow with two children, married Henry Feakes, a widower with three children. In 1657 he died leaving most of his property, more than half of which he received from Joanna, to his own children. Joanna Wheeler Feakes died shortly after her husband and her children sued to recover what had belonged to their mother.[23]

A parent's desire to provide for and protect children and spouses seems natural, and this concern runs like a thread through all the wills from the beginning to the end. Thomas Cornish's will of 1662 left his whole estate to his wife, Mary, but only until his underage children reached their majority. Once these children were grown she retained one-half the estate, a settlement given whether or not she remarried. In this provision, Cornish followed Dutch custom which gave one-half, not English custom which gave the widow one-third, as her dower right. Cornish's tools went to his son John, "as his portion," that part of an estate that went to the eldest son. Any other adult children had probably received their shares already.[24]

The town became responsible when those who died failed to provide for their dependents. Mary Wood, a two-year-old infant, became a ward of the town when her father died in 1659. Three years later the town's magistrates had agreed with John Cocheran, who had been keeping the child, to pay him £35 if he raised her until she was fifteen. He was to teach her "to read English in the Bible" and at the end of ten years give her £5 and "sufficient" clothing. The £35 might have been from her father's estate since town records do not note it as an expense. Seven years later Mary was again a town concern since John Cocheran had died. This time the constable and overseers bound her out for five years to Robert Field. She probably worked in his household. Field, in return, was to provide meat, drink, washing, lodging, and clothing "fitting for such a servant," and he was to teach her reading and the skills befitting a housewife. At the expiration of her term Mary would also receive "apparel as well linen as woolen with hose and shoes and all other necessarys fitting and becoming one of her quality." Place and position were both part of Newtown's ethos. Mary Wood's quality was probably a cut above that of servant since her father had been called "Mister" and great care was taken to see that she not be demeaned. Mary would be cared for, under town supervision, consistent with her place in society.[25]

Mary Wood's place in Newtown depended upon the wealth and standing of her father. There were few distinctions that people brought with them from England. The aristocracy had remained at home and so, by and large, had the gentry. Among those who could have commanded respect based on their Old World status were the ministers. In New England they were valued for both their education and their piety. Indeed, Darrett Rutman has gone so far as to define Puritanism as "a particular 'Christian fellowship' of ministers." In Rutman's view it was the ministers who made New England's religion different from other forms of Protestantism in both old and New England.[26]

The question of religion's role in defining a unique character for New England is complicated and answers are ambiguous. Rutman has rightly noted that "two schools of thought have grown up, one devoted to New England as a Puritan *idea*, the other devoted to the study of New England as a *society*, each tending to be oblivious of the other." Behind each school stands the towering edifice of Perry Miller's work which insisted upon the monolithic nature and overpowering influence of New England Puritanism. Only recently has Miller's influence, whether implicit or explicit, been challenged. This attack has proceeded along various fronts. First, Massachusetts Bay was not all of New England, a fact recognized at the time. In 1671 the Reverend John Woodbridge Jr. identified four different regions divided by their religious ideology. Second, even within Massachusetts Bay there were a number of theological strands, not just one. Indeed, the very nature of congregationalism made orthodoxy impossible. Third, there were common assumptions shared by all Englishmen, even those in Virginia, who, as early as 1611, instituted compulsory worship. The value placed on such mandatory attendance far outlived the law code that prescribed it.[27]

The omniscience of God and his hand in human affairs were notions deeply embedded in the seventeenth-century world view. This set of ideas cut across denominational and even ethnic lines and so hardly distinguishes New England from other areas in America. It might be argued that the difference lay in the value of community, or in the identification of the "visible church," or in the early attempts to place both religious and secular authority in the hands of those who were saved, or in the willingness to use state power for religious purposes. Unfortunately, none of these ideas adequately describes New England, or even Massachusetts. First, Englishmen and other Europeans in the Middle Colonies set up discrete towns with recognizable social, political, and geographic boundaries. Dutch towns also held town meetings, elected officers, raised taxes, and supported ministers, even if they had fewer overall privileges than New York's English towns and received them later. Second, even within Massachusetts the division of the population into the regenerate and the unregenerate was idiosyncratic. Ministers disagreed as to just how "visible" the truly saved were. In places like Newbury the church welcomed "all but the most scandalous sinners." Third, just as church membership varied, so did political participation. The extent of the disenfranchisement of non-church members has generated exceptional disagreements among scholars. Robert and B. Katherine Brown maintain that most adult males could participate; Arlin I. Ginsburg and Robert E. Wall, among others, disagree. And fourth, the notion that the state could and should maintain religious control was a common one. Peter Stuyvesant believed it, and had to be restrained by his superiors in Amsterdam. Moreover, Massachusetts' willingness to use central power to enforce religious orthodoxy, so vividly displayed against Roger Williams, Anne Hutchinson, and some hapless Quakers, was quickly muted.[28]

If the real difference in Massachusetts was the presence of a minister, how powerful was that minister and how many towns had ministers? Sudbury stripped the Rev. Edmund

Brown of "almost every function that Brown, with his sexton and curate, had been accustomed to administering in his English parish." And many places in New England went years without a minister.[29]

The English settlers who moved to New Netherlands carried with them both English religious values and New England religious variety. Hempstead's founders included a minister. Jamaica, settled by men from Hempstead seeking more land, did not, and made no early move to get one. There were few clergymen of any sort in New Netherlands, and there would be few in New York. Newtown's first minister was Francis Doughty, but he left in 1643, never to return. His subsequent career was uninspired. Governor Stuyvesant appointed him to the church in Flushing but his residence there was stormy and he later sued for his salary. In 1655 he sailed to Virginia.[30]

In 1652 Middleburgh obtained the services of John Moore. Described by the Dutch as an "Independent," meaning a Church of England dissenter, he was licensed in New England but never ordained. He could preach but could not administer the sacraments. In 1655 he left Middleburgh for Barbados, his congregation being in arrears for his salary. The next year he returned, but in 1657 he died. William Leverich agreed to become the town's minister in 1662. Educated at Cambridge and ordained, he performed baptisms, marriages, and administered the Lord's Supper. He would add to the religious stability of the town.[31]

Townsmen were mainly Independents with a few Presbyterians scattered about. Although styled "Independent" by the Dutch, there is some evidence that Francis Doughty and John Moore were Presbyterians. If so, they would have identified a church community larger than the congregational unit of the town. They would also require ordination by other ministers, not by the calling of a town.[32]

The Dutch around Newtown were Dutch Reformed. Initially, the Dutch trekked into New Amsterdam for services, but by 1657 the Kings County settlers had their own minister. The Dutch on Newtown's outbounds went to his services. Other religious groups were yet to emerge. The Church of England would establish a foothold only after 1700 and the Quakers were just beginning their proselytizing in New Netherland. In 1657 their arrival was distastefully described by Dominies Megapolensus and Drisius, who wrote: "Again a little while ago there arrived here a ship with Quakers, as they are called. . . . They left several behind them here, who labored to create excitement and tumult among the people,—particularly two women, the one about twenty, and the other about twenty-eight. These were quite outrageous."[33]

When specialists were unavailable, lay preachers filled the vacuum. These men, some educated and some not, undermined the authority of the church and, by implication, the authority of the state. In 1656, William Hallett, then living in Flushing, and newly elected sheriff there, allowed the heterodox William Wickendon to hold meetings and administer the Lord's Supper in Hallett's house. Indeed, according to the charges against Hallett, he not only allowed this itinerant in, but participated in the sacraments. In response, the Dutch authorities stripped him of his office and fined and banished him, although the banishment was lifted. The severity of his sentence illustrates the importance that the Dutch governors assigned to keeping control over the ecclesiastical affairs of the province. In this effort they looked more like the early Massachusetts magistrates and the later New York governors than the liberal vanguard that the New Amsterdam Chamber would force them to become.[34]

The desire for religious orthodoxy was part of a larger-felt but less-articulated need to smooth out differences among people and prevent divisions that would split neighbor from neighbor, thereby rending the fabric of community. Both individuals and the courts viewed arbitration as the best way to settle disputes. When William Lawrence and John Forman disagreed about whose fault it was that an acre of wheat was improperly reaped and shocked, the case ended up in court. However, this outcome was not what Forman wanted, according to witnesses, who testified that "he said that if William Lawrence would have attended arbitration the thing had been done withal." Richard Brutnell and William Harck could not come to terms over a land title but the court in New Amsterdam refused to rule and required that each side choose an arbitrator "who at the cost of the parties shall repair to Mespats Kill, and summon all, who have any claim to the land before them to prove their claims, and if practicable, to bring parties to an agreement." [35]

All the colonial settlements, not just Newtown or the English in New Netherlands, felt the need to reconcile differences. Langdon Wright, in a recent article suggestively titled, "In Search of Peace and Harmony: New York Communities in the Seventeenth Century," says, "Like their New England counterparts, New York towns valued peace and harmony." He includes Dutch Flatbush among his sample. And how could it be otherwise? Society had no real means of enforcing its will. There were no armies or police forces in the colonies. Peace depended on agreement, and everybody recognized this even if they could not always succeed in attaining it. [36]

Arbitration could fail. In the feisty, at times individualistic, society that their English heritage permitted and that Dutch tolerance encouraged, both individuals and towns could react badly to authority. Most of this aggressiveness was channelled through the town courts. Keeping local disputes local had two consequences. First, the towns became responsible for their own well-ordering, thereby giving them power and legitimacy. In 1655, for example, Thomas Stevenson sued Thomas Reade in the municipal court at New Amsterdam. "Parties being heard, the Court, (inasmuch as they both reside within the jurisdiction of Middleburgh, and as the said Court can arrive at a better understanding of their affairs in question) refer the parties to their aforesaid tribunal." Second, the Dutch inadvertently cut themselves out of local adjudication and deprived themselves of a useful tool through which to exercise social control. As in Connecticut, townsmen would look to each other for the solution to most minor problems, yet they could choose to involve those higher up if it were in their own interest.[37]

The Newtown court record begins in 1659 although other evidence shows that the court functioned as early as 1655. Between 1659 and 1664 some sixty-eight cases bearing date, plaintiff, and defendent were recorded. Of these, seventeen were left unresolved, four were nonsuited, thirty-eight were awarded to the plaintiff, suggesting that the suit was just, eight to the defendent, and one to neither. Twenty-five cases involved a debt of some kind, thirteen were "actions" and cannot be specified, and the remaining thirty were a miscellaneous collection of trespass, ownership disputes, property damage, theft, defamation, and slander.[38]

The large number of debt cases (35 percent) would increase in the coming years. These and the major work of the court will be discussed in Chapter 4. The debt suits revealed unhappiness about payment but, more importantly, they established a written record of the debt in a society where not everybody could read or write. Of more interest here are suits that in their detail show a number of social forces converging. The case of *Ellen Wall* v. *John Lorison* is one of these. The problem began when Ellen Wall bought liquor in New Amsterdam which she meant to resell in Newtown. John Lorison found the liquor, drew off four porringers' worth, and, being a social creature, invited his friends to partake. Joseph Fuller testified "John Lorison and Hendr[icke] Tombore coming up the kills Joseph going along by . . . them in a canoe he saw a porringer of liquors stand . . . near the middle of the canoe he asked John Lorison whether that drink was for him John Lorison bid him drink it but he must hold down his head and it was brandy." Edmund Riley noted that "John Lorison did tell him that he did draw four porringers full of old Nell's drink," and Thomas Rise said, "John Lorison and Hendricke Tomebore came into our house and after we took a pipe of tobacco they invited us down to our landing place and there was a parcel . . . of drink in a porringer and we drunk and there was the quantity of 2 or 3 porringers more drawn and the last of all that was drawn John Lorison bid Hendricke Tombore have a care of it." The evidence was plain and Lorison was found guilty. What the testimony also shows, however, was a social ease among people, a certain prankishness, and perhaps male bonding. "Old Nell's drink" went down male throats.[39]

The fun stopped when the women got into the act. Ellen Wall not only lost brandy but she faced the wrath of Lorison's wife. According to one witness, "I stood in my lot and see Mary Lorison strike Ellen Wall and thrust her down[.] Ellen rose up again [and] John Puddington's wife thrust her down again, the next day I see her face black and blue and further . . . heard Mary Lorison and Ellen call one another whore." John Lorison then sued Ellen Wall for slander since married women being legally under the care of their husbands did not sue in their own names. The court ruled that both women be fined and "for future time to refrain such drunken bouts."[40]

Theft was condemned in colonial Newtown, but slander and defamation were potentially more serious crimes in a small-scale society that relied upon personal contact and reputation for its assessment of worth and trust. Burton Benedict notes that this type of society is one in which the kinship, political, religious, and other systems coincide, and, that, therefore, each individual plays many roles and occupies a number of statuses. The ties that bind are kinship, friendship, and neighborliness. To impugn a person's good name, to call one a "rogue" or a "whore," was to declare that he or she was of "evil report," hence unfit to share in the benefits and responsibilities of civil society. Moreover, reputation not only bounded social and economic discourse, it also denoted "quality," the place a person held in society, and thereby marked where one stood and how one was treated. Those who unjustly undermined a person's good name had to admit their error publicly. Thomas Lawrence was forced to admit before the town court:

> This may satisfy any whom it may concern that whereas I Thomas Lawrence have said that Thomas Robards testimony being read before the Governor that either the testimony or the said Thomas Robards should be perjured in defaming him in this manner I am sorry for it and know no such thing by him.[41]

John Lorison stole brandy from Ellen Wall and had to pay damages, but there his punishment ended. Ellen Wall and Mary Lorison not only paid fines but were shamed before the court. Indeed, shame was another weapon in the peace-keeping arsenal of this small-scale society. The case of John Forman shows how many levels of meaning could be contained in one set of actions. In 1660, John Forman stole grain from Captain Coe's mill, just as John Lorison stole brandy from Ellen Wall, but Forman not only had to restore the grain, he had to "walk from Mr. Doughty's house with two rods under each arm and the drum beating before him until he comes to Mr. Jessup's house and there to have his liberty." All of Middleburgh undoubtedly turned out to watch this public and humiliating spectacle.[42]

John Forman had stolen corn, but, worse, he had transgressed the society's sense of place. On the 1660 voluntary wolf bounty, Mr. Coe was first and John Forman, then aged about twenty-nine, was in the bottom 20 percent. John Lorison, on the other hand, was in the top 10 percent and Ellen Wall was not on the list. Even the honorific title "Mr." shows that Coe was a man who represented the "quality" of Newtown. Because he was poor and stole from one held in higher esteem, Forman had crossed unspoken social boundaries. His shameful march through town was public punishment for this latter breach of the social order and shows how seriously townsmen took that order.[43]

By the English conquest Newtown was an agricultural village remarkably like the Massachusetts and Connecticut towns from which its population had come. Dutch toleration permitted them wide latitude to manage local affairs and settle their own differences. What it did not do was grant Newtown a representative assembly or protect either life or property to townsmen's satisfaction. This lack they protested in terms that they would use again when government undermined non-negotiable liberties.

Closer to home, townsmen grew their crops, plied their trades, and orbited within the economic sphere of the metropolis of New Amsterdam. They valued religion, harmony, and a hierarchical social order that law and custom protected. At the same time, Newtowners, like New Englanders, realized that there was little need to draw boundaries too narrowly. They must have felt the new regime would allow them even greater latitude when Dutch sovereignty gave way to English on that August afternoon in 1664.[44]

PART TWO

1665 – 1691 :

The
English
Conquest

CHAPTER 3

The Foundations of Anglo-American Structures

The English conquest of New Netherlands changed the nationality of all those living there and had long-range implications for Newtown. Its immediate impact was less striking, due in part to previous Dutch toleration for local autonomy and also to the English governor's weaving of existing organizational forms into New York's new governmental structures. Dual localism saw to it that town affairs usually remained town affairs except when townsmen requested outside help. Daily life continued unchanged, and Newtown, recognizing that not much was new, neglected to even note the conquest in the town minutes. After all, the townsmen had declared themselves loyal subjects to Charles II six months before, and they saw no need now to repeat their allegiances.

Government under the Dutch had been rather simple; under the English it became more complex. In March 1665, Governor Richard Nicolls ordered the towns to send deputies to Hempstead "to settle good and known laws within this government for the future, and receive your best advice and information in a general meeting." This law code, which was already drawn up, was known as the "Duke's Laws." A skillful blend of English, New England, Virginia, and Dutch practices, it smoothed the transition from Dutch to English rule. Newtowners, being transplanted New Englanders living under the Dutch, saw much in the Duke's Laws that was familiar. What they did not see, but had expected, was a representative assembly.[1]

Richard Betts and John Coe, Newtown's representatives to the Hempstead Convention, sat with their peers and heard Governor Nicolls' reorganization of government. The "good and known laws" regulated a wide variety of activities, from the registration of births to the branding of horses and mares. Of more immediate importance to Newtown, Betts and Coe were exhorted to clear the title of the town's lands and bring in patent, bills of sale, and a survey of the boundaries.

Governor Nicolls did more than institute a law code. He also reorganized the judicial structure. First, he instituted the office of justice of the peace. The evolution of that office had begun in the fourteenth century and reached the form known to the Newtown English somewhere between 1558 and 1640. Justices were local notables appointed by the Crown to keep order. Their principal tools for doing so were their good names, their connections with the neighborhood elite, and their increasing jurisdiction over other officials at the town and county level. The evolution of the justices' power in New York recapitulated, albeit within far fewer years, the rise of the justice in England. Under the Duke's Laws, justices had few responsibilities. They could issue warrants; the eldest justice, in the absence of the governor, deputy governor, or council members, could pronounce sentences or decrees; and, most potentially important to towns, any justice could "preside as chief in any of the town meetings within the jurisdiction where he dwells." In these early years New York justices did not see fit to so preside and so made little impact on the governance of the town or the administration of justice at the local level.[2]

Second, Governor Nicolls reorganized the province into shires and ridings. Newtown was part of Yorkshire and lay in the West Riding with the Dutch towns of Kings County,

Gravesend, and Staten Island. This system created a new judicial hierarchy. The town court remained, but above it sat a
Court of Sessions and above that the Court of Assizes, which
included the governor and the council.

In July 1673, the Dutch recaptured New York and reestablished the former Dutch system of government. Some
thirteen months later the English retrieved their colony
through the Treaty of Westminster. It would remain English
until independence.

In 1683 the English again reorganized government. They
replaced the shire and ridings of Nicolls' day with counties. These counties, which would also form New York's election districts, were much smaller than either Yorkshire or the
three ridings and so allowed officials within them tighter control. They also divided the population along clearer ethnic
lines. Kings County included the old Dutch towns. Rich-
mond, Queens, and Westchester were predominantly English. Newtown was now part of Queens County and in January 1684 elected Samuel Moore and Thomas Stevenson to
meet with representatives from the other five county towns to
choose a county treasurer.

The increasing needs of colonial society required greater
specialization. Queens County created two administrative
units with different functions and different personnel. The
county board of supervisors, instituted in 1686, taxed, cared
for the county court house, assumed responsibility for vagrants and felons, and doled out bounties on vermin. It also
audited the county books and paid the salaries of the two representatives Queens County sent to the General Assembly
once that body was organized. New England towns would be
the lowest unit of political representation but in New York the
county was the level that elected delegates. New York was
tardy in creating an assembly. Neither Charles II nor James II
was happy about this kind of local autonomy and both had
hoped to prevent it in New York. However, an unexpected

consequence of their failure to do so might have been the political health of the towns.[3]

The second administrative unit was the county court. The town court remained the lowest civil court; its days, however, were numbered. Over the next eight years its civil jurisdictional boundaries first narrowed to cases worth less than forty shillings, then widened to those worth five pounds; criminal jurisdiction was apparently abolished. Furthermore, its bench was altered, first being restricted to three appointed commissioners, then being opened to three elected commissioners. As Goebel and Naughton note, "the effect of the change was to facilitate the eventual shift to an administration of petty local judicial matters by justices of the peace." Above the town court sat the Queens County Court of Sessions, the Court of Oyer and Terminer and General Gaol Delivery, and the Court of Chancery, composed of the governor and the council.[4]

The General Assembly and the various reorganizations of the judiciary were short-lived. In 1688, James II added New York to the Dominion of New England, which was governed without the benefit of an elected assembly. Events soon overcame this consolidation in the form of England's Glorious Revolution. James fled the throne leaving provincial government with no legal authority until the accession of William and Mary. New York, left leaderless by the flight of Lieutenant Governor Nicholson, became embroiled in the quasi-civil war known as Leisler's Rebellion. In January 1690, William III appointed Henry Sloughter Governor of New York. On March 19, 1691, fourteen months later, he arrived. Sloughter arrested and executed Jacob Leisler and then again revamped the political and judicial structures of the colony. He reconvened the General Assembly and changed the court system. Appointed justices of the peace, who would now deal with petty civil cases, replaced the elected town court. A Court of Common Pleas was added to the Court of Sessions, and a new Supreme Court of Judicature replaced the Court of Oyer and Terminer. Sloughter's changes would be the last tampering with the forms of government until after the Revolution.

The various reorganizations of New York's legal, administrative, and legislative structures changed Newtown's relationship with other towns and the province as a whole, but they made little immediate difference to the town. Newtown utilized outside administrative and judicial units to secure town rights and interests as it had done all along. The most important of these was the right to the land itself.

Newtown's patent and boundary problems began almost at once because the 1642 charter was invalid and Peter Stuyvesant had never granted another. Newtown was left with only its 1656 Indian bill of sale to prove its claims, but because townsmen still owed the Indians their second installment the Indian deed was yet unclear when Governor Nicolls began calling for grants and receipts at the 1665 Hempstead Convention. Newtown finally paid for its land, and in July 1666 the signatures were acknowledged. The Indian deed gave Newtown the right to the land and Nicolls granted the town a charter in 1667. Inadvertently, the Indian deed was not recorded in the provincial land records even though it was signed and dated by the governor. This neglect caused problems later.[5]

In 1684 the English government commenced the laborious, thankless, and fruitless task of making the colonial governments pay for themselves. In New York this meant an examination and reconfirmation of all old patents and the negotiation of the token and symbolic payment known as the "quitrent." The quitrent, an English institution dating back to at least the fifteenth century, was a mechanism through which those who held land recognized the sovereignty of the king. Its meaning extended beyond the small amount of money that changed hands. By paying it, townsmen acknowledged English legitimacy, a concession never wholeheartedly made to the Dutch, and their own identification as Englishmen.

In 1686 Newtown received its patent. The final version confirmed the 1667 Nicolls charter and Indian deed and named a total of 113 freeholders and inhabitants "of said town." Among those 113 were the Dutchmen and Englishmen holding land on the outbounds. They were now formally inhabitants of Newtown.[6]

Questions of boundaries were closely related to patent rights since the town charter established the boundaries. Basic to these rights was control over what people quickly realized were finite natural resources. Newtown's excessive concern with the town bounds began early, ended late, and involved every appropriate agency of provincial government. Boundary disputes embroiled Newtown with Jamaica, Flatbush, Brooklyn, and Bushwick, but the Bushwick line was the major problem. The boundary dispute with Newtown's predominantly Dutch neighbors was again more than it seemed and layered with meanings that served symbolic as well as material functions. Dragging on for almost one hundred years, it reaffirmed Newtown's corporate identity. It also showed a possessiveness for territory and displayed a jealousy of rights and autonomy that augered ill for those who would encroach later. Finally, it suggested that provincial power was limited and that townsmen felt free to assert their disagreement with those in authority.

Initially, the difficulty centered upon Thomas Wandall's 1661 claim to some meadows between the kills dividing Newtown and Bushwick. By 1665, these meadows had become a town concern, when Governor Nicolls ordered "that the meadow ground in question between Bushwick and Newtown, shall remain to the inhabitants of the town of Bushwick." Nicolls based his ruling on the Indian deed of 1656, but Newtown read the same deed differently and declined to accept his decision. In 1669 they decided to take their case to the Court of Sessions and appointed three trustees to stand in the town's behalf.[7]

The Sessions called for arbitration, but nothing happened and Governor Francis Lovelace then called on the two towns to appear before him with their papers. The case was referred to the Court of Assizes, which ordered a survey of the area in question. The Assizes decided for Bushwick, and Newtown was left with the costs of the suit. Newtown petitioned the New York Council for another survey, which was completed in 1672. In the end, these 1672 boundary lines would set the limits between Newtown and Bushwick, but not before another century of contention, which began but one month later.[8]

Newtown's nerves, pocketbook, and dignity were already frazzled when the provincial government called in all land patents in 1684. Newtown and Bushwick officially renewed their quarrel and Newtown commissioned yet another survey. Once the new line was drawn, Newtown placed settlers along it. Leisler's Rebellion apparently took people's minds off land problems, but when stable government returned the grievances resurfaced. This long land dispute raises questions about authority's ability to resolve conflict and restore peace. The New York provincial government was either unable or unwilling to enforce its decision and Newtown knew this.

Newtown's experience with boundary disputes and with provincial authority's inability to stop the dissension was shared by other towns in both New York and New England. While Newtown's limited size of approximately 16,000 acres might have contributed to its feistiness, even large towns fought with their neighbors over boundaries. Jamaica, with 53,000 acres, quarrelled with Flushing, Newtown, Hempstead, Flatlands, Flatbush, and Brooklyn. Dedham, Massachusetts, with some 120,000 acres, quickly lost the right to this huge grant and by 1673 shared it with two other towns. Even so, the amount of land held by Dedham would seem adequate. Yet, as early as 1651 Dedham and her daughter village, Medfield, fought over the bounds, and the next year Dedham took on Dorchester. In Connecticut the same pattern persisted. Town grants were bountiful. Indeed, by 1675 twenty-five towns averaged 106.3 square miles, or some 68,000 acres, and still "the endemic boundary disputes among the towns reveal the depth of the desire of town planters to secure all the land possible." No provincial government seemed willing to exercise authority over what must have been seen as town business. Whether called "persistent localism" or "dual localism," the central government's sense of its own responsibility excluded the touchy question of land boundaries. When Governor Edmund Andros breached this fine line in 1686 he succeeded in uniting the widely disparate forces that overthrew the Dominion of New England in Massachusetts.[9]

Townsmen's willingness to fight for so long over a few acres of disputed meadow reveals how vitally important both land and the idea of land were. Town decisions show which lands were considered most important or were in most limited supply. Meadows were regulated first, not only in Newtown but elsewhere. As early as 1667, townsmen voted that nobody could sell the meadows "from his accomodations to any stranger of another town." In 1668 all remaining common meadow was laid out, and in 1669, in recognition that meadow lands would no longer be available, the town "voted and agreed . . . that there shall be forty acres of Traines Meadow reserved for poor men which have no meadow to be disposed of to them by purchase by those who shall be appointed thereto by the town paying their proportion of the town's debts." In Jamaica, land allotments were pegged to the size of meadow holdings. By 1690 the town granted no further meadow lands, or the uplands to which meadow entitled settlers. In 1670 Newtown forbid townsmen to sell wood to strangers, while in that same year townsmen ruled that no man could cut or sell timber or firewood unless he had planted two acres of corn. These timber restrictions reflected scarce resources that were one consequence of placing town sites on cleared fields and abandoned Indian villages. As Thomas F. Gordon noted in his 1836 *Gazeteer*,

> The western end of the island, when settled by Europeans, was, in great measure, bare of timber. The Indian practice of burning over the woods, in order to clear the land and provide food for deer and other game prevailed; consequently there was no underwood, and large trees were so scarce that early and careful measures were deemed necessary for their preservation in almost every town of the island.

And yet, how limited was too limited? Rowley, Massachusetts, sat "on the edge of a vast forest wilderness" and still passed early and severe restrictions on timber. If as much were known about Newtowner's origins as about Rowley's, some of these regulations might also prove to depend more on past experience than any immediate reality.[10]

Initially, as in most of New England, all land within the patent belonged to the town as a corporation, not to individuals. By vote of the town's inhabitants some of these lands had been divided up into private house lots, commons, and open fields, but most acreage was held back. This reserve remained part of the town proprietary and could be used or disposed of only with the consent of the townsmen.

Town lands were exchanged for various services. They were given away in order to lure craftsmen whom the town needed, pay off loans made to the town, and pay for services done for the town. In 1674 Newtown voted that no strangers would be given land until all the inhabitants had their proportions, "except it be to some useful tradesman." The same need for local industry led the town to make a grant on Lodwicke Brook in 1691 to Thomas and Edward Stevenson for a fulling mill. Those newcomers given home lots were denied purchase rights. They had no claims to parcels of common land, and they could lose their land if they moved. In 1678 the town voted Richard Osborn twelve acres, but only if he settled in Newtown, at which point it was his to use or later even sell. Otherwise, the land reverted back to the town.[11]

Specific needs of the town, like services and loans, were also met by disposing of land. In 1665 the town paid James Lorison for work done on the town house by giving him meadow land. In 1668, when the town needed to pay Robert Coe for the money he advanced it, it voted to sell a piece of meadow rather than levy a tax. Thereafter, until 1723 when all town lands were gone, the pattern, or at least the preference, was to sell land to pay extraordinary town expenses rather than to raise taxes. These sales were to townsmen, not to strangers.[12]

The disposal of public land in exchange for goods and services was practiced everywhere. Sudbury used river meadow to "gratulate" town officials for time and service rendered, and Hingham agreed "to use town lands by granting them 'unto whom the Town is in debt.'" Andover sold forty twenty-acre lots between 1668 and 1686. Hempstead, Queens County's largest town with 114 square miles, voted to sell land in 1691 and 1710 to pay for boundary disputes, while Eastchester, New York, granted land to both a smith and a weaver if they remained in town. Such use of public resources for the common good is hardly surprising. However, land was a limited commodity, and when town resources dried up the towns would be forced to levy taxes—to take actual goods—to pay for improvements or services. Most studies have clearly shown that town meetings atrophied in the eighteenth century. Part of that process must be related to the loss of free land and the leeway that it gave townsmen.[13]

The decision as to what to give and what to sell lay with the town as a whole until 1683 when the purchasers held their first meeting. The purchasers, who formed among themselves an interest group, were those who had subscribed to the Indian rate of 1656 and their heirs, and those who had bought purchase right from persons who already held it. The number of shares owned seems to have been based solely on the amount of money originally paid and was phrased in terms of shillings: one held a six shilling purchase right, or a ten shilling right. Other places allotted these rights differently. In Dedham and Sudbury, size of family, status, or skill were also considered. In Windsor, Connecticut, only the movable property one brought in mattered, while in Andover, a proprietor's lots were "proportionable to his estate." Newtown seemed to value only the size of an inhabitant's original investment, but it made no difference, for all of these purchase right systems including Jamaica's, which doled out meadow, not house lots, built inequality into land redistribution, hence inequality into the social order. Purchase shares determined the amount of land received in each land division. In Newtown, extra expense also went with larger purchase rights. Early taxes, and all of the purchasers' later expenses, were based on the number of shares held in the purchase.[14]

Newtown's land distribution, which favored small plots, was conservative even by New England standards. Between the first land division prior to 1662 and the next formal land division of 1679, the town disposed of small plots and various swamps and meadows. Juniper Swamp was given in lots thirty rods wide to anyone who would clear it. The South Meadow was laid out according to the amount men paid in a 1667 tax list, and Smith's Meadow and Island were sold outright. Indeed, until 1679, the town's distribution of land seems haphazard—a bit of upland here, a piece of meadow there—but "at a town meeting the 13th of September 1679 it is voted" that the town make a division of land based on patent right.[15]

The 1679 division allowed each holder two acres per shilling purchase right. A 1683 purchaser list shows these rights to have ranged from twenty to one hundred and forty acres. In 1684 the town held a further division giving one acre for each shilling right. The last division took place in 1695.[16]

Part of Newtown's reluctance to give land had to reflect

the limited acreage the town owned, but part of Newtown's choice must also have been cultural. Of David Grayson Allen's five towns only Watertown "indulged" in a wholesale dispersion of land. First grants in Rowley and Hingham averaged 23 acres, Newbury averaged 80 acres, and Ipswich and Watertown 97 acres. In Watertown's first six years of grants, townsmen gave themselves 16,000 acres, an area the total size of Newtown. Dedham, on the other hand, only parcelled out 2,000–3,000 acres in its first twenty years. Andover's land grants show the process of early control breaking down into more liberal dispersion. House lots averaged between four and twenty acres, with each succeeding grant based on the size of the house lot. The first two allotments yielded one acre of upland for each acre of house lot. By 1658, the third division, Andover granted four acres per house lot acre, and in 1662 townsmen gave themselves twenty acres per house lot acre. With various meadow and swamp allocations, a four-acre house lot yielded 122 acres of land, while a twenty-acre house lot brought 610 acres. Newtown never gave away this much land.[17]

The differentiation of townsmen into two distinct categories, purchasers and inhabitants, reflected two processes already underway. The first of these was the growing complexity of local life with its concomitant need to draw sharp lines between those who held certain rights, in this case to land resources, and those who did not. In the more simple past either everyone held such rights and shared common status, or those who did not hold such rights were few and universally known. The second process was one that accorded status and future wealth according to economic rank alone, and saw land and rights to land as commodities. William Bradford of Plymouth saw this trend and bitterly noted that men wished to move "not for want or necessity so much . . . as for the enriching of themselves." Studies of Massachusetts and Connecticut have labelled this change the transition from "Puritan" to "Yankee" and have dated it somewhere in the latter seventeenth century.

These generalizations probably mislead, since they obscure the differences among New England towns and the long history of the processes themselves. Newbury, Massachusetts, perhaps an anomoly, was, according to David Grayson Allen, the home of "a new man . . . , one in which at least old ways of forest and field were being pushed aside for the desire of greater capital accumulation." Newbury differentiated proprietors from the town meeting as early as 1642. In Connecticut, maybe because of its towns' larger areas, the distinctions came later. Lyme in 1698 and Branford in 1700 held separate proprietor meetings. Other towns followed.[18]

Once town lands were sold or divided to townsmen they became commodities available to anyone. Newtown passed laws in 1667 and 1687 forbidding the sale of land to strangers, but the land records show that land was sold to men from other towns. Even before the lots were actually surveyed, the rights to them were marketed, and by 1667 both Newtowners and outsiders were buying up individual lots and consolidating them into larger holdings. Jamaica's experience was similar. In 1661, 1664, and 1688, the town passed legislation giving itself the authority to admit strangers. These laws were made to protect the town from the indigent, not to keep out newcomers. Indeed, Jamaica welcomed the able-bodied and by 1670 had attracted sixty-two new families. They fanned the local land market which saw 275 transactions between 1656 and 1690.[19]

The private land market bypassed town authority, but even more pertinent to the loss of town control in Newtown was the town's willingness to settle people along the town boundaries in 1664, 1684, and 1687. While the majority of people still lived near Horsebrook Creek, small clusters of settlers moved to town lands adjoining Bushwick and Jamaica. This willingness to exchange control over people for control over land was probably fostered by the relatively small area of the town which permitted easy access to the town meeting house, the geographic limitations of western Long Island, the relative security from hostile Indians, tolerance for religious and ethnic diversity, and the initial settlement pattern of town and individual outbound plantations. Newtown was never really a frontier town, and only the outbounds lay beyond the chartered borders. Once these became part of Newtown under Governor Dongan's patent of 1686, there was no room for expansion. Each town began where the previous one ended.[20]

The erosion of the nucleated village would seem, more than most processes, to differentiate Newtown, even New York, from the communities of New England. However, Massachusetts and Connecticut towns displayed a wide variety of behaviors, among which were both the willingness to permit people to leave villages and move on to more isolated compact farmsteads and its opposite, tremendous resistance to any move away from the village center. In Plymouth, dispersion began within the first ten years and continued in the face of a vocal but impotent opposition. In Andover, the change began within the first twenty years, as it did in Salem and Newbury. Windsor, Connecticut, saw the same pattern emerge, as men settled in two separate areas along the Connecticut River within five years of the town's founding, and along both sides of the Farmington River within twenty years. In Jamaica, most people stayed near the heart of town, but some did not. Those who wanted to move did so without opposition from the town.[21]

The unwillingness of some New England townsmen to allow people to move out from their original home lots in the town center sprang from a variety of separate but related impulses. Past experience, ideology, self-interest, and frontier realities were all factors. In England, open-field agriculture led to nucleated villages but enclosed-field did not. Settlers initially established a lifestyle familiar to them, even though, as in Andover, they might modify their behaviors a short time later. The settlers who came for ideological reasons wished to establish disciplined religious communities built around a particular minister, or they wished to exercise strict control since, Richard Bushman suggests, they feared that isolation would lead to morally suspect behavior. Movement away from the town would dilute community control. Also, townsmen realized that those leaving towns for the outbounds were less committed to town afairs. Indeed, those farthest out would resent paying for services they rarely enjoyed. Many New England squabbles involved small groups seeking an independent status, which either freed them from town taxes or granted them their own lands. Salem, which had already lost four townships by 1668, tried to stop the process in the late 1660s: "From this early and fundamental divergence of interest sprang more than a century of conflict between the Townsmen and the 'Farmers.'" And, finally, some towns recognized the physical dangers of living near the borders. In the 1640s Sudbury was a frontier village with a town watch and nightly patrol against surprise Indian attack. In time, memories of life in England with its field systems, manorial forms, and religious persecution would fade, the immigrant generation and its ministers would die, and the Indians would retreat further from the coast. Remaining to bedevil the larger towns would be questions of representation, taxation, and community services. Newtown, because it was so small, and also, perhaps, because it freely allowed villagers to go beyond town boundaries for their religious needs, never faced this problem. Indeed, only Hempstead, the largest of the Queens County towns, would later feel the pressures of those wishing to hive off and form their own separate political unit.[22]

Newtown provided all townsmen with the administrative services they required. Before 1691, the town court and the town meeting shared local administration. The town court, established under Dutch rule, continued in much the same way under the English and must have eased the change from Dutch to English sovereignty. The magistrates, now called overseers, were still elected by townsmen and served as a petty civil court hearing cases involving less than forty shillings (about the same value as the Dutch fifty guilders). This court must have been one of Newtown's most useful institutions, and one that kept local concerns local. It was certainly one of its most responsive, meeting about five times a year. Furthermore, the court followed the agricultural rhythms of the townsmen, sitting least frequently in June, August, September, and October, and most frequently in February through May. Newtown's court not only met often and at convenient times of the year, but also resolved its cases quickly. Of the 405 cases the court heard between 1665 and 1691, 355 were determined at the same court. The remaining 50 were settled as soon as possible, 46 of them during the following court.[23]

The court's main function was to decide cases, but it also had other duties as befit a generalized institution. Along with the town meeting it regulated fencing and highways, and occasionally appointed surveyors, fence viewers, and highway supervisors. The court also issued warnings to those late in paying taxes and court fees. More important than its petty administrative labors, the court acted as protector of the public good. On October 2, 1668, the court forced John Scudder to remove his dam, despite Scudder's obvious reluctance:

> Whereas there hath been complaint made to this court against John Scudder Sr. by several of the inhabitants for making a dam which has and still does stop the passage of the water at or near Fowlers Bridge or run which is a great annoyance and it is conceived a great cause of so much sickness among them, the court does therefore order that the said John Scudder shall forthwith cut the said dam whereby the said water may have free passage through it under the penalty of five pound sterling.[24]

The town court was one branch of town administration; the town meeting was the other. The town meeting is one of

68

the better-studied aspects of colonial community life, and yet, even here, the picture is one of widely divergent patterns and complexity. As with almost every other colonial institution, English patterns seem to be the major influence on American choices. Rowley, Massachusetts, settled by families from a stable open-field society, vested power in the town. They met often, an average of five times a year, and used selectmen as administrators, not initiators. Newbury, a town born in contention, whose founders came from many different but economically unstable areas in England, met four times a year but gave power to its selectmen. The inhabitants of Watertown, who had known economic instability, met two or three times a year. They relied upon selectmen who sat about three times as often as the town did. Dedham, at least through 1689, met only twice a year, but its selectmen gathered almost every month to make most of the town's decisions. Dedham's most recent chronicler did not look into Dedham's English antecedents, but if David Grayson Allen's study showed a definite pattern between towns, then Dedham's people came from an economically unstable area.[25]

New York towns also show diversity, but less is known about their English origins. Undoubtedly, New York's patterns can be related to English precedents. Between about 1670 and 1709, Easthampton met 6.9 times a year. Oyster Bay met an average of 3.58 times a year, Hempstead 3.83 times a year, and Jamaica 4.84 times a year. Newtown also had an active internal political life, and between 1665 and 1691 met eight-one times, for an average of three times a year.[26]

The years of greatest concern for Newtown were the period just before the English conquest in 1664 and the period in which the town charter was rewritten in 1686 and 1687. The town convened fourteen times in 1686 and eight times in 1687. Oyster Bay and Hempstead were also most active in the 1680s, since the repatenting of land was a problem for them too. Jamaica met more times than average in the 1680s but her peak years were around 1660, 1673, and 1689. Perhaps the presence or absence of selectmen or townsmen also made a difference in New York. The case is not so clear as it is for Dedham and Watertown because Newtown had no such officer.[27]

Town meetings decided public issues like the height of fencing, but their major function was the yearly election of officers. These elected officials were either part of the regular town administration, which mainly concerned itself with the town court and taxes, or were chosen for specific tasks. Between 1665 and 1691, regular town offices expanded to include an assessor, collector, and supervisor. All three were involved with taxation, the supervisor being Newtown's representative to the county board. All three had also been ad hoc offices before they were institutionalized. That more complex town administration was necessary for taxation was no accident. The power to tax is the power to control. These taxes were paid to the province, the county, and the town. More than any other single development, increased taxation shows how the province and the county drew in the town, and how the town embraced its inhabitants. It is hardly caprice that taxation would be a central issue later.

By 1690 the town's yearly elected establishment consisted of a constable, overseers (the old Dutch magistrates who continued to comprise the town court bench), a town clerk, and the assessor, collector, and supervisor. In 1691, with the abolition of the town court, the overseers were phased out. Ad hoc officers, probably chosen for their overall competence, did those jobs that circumstances dictated. Drafting the bounds and patent in 1666 fell to Thomas Lawrence, Ralph Hunt, and John Burroughs. Gershom Moore, Robert Field, John Coe, John Ketcham, and Francis Doughty negotiated with the minister, Mr. Leverich, about his salary. Meeting with the governor or other towns, levying taxes, even binding the town minutes together, were specific tasks that required someone to do them. That someone was usually a person who was also entrusted with elected office. The years 1684–1687 were especially busy with patents and boundaries, and in those four years the town created twenty-six ad hoc committees. Over-all, between 1665 and 1691 Newtown averaged 1.8 specific ad hoc tasks per year.[28]

Townsmen's reliance on ad hoc committees shows clearly their attitudes toward power and authority. By only vesting authority in temporary bodies, townsmen were saying that power resided in the town, not in certain men or in particular offices. Even then, townsmen might put aside a committee's recommendation, which suggests a critical intelligence rather than blind deference. Newtowners refused the first draft of Joseph Sackett's patent in 1686 and appointed four others to help him write another.[29]

Some Massachusetts towns relied far less on the flexible ad hoc system. This was due partly to their much larger number of regular town officers. In 1668/9 Rowley required twenty-one men to serve as constables, town marshalls, select-men, overseers, pinders, clerks, judges, and sealers of leather. Hingham needed fewer men, choosing only selectmen, com-missioners to hear small causes, deputies, and waywardens. Interestingly, Hingham chose others year by year—a pound-keeper, a herdsman—but not as regular officers. They also utilized ad hoc committees, which were "created by the town and competed with the selectmen for power and responsibil-ity." Where selectmen acquired power ad hoc committees were unnecessary, but when towns turned from selectmen, as did Dedham and Watertown in the 1680s, ad hoc committees filled the void. Between 1636 and 1689, Dedham averaged five ad hoc committees per decade. Between 1689 and 1736, this figure rose to seventeen. Similarly, Watertown chose three such bodies in the 1660s and only one in the 1670s, but fifteen in the 1680s and twenty-one in the 1690s and first decade of the 1700s. Changed forms of local government suggest changed attitudes toward power. These New England towns and Newtown seem to have shared the basic notion that power resided in the electorate, and that this body doled it out when necessary.[30]

By definition, ad hoc offices were of limited tenure, but during the years 1665–1691, so were most of the others. Officers rotated, constables serving an average of 1.7 years. Only the town clerk kept his position for any length of time, a pattern that would persist until 1776 (see Table 1). The average total number of years in office for all thirty-eight of those who held office was 5.4 years. Public office, it seems, was open to a range of people, who needed no special skills while serving.[31]

Given the frequent number of town meetings and the liberal use of ad hoc committees, the high turnover of officers in Newtown is not surprising. It does, however, mark a change from the Dutch period, when townsmen kept their town leaders in office. The Massachusetts' towns show a pattern identical to the one their town meetings would suggest. Rowley had a high turnover; Watertown had a low one. Years of experience and economic position also follow suit. Rowley's selectmen had little experience and were scattered throughout the tax list. Watertown's selectmen had many years of experience and were "usually very wealthy and often economically remote from the common townsmen who lived in the community."[32]

Newtown's thirty-eight office holders who served in all town offices between 1665 and 1691 fall somewhere between more egalitarian Rowley and more stratified Watertown. Ninety-five percent of them were English; the Dutch would hold office later. They were also comfortably off by local standards. Those who were in the town when surviving tax lists were drawn up were among the wealthier townsmen. Eighteen officeholders, or 49 percent of the total, appeared in the 1666 rate. Of these eighteen, 17 percent were in the wealthiest 10 percent, and 69 percent were in the top quarter. Only one officer was in the bottom half, and he was Samuel Moore, a young man who would do well later. By 1683 more officers were being taxed, as 68 percent show on the rate list. These officers were again the more substantial citizens, with 32 percent in the top 10 percent and 52 percent in the top quarter. This percentage is lower than in 1666 and probably

TABLE 1

Tenure in Town Office, 1665–1691

OFFICE	AVERAGE NUMBER OF YEARS
Constable	1.7
Magistrate (overseer, commissioner)	2.3
Town clerk	5.4
Assessor	1.8

SOURCE: The town minute books.

reflects the growing population of the town and the larger pool of potential officeholders. Again, only one person, John Lawrence, is in the bottom half of the list, and, like Samuel Moore, he was a young man who would do well later. Moore had meanwhile moved up to the top 20 percent.[33]

Another wealth measure that suggests that the more successful townsmen held office is slave-holding. About 35 percent of the officeholders owned slaves, but only 25 percent of all townsmen in the 1698 census held bondsmen.[34]

Tax lists and slave-holding are crude economic measures, but they do suggest that Newtown chose its officials from the upper half of its economic spectrum. Wealth itself, however, was no guarantee of office or long tenure in office. Even those in the top 10 percent of the lists never automatically served in ad hoc office, held a large number of offices, or spent long years in town office. Of the nine men who made up the top of the 1683 tax list, four held no ad hoc offices, two held no regular offices and none held mor than three different offices. Only one man served more than a total of four years in town service. In contrast, 27 percent of the thirty-eight officeholders held more than three offices, and they each served an average of 5.4 years in office.

A solid sufficiency bound Newtown's officeholders together, but it was not enough by itself. Perhaps as important as any other attribute was amicability. Newtown's leaders kept out of the town court, and those frequently involved in litigation rarely held town office. Thomas Wandall's career is a case in point.

Thomas Wandall was one of Newtown's first settlers, buying land in Maspeth Kills perhaps as early as 1648. He did well, and in 1675 stood first among the town's taxpayers. A man of many economic enterprises, including renting property, shipping, and farming, Wandall was a respected member of the province. This prominence led to several appointments at the county and provincial levels. In 1663, under Dutch rule, the New Amsterdam court used him as an expert witness to value a sloop. After the conquest, in 1668, he served on a jury for the murder trial "upon the life and death" of John Coperstaff, and the next year Governor Francis Lovelace placed "Mr. Thomas Wandall of Maspeth Kills" on the commission to adjudicate the boundary dispute between Westchester and various individuals. No evidence exists that he served less than well in these tasks. But townsmen (and indeed, the New Amsterdam court) knew another side of Thomas Wandall. The third most contentious man in Newtown, he appeared in the town court thirty-three times, eighteen as plaintiff. A driver of hard, if not harsh, bargains, he made life miserable for any who came under his control or fell into his debt. The town rewarded his unneighborly, uncharitable, and aggressive behavior by withholding town office. Wandall served only five full years and, although he was elected overseer in 1665, he was not then chosen constable, the next rung of the leadership ladder. Wealth, outside standing, and a far-flung economic network, the pillars of deference and usefulness, were not sufficient. Townsmen wanted leaders who could compromise, who could live and let live within the constraints of the small-scale, face-to-face society that Newtown was.[35]

Town leaders shared characteristics other than wealth and neighborliness. Church leadership is not well documented for these years, but some other outside activities are. Of the thirty-eight officers, five were appointed by the governor as justices of the peace. These men all served in town office and all served in other offices with longer tenures. Justices averaged 23.4 years, as compared to the average 5.4 years of the townsmen. Like England's justices of the peace, they were Newtown's political middlemen, linking the town with both county and province. Newtown had a sixth justice in these years. He was elected justice of the peace by the town during Leisler's governorship and his case is the exception that illuminates the rule.

Samuel Edsall was born in Berkshire, England, but by 1655 he had moved to New Amsterdam and married a Dutch widow. An entrepreneur, he pursued the trade of beaver hat maker while acquiring lands in New Jersey, to which he moved. In 1668 he served on the New Jersey Council. At some point his daughter married Jacob Milbourne. She died and Milbourne married the daughter of Jacob Leisler. Edsall's first wife also had died, and he married the Newtown widow of Cornelius Berrien. By 1689 he lived in Newtown. Edsall's record of public service and his close ties to Jacob Leisler, on whose council he sat, made him a logical leader. Newtown responded by electing him justice when Leisler called for election of that office. He had not held previous Newtown office but would hold five ad hoc offices later. He died around 1700.[36]

Samuel Edsall was unique. No other townsman would rise to Edsall's prominence. Newtown, acting very much like Edward M. Cook's third-order towns, sent no other councilmen or assemblymen to the provincial capital. Townsmen did combine militia duty with office-holding. Fourteen, or 38 percent, were elected by the town to officer rank in the Newtown militia. None would use Newtown office as the base line for a provincial career, suggesting that, at least politically, New-town was out of the mainstream.[37]

Newtown's most active officeholder in these years was Content Titus, who served thirty-six years in eight offices. Titus was born in 1644, in Weymouth, Massachusetts, and came to Newtown by 1672. His first wife, Elizabeth, was the daughter of Reverend John Moore; his second wife was Mary Samway of Huntington, Long Island, whom he married in 1711. Titus had at least seven children before he died at the age of eighty-six.[38]

Content Titus styled himself a yeoman, and then an es-quire. He bought and exchanged land and was also a New-town purchaser. His will, made out in 1728, when he was ad-mittedly old and feeble, listed land, at least two houses, and slaves. His inventory of 1730 contained six slaves, a feather bed, £15 worth of clothing, and various farm animals and equipment. He owed £54. On the tax list of 1683, when Titus would have been in his prime, he ranked eighteenth out of eighty-nine.[39]

Titus first held office in 1679 when he was elected over-seer. In 1681 he was constable, and in 1686 supervisor and col-lector. In 1693 he was chosen assessor and in 1712 trustee. He had been first a congregationalist and then a Presbyterian, serving as one of Newtown's first church elders. Titus also represented the town to the outside. An ad hoc officer twenty-one times, his tasks included meeting with the governor con-cerning the patent and quitrent in 1686 and searching for a minister. By 1700 he was also a justice of the peace.[40]

Newtown's deputies met the deputies of the other towns and Newtown's justices sat with other Queens County jus-tices, but only rarely did the town or individual townsmen play any role in the provincial political structure. Townsmen's overwhelming concern with their own welfare, their "per-sistent localism," meant that provincial issues were of interest only in the most personal immediate sense. This was true in

1665, when the province changed hands, and it would be true in 1689 during Leisler's Rebellion. The fewer local implications these problems had, the less time the town took with them. Two examples show this tendency clearly, one from 1668–1669 and the other from 1683. In 1668 and 1669, Governor Francis Lovelace called in town patents and set the prices at which produce was valued for paying taxes. These rates were lower than the market rates for grain, beef, and pork. In November 1669 taxes were levied at the rate of one penny per pound of assessed value. This impost, raised without an elected assembly and paid in goods valued at less than retail prices, sparked protests. Governor Lovelace sent his pained response to Hempstead with copies to all of the other Queens County towns, Newtown included.[41]

Apparently eight English towns, including Newtown, sent petitions to the Court of Assizes. All subscribed to Hempstead's list of ten grievances. The first of these asked for representative government "as other his Majesties subjects in America do enjoy which privileges consist in advising about and approving of all such laws which the governor and his council as may be for the good and benefit of the Commonwealth." The second asked that towns have clear title to their lands freed from controversy with other towns and private individuals. The third asked that prices be regulated, the sixth that the New York ferry be better maintained, and the eighth that corn prices be standardized at the rate set by Governor Nicolls. The other provisions did not affect Newtown.[42]

The 1669 set of grievances were somewhat similar to the 1653 Remonstrance. Both asked for political representation and the economic security that clear land titles brought. What is more interesting is that Newtown's surviving town records make little mention of the whole affair. Jamaica's town minutes recorded that on February 3, 1668/9, their deputy would meet with men from the neighboring towns to draw up a petition to the governor about the price of corn "and other things as they shall see convenient." Hempstead, a few days earlier, had done the same. On September 23, 1669, seven months later, Newtown "voted that Lieutenant Ketcham shall go to Jamaica to meet with the deputies to treat concerning country affairs." Jamaica followed suit and elected Nathaniel Denton its deputy to convene with those from other towns to petition the governor at the next assizes about boundaries and other "grievances of the country," and to meet with the governor. Nothing more is said. However, 1669 was an unusual year in Newtown. Not only were there potential provincial difficulties, but also a bewildering host of local ones.[43]

Problems began in 1668 when widespread malarial and typhoid fevers broke out, not only in Newtown but throughout the countryside and city. Newtown's response, noted above, was to force John Scudder to empty his stagnant pond, which Newtowners believed caused "so much sickness." Townsmen, however, also let out their frustrations in other ways. In 1669 they threatened both the town meeting and each other. While nothing actually happened, the court record of June 8, 1669 shows the discontent very clearly:

> The deposition of Nathaniel Pettit sworne in Court testifieth that he being at the mill Gershom Hazard came there and warned the people to a town meeting the next day and he asked John Ramsden if he was warned to the town meeting and he said no neither he nor John Lorison and George Wood did not use [sic] to be warned but he would go and make such a disturbance there, that there had not been the like this good many years and he did not question but there was several persons would join with him.[44]

If disrupting a town meeting was too drastic to carry out, disrupting the neighbors was not. Townsmen harassed one another in that most local of arenas, the town court. In 1669, seventy-four cases, more than twice the number of any other year, came before the town court. All four suits over debt for unpaid taxes occurred in 1669 showing townsmen's dissatisfaction with government. Seven of the nine appeals of the town court's decisions, ten of the twenty-seven property damage suits (37%), four of the fifteen cases of broken contracts (27%), and one-quarter of all neighborly boundary disputes (three out of twelve) took place in this one contentious year. John Demos hypothesized that Puritans channelled aggression, generated by close living quarters, outward against their neighbors through litigation. As will be noted in Chapter 4, his hypothesis is not sustained by the court records overall; however, court records for 1669, 1670, and 1671 do suggest that for some the accumulating insecurities of land patents, taxes, and illness, required action. Any one of these problems might have caused only annoyance. Coming together, they provoked a small number of townsmen to act out their frustrations in the town court.[45]

Town unwillingness to become very involved in provincial concerns, or to change in the face of what seemed to be new institutions, is also evident in the 1680s. Robert Ritchie says that Governor Dongan "forced an unwelcome change upon the smaller towns" by compelling all settlements of the province to repatent their lands. These patents, in turn, reorganized town government by appointing trustees who called and led the town meeting, but only after acquiring a warrant from the justice of the peace. Newtown had to repatent lands, and in the process acquired the outbounds. This effort required both town meetings and ad hoc committees, but the town minutes from 1684 to 1687 show that the big issue was land, not political reorganization or the loss of autonomy. The repatenting of the town opened old boundary disputes that required town action. Townsmen also tried to settle people along the boundaries, thereby demonstrating that possession, if not law, entitled the town to those few acres. And they negotiated a quitrent. But nowhere were trustees mentioned, nor did the minutes suggest that town meetings required a justice's warrant. The town would elect trustees, but later, and their power never included managing the town meeting.[46]

The Glorious Revolution and Leisler's Rebellion forced Newtown to become even more involved. But here again that involvement was as minimal as townsmen could make it. The major events of Leisler's Rebellion took place in New York City and Albany, not Long Island. Langdon Wright, who studied each of the towns, found that the Dutch towns of Kings County suffered the most disruption. Town records are missing, but the county court minutes show that the courts did uncharacteristically little during that period. The rebellion in Queens County was less pronounced. Wright notes that there were no "major" political divisions there, "and that the inhabitants reacted to it more or less in unison, giving modest aid to Leisler in 1689 and early 1690; then in late 1690 resisting his repeated calls for money; and finally becoming completely disenchanted by his use of force against protesters." Suffolk County, which comprised eastern Long Island, traditionally took its cues from Connecticut. Suffolk supported the Glorious Revolution but not Jacob Leisler. Distance from New York City, and Leisler's increasing problems with the French, Albany, and discontent closer to home, spared them his wrath and his dominion.[47]

Newtown exemplified the pattern that Wright found throughout Queens County. News of the larger issues of the Glorious Revolution and the overthrow of James II never appeared in the Newtown minutes. Provincial affairs rarely did. The first notice of unusual activity was Newtown's response, on June 11, 1689, to a proposed meeting of deputies from the neighboring towns, "there to act as they shall see cause for the good and benefit of the country." Four days later the town met again, this time to agree to maintain two soldiers at New York and to send deputies to elect a Committee of Safety. All these decisions were in response to calls by Jacob Leisler, and none were questioned in the town minutes. The town's attitude at this point was pragmatic. The two soldiers would be hired, "so cheap as they can"; the deputies were to be established members of the Newtown militia.[48]

By October, Leisler was facing increasing opposition from those who felt that his administration lacked legitimacy, and he issued a call requiring towns to elect new civil and military officers. Newtown again complied with this request, but chose her former leaders except for the election of Samuel Edsall as justice of the peace. Two months later, "at a meeting ordered by Governor and Council to make choice of new military officers" the same men were chosen again though their ranks were slightly reordered. Newtown obviously had no quarrel with its leaders and saw no need to remove them. It also seemed to have no inclination to question Leisler's authority to call the election in the first place.[49]

In March 1690 the town again was called "by virtue of a warrant derived from the Lt. Governor and Council" to select deputies to choose Queens County's two representatives to a meeting in New York City. In May and June it elected tax collectors to raise the rate as Leisler's government demanded. Suddenly it was all over. The town records no more about Leisler or the new governor, Henry Sloughter.[50]

For some townsmen, the Leislerian controversy lingered a bit longer. Samuel Edsall had been an active Leislerian and member of the council. He was tried and acquitted by the same Court of Oyer and Terminer that sentenced Leisler and his son-in-law, Jacob Milbourne, to death. Joseph Sackett, fearing that he would be prosecuted for his role in collecting Leisler's tax, asked to be relieved from this responsibility. And some, including Samuel Moore and George Wood, petitioned the assembly for pay. They had raised men against Leisler. There were anti-Leislerian forces seething in Queens County. These men were meeting and taking up arms, a treasonous activity that moved Leisler to call for a show of strength. The antis rallied, citing Jacob Milbourne and Samuel Edsall as "two . . . villains with their collected rabble," the latter further described as "the most wicked and poorest of the sons of men." Verbiage aside, however, the Leislerian episode scarcely altered Newtown's internal peace or its relationship with the province.[51]

Nor did Leisler's Rebellion change the town's ethnic harmony. The presence of an older Dutch population along the outbounds could have produced tensions. Certainly, ethnicity was recognized. In 1664, when Hendrick Hendricksen Obe sued Sara van Brugge for a hogshead of tobacco, Obe's wife declared that an Englishman had delivered the tobacco. Five years later, Governor Lovelace wrote to Justice Richard Betts about some Indian problems: "Upon the complaint of an Indian that some Englishmen came this morning to his wigwam at Maspeth Kill out of which they took two Indians prisoner and also carried away two guns." The offenders were not labelled "Europeans" or "whites" but "Englishmen." However, these distinctions produced no animosity, judging from the records of the town court, the one place where it would most easily have surfaced. Both English and Dutch used the local court, chaired by English magistrates. Of the 266 individual names in the record 36, or 14 percent, seem to be Dutch. These non-English were plaintiffs 66 times and defendents 67 times. In a sample of 59 ethnically mixed cases (one-half the Dutch names), Dutch plaintiffs won 18.5 percent of the time and Dutch defendants 5 percent of the time. English plaintiffs in these cases won 16.9 percent of the time and English defendants 6.8 percent of the time. In the remaining cases no winner was noted. The court minutes show that Dutch and English fared equally well. Each nationality won 14 of the 59 cases. More important than these figures is the absolute lack of ethnic prejudice in these cases. No slurs or slanders were based on ethnicity in either testimony or the charges themselves.[52]

Most historians agree that Jacob Leisler appealed to the Dutch. Thomas Archdeacon feels that Leisler represented an earlier elite that the new English administration bypassed. Robert Ritchie found that while the New York City Dutch supported Leisler, so did others. They shared close family ties, middle-level economic status, and political marginality. John Murrin, who called the Leislerians "an ethnic Dutch movement," traced them back to those suspicious of the 1683 Body of Liberties. Disagreeing with Archdeacon, Murrin claims that Leisler moved "not to secure political careers for himself and his close associates, but to forestall a sellout to the papists." Joyce Goodfriend, whose work on ethnic pluralism in New York City encompassed all groups over a reasonable period of time, disputes Archdeacon and the notion of fast ethnic change and its dislocations. According to Goodfriend there was change from 1664 to 1700, but it was gradual. "The Dutch, who comprised the majority of old settlers, lost ground slowly, but they were not shut out of economic and political life." They continued to occupy "a central place in the local social order with Dutch communal institutions overshadowing all others in the city." In the Newtown countryside the Dutch apparently felt no need to join an "ethnic movement." Their behavior was indistinguishable from their English neighbors, and, since few issues were involved, why should they behave differently? Newtown men of substance avoided calling attention to themselves as either pro- or anti-Leisler. As long as little was required of them, and their local liberties held fast, they went along with whoever seemed to hold the reins of government, and it made little difference whether he was Dutch or English.[53]

CHAPTER 4

The Economic
and Social Order
under the Duke of York

Townsmen's seeming indifference to the political changes surrounding the Glorious Revolution represented a wait-and-see wariness toward the government. They were bound to devote more time to their private concerns, taking part in larger issues only when their well-being was threatened. This well-being was based on land.

A few townsmen, like William Hallett and Captain Thomas Lawrence, bought land directly from the Indians. Lawrence purchased only eight or nine acres, but Hallett was more ambitious. While the size of his holding remains unclear, it was larger than 150 acres and cost "fifty-eight fathom of wampum, seven coats, one blanket, and four kettles." Hallett and other townsmen also owned lands outside Newtown. Many of Newtown's inhabitants had lived elsewhere and had been granted lands in their former villages. Hallett held a twenty-acre meadow lot in Jamaica, parcels in Flushing, and, through his wife, claims to Greenwich, Connecticut.[1]

The town's limited land resources were granted to individuals by town vote or by wholesale land division. Once in private hands, these lands became private property that could be exchanged, given, bought, sold, or willed. For the 110 years between 1665 and 1775, 1499 land transactions, excluding bequests and gifts from the town, survive. Of these 1499, 351, or 23 percent, took place between 1665 and 1691.[2]

Of the 351 land transactions, 4 percent were exchanges, meaning that townsmen were swapping land with one another. While few in terms of the percentage of total transactions, these exchanges represent 31 percent of all the exchanges that ever took place in Newtown. Neighboring Jamaica shared Newtown's pattern of land exchanges. This consolidation of lands and the attitudes which underlay it were also part of New England's behavioral range that, in turn, reflected English origins. Townsmen in Newbury, Ipswich, and Watertown all perceived land as a commodity to be bought, sold, and traded. In these areas, as well as in Newtown, the push was toward compact farms through consolidation of the individual holdings that the town had parcelled out in widely dispersed strips.[3]

The exchange of strips of land signalled the end of experiments with open-field farming. Newtown, which never was committed to an open-field system, quickly lost what little interest it had. Whereas, in 1667, eleven townsmen had voluntarily agreed to plant "in one common field," each maintaining a portion of the common fence, this was the last mention of open fields. Shortly afterward these lands must have been given to the individuals involved.[4]

Those who look for conservatism and community in New England often cite the frequent establishment of open fields as evidence supporting their findings, but, while open fields sometimes coexisted with closed fields, there was a move away from this form of economic and social organization. Sumner Chilton Powell noted that in Sudbury, "younger sons . . . were undoubtedly influenced by the fact that the Watertown farmers, by 1655, had almost completely changed to individual farm management." In Andover also, the change began in the 1650s and, by 1662, "it was evident that the open-field system of the first two divisions was permanently abandoned."[5]

Gifts, which made up another 8 percent of transactions, and exchanges comprised a relatively small part of the land transfers. As Greven found in Andover, a father might let his sons use the land they would inherit, but few who owned land wanted to give it away free and clear. William Hallett Sr., with his large land holdings, by local standards, was an exception. In 1688, aged seventy-two and recognizing that both William Jr. and Samuel were settled adults, he gave them each the 150-acre farms upon which they already lived. This generous bequest still left him enough property to sustain himself and preserve his independence.[6]

Most townsmen purchased their land. Of the 351 land transactions in this period, 84 percent were sales. This figure is close to the 87 percent for all Newtown sales. Perhaps even more important than these raw figures, however, are the kinds and amounts of acreage sold. Each townsman needed a home lot upon which he built his house, barns, and other outbuildings and planted a garden and orchard. Beyond the house lot, but not necessarily attached to it, the farmer needed upland, meadow, and woods. He might also have some swamp. Whole farms, meadow, upland, and upland and meadow combined comprised 83 percent of these transactions. People were either buying and selling farms or putting farms together. This ability to fashion a farm piece by piece would diminish over time. While 26 percent of these transactions were for meadow, only 15 percent of all transactions involved meadow. Indeed, meadow, the scarcest of crucial land forms, would be the first type of land to disappear from the market. On the other hand, upland, given in these years through various town land divisions, would not reach its sales peak until later. Twenty-five percent of the 1665–91 conveyances were upland, but the total percentage is 30 percent.

The size of the holdings conveyed also showed distinctive patterns. Of the 152 conveyances that noted size, over one-half were for plots ten acres or less, and 79 percent were for plots twenty acres or less. These conveyances are a bit smaller than the transactions as a whole. The most striking difference shows in the 21–50-acre range where the sample shows 11 percent and the total 19 percent. Only six transactions include lands of over one hundred acres, and two of these are Hallett's. Newtowners in these years were not selling or buying large properties. Meadow lots and home lots were usually small, and even the farms were modest. This pattern is further support for the rough equality the tax lists show. Farming on a grand scale never existed in Newtown, even for those better off.

Gift and sale are two ways to acquire land. Inheritance is the third, and probably the surest. Lands changed hands legally at death, even if the real occupation of property preceded the owner's demise. Between 1665 and 1691, twenty-five wills were probated. Of these, twenty-one mentioned land.

Sons were favored to get land in the redistribution of Newtown property. In the largest number of cases, as in New England, all sons received some acreage. This provision for all living male heirs, made possible by adequate land holdings, put into practice what English yeomen also tried to do. Both Margaret Spufford, who studied land and inheritance in Cambridgeshire, and Cecily Howell, who looked at the Midlands, agree that fathers tried to provide for their wives and all of their children. In the process, "the sharp legal distinction between unigeniture and partible inheritance becomes somewhat blurred." Indeed, as land became more limited in the eighteenth century, townsmen would fall back upon the English (and possibly Dutch) practice of leaving one son the land, but saddling this legacy with bequests for the other heirs, or selling the land and distributing the monies which it brought. In Newtown, only Abraham Rick, who wrote his will in 1688, left all of his lands to one son, and that son, Abraham, was to pay the legacies to his brothers and sister. This request, and the estate that went with it, were peculiar for a number of reasons. First, Rick, or Riker as the family would become known, was Dutch, and the Dutch usually provided for all sons. Second, Rick was a comparatively prosperous townsman. In 1667, when he would have been in his fifties, he ranked nineteenth of seventy-eight on a tax list. Yet his estate of £13 13s. was hardly worth inventorying. He had probably already distributed most of his property before his death since he was past seventy and left his children only twenty-five to thirty shilling legacies. His son Abraham, who inherited his Newtown estate, was his fourth son, not his first or his last. Indeed, both his first and last sons took the surname Lent, not Rick or Riker, and both, along with their brother Jacob Riker, moved to Westchester County. The third son, John, later moved to New Jersey.[7]

There is little evidence to suggest that fathers overtly used the land to control their children. Only James Way Sr. made any threats, and there it is clear that he was concerned not only for his son, but for his son's family. Way noted that "my will is that except my son Francis do turn and amend his life his said part is to remain in those man's hands as I shall depute and think fit for the relieving of his wife and children." Philip Greven's emphasis on patriarchal control through property fails to surface in either Newtown or various other places. Linda Auwers Bissell found that prospects for inheritance had little to do with marriage age, a connection that Greven saw as proof of paternal authority, and that Windsor had few prodigal sons. She goes so far as to state that there was no evidence of economic manipulation, as described by Greven. Joyce Goodfriend suggests that the New York City Dutch married earlier and had fewer constraints than their Andover counterparts. She found only one instance of a father disinheriting his son for disobedience.[8]

Women possessed little land in Newtown. In 25 percent of the wills land was left to all children including daughters. Wives did less well. In only 12 percent of the wills did widows acquire real property that then became theirs to dispose of. Instead, they were given the use of land until their death or remarriage. Three women noted land in their wills, but it is unclear if they actually controlled the property or were just reiterating their deceased husbands' wishes. Elizabeth Burroughs gave to her son, John, "all that his father John Burroughs gave him in his will," and a look at John Sr.'s will shows that his wife never actually owned the farm but had its use until either young John came of age or she remarried. During her widowhood the land could not be sold, even though she no longer managed it after her son reached his majority.[9]

The twenty-five wills which survive for this period contain only two wills by Dutchmen who left widows, but work by David Narrett suggests that, initially, Dutch and English inheritance patterns differed. As the Dutch became more acculturated, their widows were given less of the estate, in conformity with English practice. In the two Newtown wills, one Dutch widow, Johannah Berrien, got all of the personal goods and one-half of the lands and chattels of Cornelius Janson Berrien. Hannah Buckhout fared less well. The only property left for her sole use was "liberty of five pounds . . . to any friend or friends she shall think fit."[10]

Women were outside of the mainstream of land ownership, but so, in this agrarian community, were some men. The problem lies in determining how many. Robert Ritchie, utilizing the 1683 tax lists, which gave the acreage of upland and meadow actually laid out to townsmen, found that for the colony as a whole, 15 percent of English townsmen and as many as 24 percent of Dutch townsmen were landless. Unfortunately, these figures are problematic since people might be landowners at one time but not at others. Newtown's 1675, 1678, and 1683 tax assessments list land. In 1675, seven, or 8.5 percent, of the taxpayers (not all the inhabitants) were landless. However, by 1678, three years later, three of these men had acquired some real estate; one had moved; one had disappeared from the records and two remained landless, not only on this list but also the next and in the land transactions. One of these men, Eleazer Leverich, son of the town's well-respected minister, had other problems that suggest he was less than able to care for himself. Sued for divorce in 1670 on the grounds of impotence, he lost both case and wife, and eventually moved to Newtown, where his family lived.[11]

The 1678 tax list, which contains 102 names, 21 more than the 1675 list, has 16, or 16 percent, of its taxables landless. Four will have land by the 1683 list, 2 had paid taxes on land in the 1675 list, and 4 others show up amidst the land transactions. Of the 16, then, 10 have land at some point, 3 disappear, and 3 men listed as landless in 1678 continue to be landless in 1683. Of these 3, 2 had already appeared without property in 1675. By 1683, the number of men enrolled on the tax list had dropped to 90. Seven were listed as without real property, but 2 had owned land in the 1678 list, and an additional 2 others appeared in the land records. Only 3 of the 7, 2 still holding over from 1675 and 1 from 1678, seem never to have held land. In sum, of the 25 who appeared on at least one tax list as landless, 15, or 60 percent, can be traced as land owners at some point in their careers.

Those without land would have to rent or work for others. Information on tenantry is lacking although some renters surely existed. Those who supplied Newtown's labor could be free, servant, or slave. Free labor was hired by the day, or week, or for some specific task. In 1669, Thomas Wandall hired Swaine Andreis to work during hay season. Andreis was paid at a daily rate but took his wages in commodities, namely, shirts and cans of rum. Nathaniel Pettit dressed flax for John Firman. Townsmen also utilized more permanent helpers than local day laborers. Some yeomen had indentured servants. Robert Williams was indentured to Mr. John Rider, while James Way's inventory noted both a maid servant for seven years and a boy servant for two years. Some had Indian and black slaves. Indeed, by 1687, these bondsmen outnumbered servants forty-nine to thirty-one. Both numbers would increase by the 1698 census.[12]

Male slaves served as farm laborers and were often given to sons or left with the widow to help her on the farm. In 1688, William Hallett gave Haney, Ginny, and the mulatto boy, Sam, to his son Samuel. John Alburtis specified that his two sons were to have his two "Negro boys," while Theophilus Phillips noted that his Negro was to live with his widow for ten years before going to his eldest son.[13]

Blacks were not the only slaves in Newtown. Indians also made up a part, although a very small part, of the unfree labor force. Jonathan Strickland's Indian boy was part of his estate, just like any horse or cow. He was valued at £10 in 1691.[14]

The presence of a slave force in Newtown had both economic and social implications. Just the appearance of slaves meant that townsmen had access to that far-reaching and sophisticated marketing system known as the slave trade. The terminus through which Newtowners would purchase slaves was New York City. Moreover, buying a slave implied that townsmen had goods or credits of sufficient kind and amount to pay New York merchants. No other commodity shows townsmen's integration into a transatlantic economy so clearly as black slaves.

Slavery was also part of townsmen's world view, and Newtowners accepted without question a separate, servile population. No will set slaves free or took any notice of slaves possessing rights. Slave holdings were broken up at the death of the master rather than kept intact. This meant not only a dispersal of slaves among the white population in each generation, but also the reordering of a slave's social and familial life. The same was not true of white servants, who would serve their time and gain their freedom. Indeed, gaining freedom probably caused the demise of a servant population since servants would have to be replaced. As the Chesapeake settlers learned, "as life expectancy rose, the slave became a better buy than the servant." By the end of the seventeenth century this process was well underway in Newtown.[15]

Slaves represented substantial percentages of the total value of those inventories in which they are found. James Way's Negro man, valued at £30, was his most valuable possession. The same was true for Elizabeth Stadum, Cornelius Janson Berrien, and John Alburtis. The inventories show the agricultural base of Newtown's economy, which depended upon mixed agriculture supplemented by small numbers of livestock. John Burroughs' inventory included Indian corn, oats, hay, and tobacco. John Graves had four acres of winter wheat, one and one-half acres of summer wheat, and three and one-half acres of meadow. James Way also had cider.[16]

Animals included horses, oxen, cattle, sheep, and pigs. The 1675 tax list shows that eighty-two townsmen owned 104 horses, 131 oxen, 508 cattle, 519 sheep and 164 swine. Eight years later ninety townsmen owned 136 horses, 167 oxen, 709 cattle, 464 sheep, and 100 swine. John Burroughs kept eight hives of bees.[17]

Newtown's economy was mixed farming, but in the years 1665 to 1691 some experimenting was done with sheep and a fledgling wool and cloth industry. The tax lists clearly show the importance of sheep. In 1675, at least forty-nine, or 60 percent of Newtown's tithables, owned sheep. Some, like John Firman and Thomas Robarts, only held one or two animals, but Thomas Wandall was taxed for a flock of eighty-one sheep, and both Gershom Moore and John Ketcham paid for thirty. By 1683, townsmen owned fewer sheep overall, but 64 percent of the men on the list owned at least one animal. Wandall's flock was down to forty, and only John Smith held as many as thirty. These men might well have come from sheep-raising and textile areas in England. Indeed, textiles also appear in the inventories. James Way Sr.'s inventory contains the usual animals, wheat, yokes, cart chains, and household goods, but it also notes woolen yarn, 21 yards of homespun cotton cloth, 9 and one-half yards of homespun cotton cloth, 27 yards of homemade wool and cotton cloth, and 43 yards of oznaburg, a coarse linen. The large holdings of cotton are further evidence, in addition to slaves, of Newtown's integration into the Atlantic mercantile community, since, as David Grayson Allen points out in a discussion of cotton in Rowley, "no place closer than the Barbados could have supplied them with it during much of the seventeenth century." In 1691, recognizing the potential benefits of a local fulling mill, the town gave Thomas and Edward Stevenson Lodwicke Brook and sufficient land on it for the mill. This mill, land, and stream were theirs, "as their own right to have and to hold to them and theirs for ever" in exchange for doing "the town's work first and as reasonable as other workmen do." These strictures represented town responsibility and concern. The Stevensons would keep the mill for a few years, but it never became their sole source of income. By 1723, it had ceased to exist.[18]

Newtown offered little besides agriculture as a full-time occupation; however, townsmen could work at other skills on a part-time basis. The crafts townsmen plied were fairly simple: blacksmith, tailor, mason, carpenter, and brickmaker. All brought in extra money, or more likely, credit towards goods. Women also contributed to the household economy. For example, Goodwife Owen apparently fed and washed the clothing of John Napper and Richard Osborn for a summer, for twenty shillings each. Yet, what did forty shillings mean? Was that a lot or a little? In 1683, Mistress Owen could have purchased 10 bushels of wheat, or 6 sheep, or 2 pigs, or 120 pounds of beef. In 1667, a day's labor was worth from two to five shillings. However, in 1670, John Alburtis made himself twelve shillings for two days of cutting and thrashing peas. In 1669, a man with a team of oxen earned five shillings a day. Some prices show how far those monies might have gone. In 1682 rum sold for eight shillings a gallon and wool for 1s. 6d. per pound. Two years later a yard of blue and white oznaburg sold for one shilling a yard, so that five yards of cloth equalled about one bushel of wheat. That same year a sheep sold for eight shillings, which equalled eight yards of cloth, which equalled one gallon of rum.[19]

Newtown's yeomen were tied into and would remain part of the general economic life of colonial New York. During the Dutch period they had access to the New York City market. This economic niche remained open throughout the colonial period and was further expanded by market and fair days. In 1673 both a market and fair were ordered for the first Monday, Tuesday, and Wednesday in November at the Brooklyn Ferry, and a second market and fair were ordered on the first Thursday, Friday, and Saturday in November in the city. Taxes were also payable in wheat, rye, peas, corn, oats, beef, and pork at fixed rates in lieu of scarce hard money.[20]

Lack of cash combined with the personal nature of a small-scale economy to create book debts that tied townsmen to one another and to outsiders. This complex pattern of payment, which occurred everywhere and at all economic levels, caused confusion when it broke down. In 1669 David Thomas sued William Wyatt for "an action of debt." The testimony of witnesses showed that Thomas demanded forty shillings, but Wyatt had offered him thirty shillings of Richard Osborne's and the rest "some where else." Thomas refused this solution, claiming "he would take no man's pay but Wyatt's." The courts agreed with Thomas—debts were not legal tender—and ordered Wyatt to pay him forty shillings. The original debt was unspecified, but William Wyatt was obviously both creditor and debtor, and he tried to use his credit from a third party to pay his debt to David Thomas. What is also clear is that Richard Osborne was outside Thomas's network of economic interaction. If Thomas had taken Wyatt's debt from Richard Osborne, and not been satisfied, he might have sued Osborne, thus further complicating the issue.[21]

A second, later example clearly illustrates how the system worked. The court entry reads in full:

I Thomas Barker do engage in the presence of the court to pay unto John Woolstonecrafts the sum of 25s. 6d. upon the account of John Bull to be paid at John Alburtis of Maspeth Kill between this date and the Last of December next ensuing witness my hand the 7th of November 1682 Thomas Barker.[22]

Debt appears with increasing frequency in Newtown's court records and also in the extant court records of other towns. Before 1675 32 percent of cases before the town court involved debt. After 1675 that percentage climbed to 55 percent. Langdon Wright tabulated court cases from five towns, including Newtown, and from Kings and Queens County, from 1647 to 1706. He found that 46.5 percent of all cases were for debts. And yet this seems to be a sign of increased economic activity and social cohesion rather than of glaring inequality. The notion of debt was much more inclusive in the seventeenth century. Instead of suggesting usury and mortgages, with their implicit economic inequalities between creditor and debtor, debt seems to be any kind of unfulfilled agreement. The exchange may be in terms of goods, labor, or even services like education. There is nothing to suggest that interest was levied. That term does not appear, although "damages," compensation for time and trouble apart from the original agreement, could be awarded to the injured party. Even the term "debt by bill," which calls to mind formal loans, can refer to the written proof of a transaction. There is no evidence of debtor or creditor "classes."[23]

The rural economy of seventeenth-century Newtown allowed little real wealth to accumulate even as economic differentiation was beginning. There are several ways to measure this economic equality. First, there are the tax lists. Wealth inequality can be measured by calculating what percentage of the wealth measured by the list is held by what percentage of the population, and how far this distribution is from total equality. A measurement of this difference between the real wealth distribution and equality is known as a Gini coefficient (see chap. 2, n. 9). Six of Newtown's tax lists can be scored for Gini coefficients. As Table 2 shows, they all fall below .5, and all but one are below .4. Although not as low as the .190 of the 1662 list, which must be based solely on land, they still seem remarkably homogeneous. Judging by the tax lists, Newtown's distribution of wealth was fairly even.

G. B. Warden has compared the Gini scores of Salem and Suffolk County, Massachusetts, Chester County, Pennsylvania, and Boston for the seventeenth century. Salem and

TABLE 2

Seventeenth-Century Newtown Gini Coefficients

TAX LIST	NUMBER	GINI
1666	66	.3687
1667A	62	.3649
1667B	78	.4231
1675	79	.3142
1678	102	.3423
1683	89	.3105

SOURCE: *Town Minutes,* I, 47, 79, 96–97, 19–20; *DHNY* II, 266–267, 298–299; New York Colonial Manuscripts 28:17b.

Suffolk County scores are based on probate wealth, the Boston and Chester County scores on tax assessments. His findings are summarized in Table 3. They suggest that inventories show greater inequality than tax lists, and that rural Chester has greater equality than urban Boston. The Newtown Gini coefficients are closer to Chester County than they are to Boston.[24]

Probate records, especially inventories, also measure the range of economic statuses. These records can be problematic, because they usually appear for an older, wealthier sample of individuals, not a random sample or the whole population. Newtown's inventories are skewed toward older townsmen, but not toward the very old. Many are in their prime years. Between 1665 and 1691, at least 55 men and nine women died in Newtown. Of these 64 decedents, only 14 left behind inventories which give property values. Five ages at death are known from the 14. Two were in their forties, one in his fifties, one in his sixties and one in his seventies. Another three had grandchildren, making them at least in their late forties or early fifties. Jonathan Strickland had an adult son by his death, but mentioned a son-in-law eleven years before his death. He was probably in his fifties. Nicholas Eddes' wife

TABLE 3

Comparative Seventeenth-Century Gini Coefficients

YEAR	SOURCE	GINI
1687	Boston	.5312
1635–1661	Salem	.4720
1661–1681	Salem	.6040
1695–1697	Suffolk County	.5070
1693	Chester County	.2598

SOURCE: G. B. Warden, "Inequality and Instability in Boston," *Journal of Interdisciplinary History*, 6 (1976), 602–603.

was born around 1641. Since wives in New England were usually about the same age, or a few years younger, than their husbands, he would have been in his late forties. Cornelius Janson Berrien still had an underage child, as well as adult children, and John Lorison had a son of about nineteen. John Graves was the still unmarried son of decedent William Graves. Only for the one woman, Elizabeth Stadum, is there absolutely no data. In sum, a reasonable guess would put only one of the deceased under age forty, with most of the others probably in their forties or fifties. This assumption is strengthened by the tax lists that show that most of the deceased were among the top one-half of the list, as befitted men in the fullness of their lives.[25]

Given that solid, substantial townsmen left behind the inventories that survive, the low value of some of these inventories is striking. Omitting land values, which only appeared in the four estates listed before 1679, the inventories ranged from the £14 of Abraham Rick, to the £258 of Cornelius Janson Berrien. They had a mean value of £98. Five inventories were under £50, the legal point at which an inventory must be taken, and five were over £150.

Land, obviously, made up a good part of an estate; indeed, more than half for William Graves and Thomas Ro-

98

barts. And yet, from 1665 to 1691 what separated the higher
from the lower inventories, and probably the better-off from
the less well-endowed townsmen, was the quantity and variety of everyday goods rather than the ownership of rare luxury items. The wealthier had chests and tables and more
clothing, and Elizabeth Stadum had a black silk gown. But
there is no mention of plate, jewelry, velvets, carriages, or
other such high status possessions. Cornelius Berrien's household goods were worth £59. The other £199 of his estate were
wheat and barley, his Negro girl, his livestock, and his wag-
ons. He owned twenty printed books valued at £1 5s. John Alburtis' inventory listed about £35 for household goods, which
included pewter dishes, an old Bible, and three old books.
Jonathan Strickland's household goods were worth about £19.
His feather bed, bedstead, and furniture composed £5 10s. of
this. Other goods included a sword, pistols, chairs, and old
pewter. He also had two canoes, a cart, livestock worth £25
1s., and an Indian boy slave. Richard Fido's household was
valued at £7. It included bedding and some pewter. Most of
his estate was in cattle and a servant with one and one-half
years of time left. Thomas Robarts' household was worth £6.
He owned a bed and bedding, a brass kettle, iron pots, and
two pewter porringers, as well as woodenware, a gun, sword,
farm implements, and £1 10s. worth of clothing. The elderly
poor could have even less. Abraham Rick had four cows and
almost nothing else, but he was an old man who had probably
dispersed his properties while he was alive. His family did
well in Newtown. Nicholas Eddes' personal belongings, besides his cattle, amounted to about £4. They included bedding, a chest, two chairs, some old trays "and other things,"
and a pot.[26]

By 1691, Newtown had some inhabitants who were less
well-off, but it is hard to know what that actually meant. The
poor would have fewer and more basic goods, and those items
might be old or broken. The poor might also have eaten less

well. In one of Newtown's few adultery cases, John Firman's wife was accused of stealing her husband's oats and peas and giving them to John Cochran. The testimony read: "Good wife Firman did several times bring a bushel or a bushel and half of meal to bake into bread and she would take home one loaf of them and let John Cochran have the rest to supply his family when they had no bread [or] corn but was fain to eat coddled appl[es] or the like." Coddled apples apparently were less than satisfactory fare.[27]

Those less well-off also had less land. The town records note the setting off of part of Traine's meadow for sale to poorer townsmen, and in 1685 some unnamed persons, styling themselves "poor inhabitants of Newtown," petitioned the governor complaining that the monopoly of lands in town kept them from procuring wood for either fireplace or fence. Yet, "poor" is a relative term, and those "poor" felt self-confident enough to petition the governor. Few people were destitute, and those who needed help were old, young and orphaned, or otherwise infirm.[28]

By law the poor were ultimately the responsibility of the town, but the town had no specialized institutions to help them. Few institutions existed anywhere. New York City did not build a poorhouse until 1735, and Newtown, without the problems of a major urban center, first appointed poor masters and built a poor house in 1784 after the British occupation ended. Without institutions to aid those unable to care for themselves, the first line of defense was the family. It helped if those needing attention had property; they were expected to pay their way if they could. Thomas Pettit, apparently hoping to avoid intruding upon his children, agreed in court that John Firman, in return for property, would maintain him "during the term of his natural life," but this arrangement either proved unsatisfactory or inimical to family interests. John Pettit, Thomas' son, "with the consent and approbation of my father Thomas Pettit and likewise the court, have received my said father from John Firman." In return for caring for

Thomas, John acquired "all my father's goods according to our agreement & also a parcel of cod or meadow with an assignment of a bill of sale for the same, & a young mare come three years old, & two yearling steers, & one two-year-old heifer which is in full satisfaction for my maintaining my father during his life." This arrangement, which sounds so mercenary not mentioning any filial affection, might well have saved old Thomas' pride. It acknowledged that he still had the resources with which to provide for himself, even if he no longer had the strength.[29]

Where there were no families, the town stepped in, sometimes helped or prodded by outsiders. In New York, the various churches were often responsible for looking after the unfortunate. The Dutch instituted this system. The Dutch Reformed church payed for "kronkenbesoeckers," or visitors of the sick, and "sieckentroosters," comfortors of the sick. The almshouse, where the impoverished elderly could go, was the deacon's house. The English under the Duke's Laws vested responsibility for the poor with the parishes, but few parishes really functioned. The Dutch Reformed, the Lutherans, and the Quakers continued to oversee care for their own; otherwise counties, towns, secular parishes, or precincts took charge. As David Schneider points out, New York's poor relief was a hodgepodge differing from place to place and time to time, each case being decided on an individual basis. Other places, like Plymouth, Massachusetts, seem equally unorganized.[30]

In 1684 Henry Sartell sold his property of a house, ten-acre lot, and some salt meadow. Within two years it was obvious to his Quaker brethren that Sartell was now unable to care for himself, and they appointed a committee to meet with Newtown and see what could be done. The committee and town agreed that the sale should be voided, and the town authorities agreed to go to court to annul it, realizing that Sartell would become the town's responsibility. As the Quaker meeting noted in their charge to the delegation, it was "to speak with the authority of Newtown to signify the condition of

Henry Sartell unto them that they may take care of him that he do not suffer want." Henry Sartell's land must have been restored, for he found a solution to his needs that spared everyone expense. In 1692, now an elderly widower, he made over his house, orchard, meadow, and personal property to his grandson in exchange for "the maintenance of me with good and sufficient meat, apparel, washing, lodging, and attendance during my natural life." In 1704 he died, presumably still in the care of his grandson.[31]

Henry Sartell must have been an old man when he died. And he probably had the company of those of like generation. The Newtown records are too sparse to calculate age at death, but evidence from New England suggests that people lived long lives. In Andover, over 60 percent of males born between 1640 and 1669, and 70 percent of males born between 1670 and 1699, reached sixty. Women died earlier. About one-half of those born between 1640 and 1669, and 60 percent of those born between 1670 and 1699, lived to be sixty. Plymouth residents also did well. Of 645 seventeenth-century deaths, 76 percent of the males and 59 percent of the females lived to be sixty or older.[32]

Care of the elderly, as well as of the young, required flexible living patterns as people moved through their life cycles. Over the course of an individual's lifetime, he would first live with his own parents. Later a grandparent might move in, as happened in John Pettit's family, or the family might go to live in an elderly grandparent's home. If he married, he would establish his own household and then have children. At some point his own parents, or a widowed parent, might live with him and his own children marry and move out. In old age he would live with one of his children, or perhaps, as did Henry Sartell, one of his grandchildren. Often wills assumed that the wife still lived in her home with the child who inherited it. Or, as in Sartell's case, the property might be given to a kinsman in exchange for maintenance.[33]

Even given the time in the life of the family when a relative lived in, the nuclear family of husband, wife, and their children was most common in Newtown. Newtown's 1675, 1678, and 1683 tax lists tithed polls over sixteen. Only 12 to 16 percent of Newtown's households listed more than one adult male. These additional men could have been widowed fathers, unmarried sons, servants, or slaves.[34]

The nuclear family was apparently the norm in other colonial settlements and in England as well. Lawrence Stone characterized the period 1580 to 1640 as the heyday of the "Restricted Patriarchal Nuclear Family," a family characterized by less reliance on kin and increased control by the father. In Plymouth, Demos found that newlyweds were expected to live apart from family, and wills left houses to one heir, not many jointly. Linda Auwers Bissell estimated that about two-thirds of Windsor families were nuclear.[35]

Some people married more than once. William Hallett Sr. married four times. Few others shared his marital experience. Of those born between 1610 and 1789, records survive for only 349 males who married. Of the 349, thirty-six, or 10 percent, married more than once, and the majority of those remarriages occurred in the eighteenth century. This figure is remarkably low—too low, perhaps. Linda Auwers Bissell found that one-third of her seventeenth-century population married more than once. Of Philip Greven's thirty-four first generation males, 32 percent married more than once. His third generation figures for 152 males ranged from 30 to 36 percent. Demos found that anywhere between 40 and 45 percent of his seventeenth-century males, and 26 to 31 percent of his females, married more than once.[36]

Marriage was a serious business. Under the Duke's Laws the couple must have gotten a license from the governor; or had the banns published three times, or read three times in church; or tacked up on the doors of the constable and two overseers. A minister or the justice of the peace could perform the ceremony.[37]

Marriage undoubtedly involved more than just two people deciding to marry. It was also an economic arrangement that redistributed property. No marriage contracts survive for Newtown, but the wills note the financial obligations that marriage implied. By law, the widow was entitled to one-third of a man's estate, "in lieu of dower," the goods she had brought to the marriage. Underlying this provision is the assumption that women were the responsibility of men. They, like children, must be cared for during their lives. Lambert Woodward noted that his wife, Sarah, was to have her proportion while she remained a widow, and James Way Sr. left his wife, Ede, one-half of all his properties until she died or remarried. A husband could manage a wife's resources as his own unless these properties specifically excluded him. John Stevenson died childless leaving his goods to his brothers and sisters, but he stipulated that his sister's "present husband, Patrick Hare, have nothing to do with these legacies."[38]

Marriage united families by joining two kinship networks. This union implied social obligations; therefore it was best to marry within one's own social and religious sphere. The possible exogamic combinations in Newtown were racial (blacks, whites, and Indians), ethnic ("Dutch" and English), and religious (congregationalist, Dutch Reformed, and Quaker). The first was unthinkable. Not a single case of interracial marriage surfaced in any of the records. Mulattoes are noted in Newtown wills, but nothing else was said. Ethnic intermarriage was possible but unlikely in seventeenth-century Newtown. Of fifty-eight marriages known to have taken place prior to 1691 in which the first and last names of both husband and wife are known, only six might be considered mixed, and of these six, two are not clear-cut. Of the four obvious cases of mixed marriages, the husband was English three times and Dutch once.[39]

Undoubtedly, ethnic endogamy was the preferred form of marriage. Joyce Goodfriend found that of 110 marriages performed in North America before 1665, 75 percent were endogamous, while the remaining 25 percent were between

Dutch, German, French, and others. Later information shows greater ethnic differentiation but some of this pattern is due to the lack of English records. Goodfriend also found that of 219 Dutch marriages, all were endogamous; of thirty-four French marriages, 77 percent were endogamous; and of twenty-two English marriages, 38 percent were endogamous. The scarcity of English women "must have played a major role in producing this unique pattern of behavior among the English in New York City." In Newtown, where English women were available, English men married them.[40]

Since religious groups and ethnic groups could be the same—most Dutch Reformed churchmen were Dutch—it follows that there was little crossing of that barrier. That leaves the Quakers and the congregationalists. The Quakers, a besieged minority, insisted that Quakers marry Quakers. When Robert Field Jr. decided to marry the widow Phebe Scudder of Hempstead, Long Island:

> [They] having laid their intentions before two several meetings of our men and women being called by the name of Quakers, and persons having been appointed by the said meeting to make diligent inquiry of their clearness from all others as in relation to marriage, and at their second coming before our meeting, all things being found clear and with consent of parents and relations the said meeting firmly consents to their proceedings. And at the house of Edward Titus . . . at a meeting of the people of God called Quakers appointed for the same purpose, the parties aforesaid Robert Field and Phebe Scudder did stand up and solemnly declare themselves husband and wife, promising to each other to live together in love and faithfulness til death shall separate.

That leaves the congregationalists who had to marry each other. Racial, ethnic, and religious barriers served to promote homogeneity, even though intra-group connections transcended town boundaries.[41]

Phebe and Robert Field, married in 1690 at her father's home in Hempstead, had no children but remained together until he died in 1735. She lived until 1743. Others found it harder to remain together, despite the premium placed upon domestic harmony and the difficulty of ending a marriage. The law recognized few grounds for the dissolution of marriage, but among these were impotence, desertion, bigamy, and adultery. The case of Eleazer and Rebecca Leverich illustrates the care and concern which the courts had for those with insoluble difficulties. Eleazer Leverich of Huntington, later Newtown, had married Rebecca Wright of Oyster Bay in 1662. Trouble began shortly afterward, "he the said husband hath not performed conjugal rights unto his wife, but on the contrary has caused her to lead a very uncomfortable life with him." In 1669, Rebecca, "by the hands of her father," since she had no legal persona in her own right, petitioned Governor Francis Lovelace to dissolve the marriage. Lovelace appointed a committee to hear complaints and gave it the power to employ anybody "skillful in such matters to make inquiry into the defect and impediments alledged." Six months later Lovelace granted the divorce, and Eleazer was ordered to pay Rebecca £25 in living cattle, "in lieu of what she brought to him at their marriage."[42]

The Leverich divorce decree makes clear the functions marriage ideally served in colonial New York society:

> that she having been his reputed wife for the space of seven years and a half, she has not in all that time received any due benevolence from her said husband according to the true intention of matrimony, the great end of which is not only to extinguish those fleshly desires and appetites incident to human nature but likewise for the well ordering and confirmation of the right of meum and tuum to be

devolved upon the posterity lawfully begotten betwixt man and wife.

Marriage thus served human as well as civil needs. Human nature propelled both men and women to gratify their
desires, and marriage provided the arena wherein those desires could be appropriately and harmlessly acted out. Moreover, but not solely, marriage insured legitimate offspring access to the property of their parents. Both lust and children
were proper within the bonds of matrimony.[43]

Not everyone restricted their drives to the marriage bed.
In 1672, Thomas Pettit appeared before the Court of Assizes
and charged his wife, Sarah, with "frequent committing of
adultery which before diverse persons she hath had the impu-
dence to avow without any apparent cause given by her husband, for the which he hath made suit that he may be divorced
from her." She refused to appear before the court, which
found for Pettit, noting that when and if Sarah were found she
was to be tried and punished for adultery.[44]

Thomas Pettit may have gotten his divorce because he
was a male. In other places there was a bias against women
who charged adultery. According to Nancy F. Cott, in Massachusetts the governor and council would grant a divorce to a
man whose wife had committed adultery, but not to a woman
whose only charge against her husband was adultery. She suggests a double standard of marital fidelity existed, at least in
Masachusetts, and probably elsewhere.[45]

The dissolution of marriage at all was unusual in most of
the colonies and would soon cease in New York. Matteo Spalletta notes that the last case of divorce in New York occurred
in 1675. Thereafter, marriage was indissoluble, a harsh fact
recognized in 1769 by Cadwallader Colden, who thought that
divorce was more easily obtained elsewhere. Massachusetts
and Connecticut, perhaps in reaction to England's ecclesiastical courts, which had jurisdiction over marriage, made divorce
a civil matter. Even so, divorce was rare. In Connecticut be-

tween 1664 and 1732, only thirty-seven divorces were granted, while in Massachusetts, only twenty-seven cases occurred before 1735. Other colonies had even fewer divorces, and where the Church of England was established there were none.[46]

New York, Massachusetts, and Connecticut recognized the same general grounds for dissolving a marriage. While impotence and adultery were one thing, simple incompatibility was another. William Hallett and his second wife, Susannah, found life together intolerable. They appeared in court in 1669, and, although the Sessions acknowledged that they could not stay under the same roof, it refused to allow a divorce. Instead, they were to live apart, he maintaining her at £15 per year. This arrangement proved too expensive to Hallett, and in June, 1674, he asked that the separation be ended. By September, the Halletts had still to resolve their difficulties and he asked that she either live with him peacefully or he be granted a divorce. In December, the court refused to rule and referred the case back to the governor. No divorce was ever recorded, nor was Susannah's death noted, but by 1684 William had remarried. Mortality had solved what human ingenuity could not.[47]

Marriage was the proper form of living arrangement, and neither adultery nor cohabitation was legal. Sarah Pettit faced jail, fine, and perhaps corporal punishment if she returned to New York. Mary Firman, who so kindly wined and dined John Cochran, fared better. She was made to acknowledge her fault to her husband before the court and to promise obedience. In 1674, Ralph Doxey and Mary Lynch, who lived together, were arrested and charged with illegal cohabitation. Apparently they married later. How prevalent either adultery or premarital sex were is impossible to say given the records, but there are few recorded cases of either.[48]

Premature pregnancy caused little trouble since the couple would most likely marry before the child was born and, therefore, be responsible for it. Unwed mothers presented a larger problem. If nobody took the burden of the child, it became a town charge. The July 1676 Court of Sessions saw a presentment by the constable of Newtown against a single pregnant woman. She claimed that John Lorison was the father; meanwhile, he had moved to Huntington. The court ordered the case be sent there. If found guilty, Lorison would support his illegitimate child. Sexual transgressions and bastardy are the nether side of adult life, but they occurred rarely. Most people behaved themselves, married, and then began a family.[49]

There are no household censuses before 1698 but that year 976 whites and blacks lived in 153 households for an average household size of 6.4 persons. If just the whites are counted, the average household size drops to 5.7 persons. Averages can be misleading, but probably are not in this case. The mode for the 153 households was 5 (26 households), and the median was 5.5. Put another way, 71 percent of all households contained less than 8 persons. The largest household, John Scudder's, held 19 whites and 4 slaves. Edward Stevenson's contained 17 whites and 4 slaves. But these numbers were unusual. In most households, 2 of the average 5.7 would be the husband and wife, while other relatives and servants would be among the 3.7. This seems to leave little room for children, even granting that not all children would be home at the same time since the oldest could well be marrying soon after the youngest arrived.[50]

The New England household looked similar. A Bristol, Rhode Island, census of 1689 distributed 421 persons among 70 families for an average of 6 people per family. Dedham had between 5.3 and 6 inhabitants per house. Robert V. Wells, after looking at 35 censuses, concluded that household size was stable throughout the American colonies in the colonial period and averaged between five and seven persons.[51]

If Newtowners were like their New England counterparts, as the wills and inventories suggest, then they lived long enough to create families, even though they lived in relatively small households. This natural increase, augmented by immigration, added to the population of Newtown, which doubled between 1656 and 1686. In 1656, there were about 308 settlers, not counting the Dutch on the outbounds. In 1686, there were about 723, counting at least some of those beyond the Indian purchase line.[52]

Newtown's population seems to have been more mobile in these years than earlier although figures are still within the range experienced by New England towns. Names from the 1667 and 1683 tax lists show that twenty-five, or 37 percent, remained as a crude persistence rate. Another twenty-two names can be accounted for through land records or genealogical materials. At least forty-seven, or 61 percent of those there in 1667, either lived in town by 1683 or had died there; 39 percent did not. Surnames also suggest a more mobile population. Of sixty-six surnames in the 1667 list, thirty-eight were gone by 1683. Twenty-nine new names appeared. Not surprisingly, those who disappear from the record are those with the least property stake in Newtown. Twenty-two, or 73 percent of those thirty taxpayers not accounted for, were listed on the bottom half of the 1667 tax list.[53]

Those who came to Newtown seem to have come from nearby settlements and not from England. Land records, which list the residence of both buyer and seller, note that people moved in from eastern Long Island, New York City, other Queens County towns, and Connecticut. They might well have been friends or relatives and were very much like those already there. Neighboring Jamaica showed the same pattern. Most of the sixty-two families who joined the community by 1670 were from Hempstead, Flushing, Oyster Bay, and Kings County.[54]

The relative homogeneity among settlers, even if people came from diverse parts of England with different local customs, and the lack of any newcomers from England after the Great Migration, had several implications for townsmen. First, Newtown never was faced with a sizable migration of those sufficiently different, either ethnically or religiously, to require integration or socialization. No one had to be reeducated. Second, Newtown, like the New England towns, but unlike the Chesapeake, found itself cut off from fresh infusions of English local culture. Like other immigrants, be they Dutchmen in New York, blacks in the rice-producing lowlands of South Carolina, or Germans in the various parts of the Pennsylvania backcountry, Newtowners found it impossible to reproduce "home." In the absence of new blood, they created a creole society shaped by English roots, memory, second-hand hearsay, and the half-hearted attempts by English governors to surround themselves with familiarity. The divergence of Anglo-America from England at the local level probably proceeded in many small, unrecognized ways, as new situations arose and old ways were forgotten.[55]

Even the Dutch, who retained some genuine cultural differences from the English, easily coexisted with them. Many Dutchmen spoke English, as well as Dutch, and attended a church derived from the same Calvinist tradition as the congregationalists. They named their children Dutch names, like Roeloff, Jans, and Tryntie. They chose godparents for their children who were fellow Dutchmen, and they married one another. Still, they shared the same agrarian adaptation, aspirations, and values as their English neighbors. John Murrin notes that western Long Island was one of the more acculturated areas, peopled by men who cooperated with the English. He calls them "Anglicizers." Joyce Goodfriend found a genuine cultural pluralism, in which legitimate differences were recognized and respected, if only because nothing could be done about them. This pluralism was reinforced by ethnically specific institutions, the most important of which was the church.[56]

Newtown was not a religious community in the same way that New England towns might be, yet the need for locally controlled, organized religion was keenly felt by townsmen. The earliest settlement had been founded by the Reverend Francis Doughty, a dissenting minister who did not remain long in Newtown. Neither did most of his successors.

Most of Newtown's inhabitants were dissenting Protestants. They formed the majority of townsmen and the nucleus of the town's religious life. The town had enjoyed the services of two ministers before 1665. The Reverend Leverich had gone from the town in 1665 after serving for three years; however, in 1668, the majority of inhabitants voted at a town meeting to recall him. Leverich agreed and stayed until his death in 1677.[57]

The following year Newtown searched around, and this time called Morgan Jones. Their choice was well-educated. Jones had attended Jesus College, Oxford, and had been ordained in Wales. A dissenter who lost his English parish in 1662, he had made his way to Virginia before coming to the attention of the town. On March 3, the townsmen voted that the constable and overseers hire him for a year "as reasonable as they can." The terms seem generous. He was promised £50 per annum in current merchantable pay, which probably means produce, and he was given meadow, upland, and the soon-to-be-renovated town house which still continued to serve a variety of purposes. These arrangements came to little, and Jones proved unsatisfactory. In 1686 he finally acquitted the town of all his debts, both from one year as their minister and as their school master. He had, by then, gone to Eastchester, where his bad luck pursued him and his two chests of books were sold by the sheriff of Westchester at public vendue. Newtown, meanwhile, did without a minister.[58]

The core of Newtown was dissenter. Surrounding this core were the Dutch-speaking freeholders who practiced the Dutch Reformed religion and accepted the sacraments from dominies licensed by the Classis of Amsterdam. No Queens County congregation existed in the seventeenth century, and as late as 1686 families who lived on the East River went to New York City, while those living closer to the Kings County

border attended church in Flatbush. Their religious commitment insured that they would interact with, and probably
marry, others whose residence, and therefore social and economic ties, transcended town boundaries and town resources.
In Massachusetts and Connecticut, where town and congregation were coterminus, town resources could usually support
only one church. Those who disagreed with that church still
were taxed for its maintenance and separation, creating a political issue dividing townsmen. Newtown's religious pluralism, wherein religious and political boundaries were openly
different, precluded this kind of strife.[59]

The Church of England made few inroads in Newtown
during the 1600s, and no Church of England minister or
teacher lived in Queens County prior to 1702. The history of
the Anglican church is tied to the political history of New
York and will be discussed in the next chapter.

In seventeenth-century Newtown, the Dutch Reformed
church appealed only to the Dutch, and the Protestant Episcopal church appealed to no one. The real threat to Newtown's
religious stability were the Quakers. Members of the Society
of Friends lived in New Netherland before the English conquest. There they had been tolerated, if not actually welcomed.
Under the English, this tolerance continued, and the Friends
were left in peace as long as they caused no disturbances.

Western Long Island was one of the earliest strongholds
of the Society and Flushing Monthly Meeting one of the first
organized in America. As many as four or five Newtown families may have belonged to Flushing Monthly Meeting, and, as
members of the Society, held meetings in their homes since no
church existed until later. The meetings shifted from town to
town in order to accomodate a widely dispersed congregation.

Quakers were close knit, perhaps because they were a
community of true believers, perhaps because they were har-
ried for their beliefs. When Henry Sartell needed help it was
his coreligionists who went to the town. Likewise, backsliding
and intemperate behavior became the concern of the whole

group. Those out of order were gently spoken to, and spoken to again if need be. At the quarterly meeting, Friends gave testimony against dancing, vanity, singing, and excessive drinking. They seemed like gentle folk, but there was another side to Quakerism, one which called for public witness against evil and gave emotional and physical expression to religious impulses.[60]

One Quaker, Thomas Case, had lived in Connecticut, but after marrying the Newtown widow Mary Meacock in 1662 he bought a house and land and moved to Newtown. The land records suggest that he prospered: the 1683 tax list shows him in the upper half. Mary and Thomas first came to public notice in 1674 when William Smith charged Thomas Case with detaining his wife. Apparently Mrs. Smith had attended meetings at Case's house without her husband's consent and against his wishes, thereby implicitly undermining his dominant place in the household. The court ordered Case to cease "entertaining" William Smith's wife.[61]

Thomas Case kept up his meetings, and he and Mary continued bearing witness. These sessions became revivals, with singing, shaking, talking in tongues, and falling faint to the floor. As one unsympathetic witness testified, they acted strange, "lying like dogs, hogs and cows." Mary Case took her mission to spread the truth beyond her own doors, and, entering the meeting house during services, said to the minister, "Come down thou whited wall, thou art one that feedest thyself and starvest the flock." The constable escorted her out.[62]

The behavior of Mary and Thomas Case was out of order. She was charged with disturbing a church service and fined. But the testimony against Thomas Case shows that more was at stake than upsetting holy worship. His trial reveals many levels of meaning by spotlighting cultural values. In the hearing against him he was accused of religious transgressions. These included unauthorized preaching and exhortation. He believed, as did all Quakers, in the immediate sense of the divine spirit, but, according to James Way, Case went further, calling himself God and foretelling that after death he would rise on the third day. These heresies were not Case's major danger to the community. Much more important were his crimes against society and the family, and it was for these, not religious error, that he was punished. He unlawfully detained wives from their husbands and both from their children. Mr. Cornell said that Case had withdrawn several from their households, and the families were "like to starve." Thomas Wandall made a similar charge, arguing in an unambiguously secular way that meetings could last for two weeks during which time many poor people stayed away from their homes and businesses. Sustaining the flesh came first; sustaining the spirit decidedly second. The Court of Assizes reacted to the civil charges. On October 13, 1675, Case was fined £20 and bound to good behavior until the next court. If he disturbed the peace he was to be jailed. By the next year, Case was in prison and three months later in solitary confinement, his frequent visitors having disturbed those living near the jail.[63]

Thomas Case eventually settled down, as did the rest of the Quakers. He disappeared from the court records and became just another townsman. He died childless in 1692 leaving all of his property to his wife and, upon her death, to his nephew William. Thomas Case disturbed the even tenor of town and family life and, as such, was a public menace. Others in Newtown also had trouble with authority and with each other although the source of their distress was secular, not religious. Their problems brought them to the attention of their neighbors and the provincial authorities. Townsmen apparently felt little reluctance to use the town court, or to go beyond the town and utilize the institutions available to them as inhabitants of New York province. Silence in the face of perceived wrong was not one of their values, but neither was litigiousness.[64]

From 1665 to 1691 the town court heard 449 cases in which date, plaintiff, and defendant can be identified. Ninety-four were unresolved, 70 were nonsuited or unknown, 29 were withdrawn, 200 were found for the plaintiff, 49 were found for the defendant, and 7 were awarded to neither. Debt accounted for 212 cases and actions for 86. In descending order, the other complaints were trespasses, disputes over ownership, property damage, broken contracts, boundary disputes, defamations, and slander. In other words, the overwhelming majority of cases concerned private property. Two-hundred and sixty-six persons appeared as either plaintiff or defendant, but they did not appear equally. One hundred and twenty-four persons appeared only once, and another forty-one twice. Thus over one-half of those in court came only once or twice in thirty-odd years. A few people were regular visitors, however, and their problems tell much about the social order.[65]

George Wood, the most frequent visitor to the town court, appeared thirty-nine times in fourteen years. His first case was in 1669 and his last in 1683. His records in court began shortly after his arrival in the town, which must have been in 1669 when he bought land and was identified in the land records as an inhabitant of Huntington. Wood was not a very successful litigant. He was the plaintiff twelve times but only won his case in three, and one of these three decisions he later lost on appeal. Five of his cases he lost outright, one he neither won nor lost, and three were not tried. He was sued twenty-seven times, more than anyone else who appeared before the bench. He fared little better as a defendant than as a plaintiff, losing seventeen cases and winning two. The other suits were either unknown, not tried, or not resolved by the court. The kinds of cases Wood was embroiled in show that he was a problem in the community. He was accused of slander, abuse, and having another falsely imprisoned. He also took those living closest to him to court six times over boundaries.

Wood must have been peculiar in other ways than being plain touchy. In a case instituted against him by Richard Fido in 1675, he refused to answer charges "upon these pretences that two of the overseers were brothers and the constable was uncle to one of them," yet, the record goes on, "none related to either plaintiff or defendant." The court found that this explanation made no sense, although it does demonstrate how closely related townsmen could be, and Wood forfeited the case. In 1669, the minutes noted:

> George Wood has misdemeaned himself by uncivil carriage and abusive words in the court to some of the members of the . . . . And he told Thomas Case that he was as good a man as he was and he would not hold his tongue in court for him although Thomas Case was a member of the court and several other miscarriages both then and at other times which was ordered to be entered.[66]

Wood's lack of restraint was sufficiently bothersome, disruptive, and disrespectful, when respect upheld social values, that in 1671 he was taken before the Court of Sessions for scurrilous language to the constable and overseers. By asking for public forgiveness, he was released on £20 recognizance. But he was before the court again in 1675 for abusing authority, and this case went on until 1677. By 1684, the last year he appears, his behavior had gotten him imprisoned in the county jail, from which he petitioned the council for release.[67]

John Woolstonecraft, who appeared in thirty-five cases, was first listed in the Newtown court records of 1669. His active years in the court ended in 1688, the last effective year of the court, and probably the year of his death. He first bought land in 1667 and was named in the bill of sale as a tailor from New York.[68]

John Woolstonecraft's history of court appearances is quite different from Wood's. He won eight cases and lost eight, in addition to which he was nonsuited for nonappearance three times. He paid for at least eleven cases over the years. Thirty-three of the thirty-five cases involved debts or actions. There were no personal attacks on anybody, nor any evidence of disrespect to the court.

The admittedly incomplete sources give three instances of Woolstonecraft's appearances before a higher court. One of these was in 1677, at his initiative, when he petitioned the Court of Sessions for a confirmation of ownership to land he bought at a public vendue ordered by the court. The second appearance, probably in 1685, was a £200 suit brought against him by John Henry of New York. The third suit involved major theft and defamation at Albany in 1667, and went against the defendant, John Woolstonecraft. If the defendant was Newtown's Woolstonecraft, he must have had far-flung communications, for he ranged from Albany to New York City. Indeed, his problems were those of the entrepreneur. He had trouble both paying for and collecting the goods and services owed him.[69]

Most of the attention that George Wood and John Woolstonecraft attracted was to themselves. Not so for John Burroughs, who in November of 1674 wrote a letter in the name of the town criticizing the government. Since Burroughs was the town clerk he had a certain authority to speak for the community. What the governor and council wanted to know was whether he represented himself or Newtown in this seditious behavior. The answer was that he spoke for both. Newtown, through its representative on the Court of Sessions, acknowledged its error and was done with it. Indeed, the town minutes are silent about the whole episode. John Burroughs, however, was in for a harder time, partially of his own making. In December, he had seen fit to write another letter, and on January 16, 1675, Newtown's constable, with Burroughs in hand, appeared as ordered before Governor Andros and the New York Council to answer charges of sedition. Burroughs was found guilty, but he was neither whipped nor fined. Instead, in a beautiful synthesis of the real and the symbolic, he was brought to the whipping post before the City Hall of New

York City "and there fastened, to stand an hour, with a paper on his breast setting forth the cause thereof to be for writing and signing seditious letters in the name of Newtown against the Government and Court of Assizes." He was also prohibited from holding any other offices. Since Burroughs died in 1678 it is hard to know if he would have been given further town responsibility. His public humiliation would presumably keep others from abusing authority and would also bring into the open those convicted of disaffection. Most important, it would demonstrate the authority and legitimacy of the state in imposing the sentence to begin with.[70]

Public apology and humiliation were tools necessary to maintain social order. Newtown still followed the pattern of small-scale personal societies that used shame and peer pressure. The town court obviously recognized the utility of this form of punishment for they used it in a variety of cases. As in the earlier period, a person's good name demanded protection, whether the charge against him was meant as an insult or as a specific comment on his behavior. When Mary Lorison and Elizabeth Moore had a disagreement, Mary vented her aggressions by slandering Elizabeth's father, Francis Doughty. He had, according to Mary Lorison, "got his living by cozening and cheating up and down the country." Doughty then sued her for defamation. Found guilty, her sentence was the public humiliation of standing before the court and admitting that she knew no such thing; that she had spoken in passion, and was sorry for the wrong that she had done him. In 1682, Miner Hendrickson implied that Thomas Lawrence branded others' cattle with his own mark. Called to answer for this accusation, he stood before the court and "does declare that he does not know any such thing by the said Lawrence and is sorry that he has related any such thing and does desire the said Lawrence to pass it by and forgive him." Lawrence was gracious enough to do so.[71]

When all the evidence is weighed, colonial Newtown was a remarkably peaceful place. So were many other towns.

Windsor, Connecticut, had little litigation between neighbors, and an intensive survey of New York's seventeenth-century court records led Langdon G. Wright to conclude that they show neither a "high or even unsettling amount of litigation." John Demos has written that Plymouth court records present "an enormous quantity of actions between neighbors." This aggressive behavior, he believes, was a response to familial tension. Unfortunately, he gives no numbers to support his statement about litigation, and the evidence from other places suggests that both the number of cases and the identity of those in court must be closely scrutinized before such a claim is made. The materials, thus far, favor harmony. In a sense, life had to be peaceful for only good will held the town together.[72]

Sensitivity to the needs of all citizens comes through clearly in the case of Gabriel Lynch. Lynch was disliked. Complaints against him included his dog biting a calf, his children stealing apples, and the goodman himself borrowing or buying hooks, hoes, and sheep without payment. In exasperation with his unpleasant ways, his neighbors conspired to bring a number of suits against him at once and pressured those more reluctant to join in. As one witness noted, they felt "now is the time or never and they was all resolved to set against him to vote him out of the town . . . because he was a very bad neighbor."[73]

Gabriel Lynch might serve as the antithesis of the social precepts which bound townsmen together. He was negligent, letting his animals and children run loose without supervision. These became the responsibility of others. He honored neither private property, the right to which men considered the foundation of their personal and social liberty, nor his word. In a society based upon personal integrity and trust he was a threat to order. Seen another way, however, the precedent of using the courts to hound somebody out of town was far more dangerous than living with a nuisance. And New England townsmen felt the same way.

While Newtown had no "warning out" system as did Massachusetts, warning out was more a means of absolving towns of reponsibility for the poor than of actually ridding them of troublesome inhabitants. Eli Faber found in Massachusetts Bay, "criminals" were readily reintegrated into the community. Linda Bissell discusses the cases of the Elmer and Crow families. The Elmers, males and females, were accused of theft, adultery, fornication, and desertion. The Crows were prosecuted for defamation, theft, "lascivious practices," desertion, and illegally impounding a neighbor's horses. Moreover, they used the courts against both neighbors and family. But at no time were they driven from the community. Perhaps the most unusual example of town loyalty was Windsor's protection of the acknowledged homosexual Nicholas Sension, who was otherwise a good and hospitable neighbor.[74]

English precedent must have lain behind local toleration and the reluctance villagers felt to eject one who was already a townsman. In New York this strong social bonding was reinforced by the wide social boundaries which Netherlands society and the Dutch West India Company promoted. But more was at stake than just neighborliness. By denying the law the power to settle interpersonal difficulties by banishment, townsmen in both New York and New England denied the state the power to persecute at the whim of a vocal minority. In Salem, this institutional void spawned tragedy, but in most places it worked. In the testimony for the Lynch case, the distaste for the intrigue against Lynch comes through as far stronger than the resentment against the man. Gabriel Lynch remained in Newtown.

By 1692 justices of the peace appointed by the governor replaced the elected town court. This was the end of an era, and certainly the end of local judicial autonomy. Newtowners accepted this change. Perhaps they felt comfortable with those townsmen, such as William Hallett Jr., who served as justices, or they might have sensed that a public trial for minor offenses and the humiliation of seeing private matters aired in public was part of a dying social order. The scale of interaction was changing, and with it the need for face-to-face public confrontation diminished. As the institutional powers of the state increased and became more specialized, the role of communal judgment, formed by first-hand observation of trials and punishments, atrophied. Minor misdemeanors were heard privately by justices of the peace, and the guilty parties were spared public embarrasment. After 1690 Newtown would become increasingly integrated into the political, economic, and judicial orbit of Jamaica and New York City. The town court would be one casualty of New York's centralization and growing complexity.

PART THREE

1692 – 1723:

Political Stability
&
Abundant Resources

CHAPTER 5

The Onset of Routine

The arrival of Governor Fletcher in 1692 brought at least some measure of political stability to New York. Both the General Assembly and the court system would remain unchanged, although, in time, the assembly would consolidate its authority. All towns continued to use both the courts and the assembly to protect their rights, fight unpopular legislation, and secure special privileges. For them, provincial institutions existed to serve local priorities.

Local needs were threatened in a number of ways and at a variety of levels. Newtown's fight to retain control of religion shows this most clearly because this dispute demonstrated emerging imperial attempts to tighten control. In this case, England's attention heralded the establishment of the Church of England in New York's southern counties as the state-supported denomination of the colony. Religion and control over the private property necessary to support religion, as translated into taxes, were basic issues in all of the colonies. In those with a strong dissenter background, such as Massachusetts and New York, the Church of England was both a denomination and a symbol of unwarranted governmental control. And it was fought on both religious and ideological grounds.

The establishment of the Church of England in predominantly dissenter New York was an English, not a local, idea, and one which royal officials hoped would make this New World settlement look more like the Old World. It was to take place in stages, the first step being the Ministry Act of 1693. Queens County was divided into two parishes, Hempstead and Jamaica, which included the three towns of Jamaica, Flushing, and Newtown. Each parish was to obtain and pay a Protestant minister. A general tax on all inhabitants would pay his salary of £60. Control of the parish was vested in elected churchwardens and vestrymen who were also to levy the taxes. If no vestry was chosen, the justices were to tax the inhabitants themselves. When Colonel Lewis Morris later told the Society for the Propagation of the Gospel (SPG) that the partial establishment created by the Ministry Act was all that could be done at the time, "for had more been attempted, the assembly had seen through the artifice the most of them being dissenters all had been lost," he underestimated the perceptiveness of the towns. Newtown bitterly opposed the Ministry Act and resolved to fight it.[1]

Opposition to the act of 1693 was organized on a countywide basis. In March, 1694, the townsmen sent deputies Content Titus and Daniel Blomfield to Jamaica to show why they could not elect vestrymen. They further decided to try "with the rest of the men of the county" to get the act repealed by the assembly. The bill remained, and Governor Bellomont further ignored a Queens County petition. Newtown, in the meantime, ignored the law and tried desperately, but unsuccessfully, to find its own congregational minister.[2]

The religious question was kept open since the governor was an interested party, both by royal instruction and personal inclination, in what was a fight between the Church of England and the dissenting towns; but even more, a battle between an imposed conformity and locally developed independence. The towns acted alone but also in concert with the imposed parish vestry now composed of dissenters. By 1702, Newtown men served on the vestry even though, according to the town minutes, no such officer was elected. They also tried to raise money for a meetinghouse in which to install an Independent minister. In 1703, crown-appointed justice of the peace William Hallett Jr., putting town loyalty before provincial duty, was cited with the rest of the ad hoc building committee for illegal fund-raising practices. However, the issue was not the funding of the meeting house itself, but who would occupy it.[3]

In 1704 the contest was joined when Governor Cornbury installed Mr. Thomas Poyer, an Anglican minister, at Jamaica. Cornbury then ordered the sheriff to evict the dissenting incumbent from the house that Jamaica had provided him, and directed the justices and churchwardens of Jamaica Parish to levy the £60 tax for Reverend Poyer. The tax went uncollected, whereupon, in 1705, the assembly passed a bill bypassing the vestry and empowering justices to collect the rate. At the same time the bill assured a salary, it also gave the governor sole power to appoint ministers to new vacancies. In effect this established the Church of England.[4]

On the face of the situation Newtown might seem to have lost the fight, and a real question remains as to just how successful Newtown, or any town, could have been in keeping its resources out of the governor's and church's control. The town minutes, by saying nothing, and the Anglican minister's continuing struggle for his salary, even upon the eve of the Revolution, suggest that townsmen were quite successful. Newtown was protecting its own religious interest by using every means available. Moreover, it was also safeguarding its right to remain small scale and locally autonomous. It would do the same when protecting its economic interests. The chief economic dangers to the town were those who threatened to take increasingly scarcer town land. These fell into three categories: neighboring towns, the colonial governor, and Newtowners themselves.

Newtown's boundary dispute with Bushwick, punctuated by smaller spats with other towns, runs like a thread through the town's history. In December, 1692, the purchasers, who had assumed most of the responsibility for protecting the bounds, voted to defend both purchase and patent "either by prosecuting in law or defending our right before any superior court or authority and to employ a lawyer one or more." Their deputies appeared before Governor Fletcher and the council in a dispute with Brooklyn, Bushwick, and Flatbush in which these Dutch towns accused townsmen of building houses on their outlands. The council called for a new survey and Newtown agreed to accept the verdict, whatever it was, but no decision was reached and the case dragged on.[5]

The town minutes duly recorded the process of appointing deputies to meet with the contending towns, of meeting with the governor and council, and of petitioning the assembly. In 1706 "rioting" broke out, occasioned by boundary uncertainties, and even though this seems to be the only violence recorded, it highlights how threatened townsmen felt. Violence was not part of the social compact and was always rare in Newtown. The vacillation and unwillingness of the Governor's Council and the various boards of inquiry to exert any authority only made things worse. No decision followed most of their deliberations leaving Newtown and Bushwick to fight it out fourteen separate times between 1692 and 1769. And even when decisions were reached the parties involved could refuse to abide by them.[6]

The unwillingness or inability of provincial government to settle the boundary issue raises a number of questions. Basic to understanding the problem is the scale of the society. As a small-scale society, the town lacked institutions that specialized in force. Furthermore, townsmen in Bushwick and in Newtown were accustomed to solving disputes through personal interaction, not outside coercion. The town and county court systems worked because they were composed of the peers of both plaintiffs and defendants. In the boundary dispute the towns acted as contending parties in litigation, but there were no peers, in the sense of equal towns, to arbitrate or judge their claims. Unlike individuals, they had few mutually dependent roles and statuses which welded them together. No forum existed wherein a town's good name would be questioned and trust withheld. An unpleasant individual could conceivably be forced out of a community, but no county or provincial body could expel a town. When arbitration, mediation, and court order still failed to resolve an issue the only way to deal with it was more arbitration, further mediation, and additional court orders. Eventually people would settle; in the meantime they kept the social fabric together by talking, even if that talk left problems unresolved.

The boundary disputes demonstrate how the town could use provincial institutions to further its own ends. It also shows how ineffective those institutions could be. The dispute did more, however. While Bushwick was a source of irritation to Newtown, Ann Bridges posed an even more serious threat and brought the town into the heart of provincial politics. At stake were not just a few acres along a boundary line, but the power of the governor to redraw boundaries and vacate patents for his own private purposes. Undoubtedly, the trouble began when the persistent squabble with Bushwick came before Lord Cornbury in 1706. The provincial surveyors looked at the line again, and this time drew Newtown's boundary too far northeast, thus creating, or finding, land not belonging to either town. Cornbury granted this parcel of some 1,200 acres to Ann Bridges, widow of his late chief justice, and her associates. Newtown fought this grant and went to court at least once in 1712 and probably more often later. In 1717 the case was still unresolved, although it seems that Newtown won in the end. Newtown had hardly enough land and a long history of fighting to protect what it did have. Moreover, it had English precedent for the sanctity of private property. That a colonial governor could blithely hope to pay off his political debts at town expense illustrates an insensitivity to local needs and an ignorance of local history.[7]

Bushwick and Lord Cornbury pressed for town lands by utilizing structures beyond the town bounds. But so did those closer to home. In 1700, nine men of Hellgate Neck, including Captain Thomas Lawrence, an old and wealthy settler, agitated for their "rights" at town expense. Instead of going to the town to demand their due, they went directly to the General Assembly where they petitioned for a bill "quieting, settling, and confirming . . . legal rights and possessions." After their bill was twice defeated, the petitioners took their case to the Court of Chancery. The town fought back.[8]

The town minutes recorded the suit as a threat to the patents of various freeholders and, "as is supposed," against the whole town, but the real contention seems to have been over the common lands and who was entitled to vote in decisions concerning them. Both sides appeared before the Governor's Council, where reliable witnesses like Captain Richard Betts, aged ninety, testified that the men on the outbounds had never been purchasers. The council found for the town and traced the problem to Colonel Dongan's Patent which "makes them one township but reserved to the original purchasers of the town of Middleburgh their distinct right to the said land to them and their heirs only." There were no further disagreements within Newtown challenging the patent.[9]

The 1700 dispute reveals more than mere dissatisfaction. On one level it says something about resources. By 1700 common lands were dwindling as the purchasers sold them off. These sales, albeit to townsmen, helped finance the boundary disputes. Indeed, the fight to maintain the bounds paradoxically left the town landless.

On another level the dispute reveals attitudes towards both town and neighbors. Going to the General Assembly was a most unfriendly thing to do. First, it cost money. More importantly, it removed the dispute from local arbitration thereby depersonalizing and objectifying the issue. This process also happened elsewhere. In Massachusetts, tacit understanding about land claims that allowed for unspoken informal neighborly usage fell before an acquisitive second generation bent on securing what was theirs. And finally, on a third level, Captain Lawrence and his associates' actions showed a shift in notions of trust. Either their claim was just or it was not. If they considered it a rightful claim they obviously felt that the town would not treat them fairly and was not worth approaching as a first step. They did not trust their fellow townsmen. If they knew that their claim was unjust, and indeed the governor and council called it "frivolous," then they had forfeit their right to equity since their whole suit was an attempt to defraud townsmen of their patrimony.[10]

The year 1683 marked the first year that purchasers were distinguished from inhabitants, but after 1683 the distinction was made regularly. As in New England, purchase right in Newtown meant a share in the town's common land, and in 1695 lots were laid out along the western boundary to each townsman according to his share. These lots would be the last of the common lands given away. Purchase right also implied an obligation to defend the boundary lines. The purchasers did this by direct taxation and by selling common lands. In 1713, £100 was raised on land "within the purchase" to defend against Ann Bridges, and at least £40 more was raised sometime between 1683 and 1723. The purchasers also agreed to sell land. In 1695 they voted to sell twenty acres for £36. In 1723, at a purchasers' meeting, they voted "to sell . . . all other vacant pieces of land that they can find in said town that is not already laid out to some one purchaser of said town." With no more common land the need for one form of status, the distinction between purchaser and inhabitant, disappeared. There were no purchasers' meetings after 1723.[11]

Newtown's fight against the Church of England, and town boundary and land problems showed how the town could both utilize and be bound by the larger provincial administrative institutions. Use of these institutions cost money which the town or the purchasers raised. But Newtown was integrated into New York province in another way. As of 1687 the town had been assessed a quitrent. This small annual financial levy, paid to the provincial treasurer, acknowledged Newtown's subordination to the crown, which, in theory, owned the land that the town used. Newtown's quitrent, which it faithfully paid, was £3 4s. a year. The money was either raised by taxation or taken from the town house rent receipts.[12]

The quitrent was an annual payment to the king, but Newtown was also burdened by other provincial and county expenditures. New York rarely taxed its inhabitants, except for war-related expenses. These years saw King William's War, Queen Anne's War, and the threat of Indian problems. The colony furnished soldiers, scouts, and built defenses and barracks. In 1709 and 1711 it raised money to send an expedition to Canada. In 1695 and 1729 it sent lobbyists to London to protest these high costs of defense.[13]

Wars cost money, but so did the tenuous peace surrounding them. The Indians required presents and trade goods that the province paid for by taxing the inhabitants. Finally, there were incidental costs of government, which included paying off the debts of Jacob Leisler and Governor Cornbury, and an occasional salary. Newtown's average share of these provincial taxes was £57 per year. These years also saw other provincial taxes that were levied as rates. In 1692 the governor's salary was raised by taxing men's estates at one penny per pound assessed value. In 1703 the colony taxed wigs, slaves, bachelors, and freemen, and in 1709 chimneys, fireplaces, stoves, and slaves. These rates would be in addition to the average £57.[14]

The General Assembly decided what totals to expend and then assigned each county a quota. Indeed, these years saw the rise of the county as an important level of government, in both New York and New England. Massachusetts established counties in 1643, Connecticut in 1666, Plymouth in 1685, and Rhode Island in 1702. The reforms of 1692 standardized functions, at least in Massachusetts. Counties became responsible for public buildings, roads and bridges, licensing taverns, and enforcing charity. They also collected the revenues and coordinated tax assessment. In New York the county not only raised its provincial levies but also its own taxes, which reflects its assumption of new responsibilities and functions. Newtown, as part of Queens County, helped to build a county house in 1709 and to provide other services, including jailing miscreants, transporting vagrants, collecting coroner's fees, setting bounties on foxes, crows, and squirrels, paying salaries for Queens County's representatives to the General Assembly and the County Board of Supervisors, and the cost of collecting taxes. From 1708, when the records began a year-by-year account, to 1723, Newtown's quota ranged between £17 and £76, with an average cost of county government of £30. Before 1708 there are few figures. Those there are suggest that £30 is a reasonable estimate.[15]

Finally, townsmen paid for local expenditures. These are complicated to assess because within Newtown were two taxing units, the "purchasers" and the town. The purchasers spent at least £140 on boundary disputes. The town paid its quitrent of £3 4s., assessors and other fees of around £3 per year, and miscellaneous expenses such as fixing the town house and buying bells, town books, and a pair of stocks. The records are sparse, but an educated guess would be an average of £10 per year.

Newtown paid an average tax bill of £97. Each townsman paid an average minimum of seventeen shillings (see Table 4). Wealthier townsmen would pay more, as would a purchaser, since he would have to help pay for the boundary question.[16]

Taxes require monies or goods with which to pay them. In Newtown, coin remained scarce and so taxes were probably still paid in grains and meats. In 1692 winter wheat was worth 4s. per bushel and tallow 4s. 5d. per pound. Pork and beef were also acceptable. The prices for agricultural produce seem fairly stable in Newtown. In 1696 wheat did sell for as high as 6s. a bushel, but, as Beverly McAnear notes, wheat declined after 1700 and only began to rise again after 1713. The usual price according to the twenty inventories from this period hovered around 4s. Corn averaged 2s. per bushel, rye 2s. 6d., and oats 1s. 5d. Adult horses cost between £2 6s. and

TABLE 4

Yearly Taxation,
1692–1723 (New York Currency)

AREA	AMOUNT
Provincial average	£57
County average	£30
Town average	£10
Total	£97
Per taxpayer*	17s.†

*Based on 112 names in the 1698 census.
† To nearest shilling.

£8, sheep 6s. each, and swine £1. Cows cost £3 in 1703 but had gone down to £2 10s. by 1716. Pork sold for 3d. a pound in 1706. Rum in 1697 was 9d. per pint, an affordable price for those so inclined. A day laborer in 1717 received 3s., a man and a cart in 1698 cost 6s. At these rates the average townsman would need four bushels of wheat, or a week's wages, to pay his taxes. Either seems like a reasonable burden.[17]

Most townsmen usually paid their taxes, thereby acknowledging the legitimacy of their government. In this sense, parting with property was a political act as well as a financial transaction. Withholding tax monies was a political message based on the use to which tax monies were put, but this hostility unleashed powerful feelings against authority. Nothing shows this more clearly than the 1719 controversy surrounding the raising of the Anglican minister's salary. The incident began in Jamaica, when the deputy constable tried to collect the minister's tax from Daniel Bull. Bull refused to pay, and, threatened with having his goods taken, he took up an ax and offered to split open the deputy's head. A crowd gathered involving twenty to thirty persons apparently armed with clubs who sided with Bull. Another sixteen or seventeen citizens supported the deputy. No violence erupted, but the encounter had the potential of getting out of hand, especially when several goodly citizens refused to aid the deputy. The justices fined Bull and his supporters for riot. The matter did not end there, however. Instead, Bull et al. petitioned the governor to remit the fines, insisting not that they were blameless but that justice in Queens County was corrupt. They charged that Deputy Richard Comes was " a notorious felon" and "a tool," and furthermore that the jury was stacked with Anglicans. The county justices responded with their own petition explaining their side.[18]

The next month the battle continued, but the grounds had subtly shifted. In a petition to Governor Robert Hunter, "several of the inhabitants" complained specifically about the justices, but in terms of a distinctive cast known as "country ideology." Briefly put, country ideology was a system of political thought that stressed the independence of those who governed. Economically secure, they would have no need for favors—they could not be bought—and they had no reason to extort those under them. They would rise above the petty concerns of small men and govern in the best interests of all.[19]

Justices in Queens County did not fit this model. The petitioners' first grievance was that the justices, Richard Betts of Newtown excepted, had thrown out the duly elected (and suitably dissenter) churchwardens. This was done, the petition explained, not for reasons of conscience, but out of private interest. For example, the Anglican minister owed Justice Whitehead money for wood, and Whitehead would only get paid if the Reverend Poyer did. Whitehead, it continued, was "a common pleader for money at the petty courts," and had "taken upon him to assess his Majesty's subjects of Newtown for a debt he alleges the town owes him, and keeps daily teasing and vexing the people before petty Justice courts." Justice John Smith of Newtown was a man of "very small and inconsiderable estate," and Justice John Hunt the petitioners could

not look upon as "other than an instrument of very great hardships and cruel severities upon his poor neighbors in Newtown." Among his other misdeeds, the justice had been both
the constable summoning and the justice trying, contrary to
law. The petitioners claimed to have proof of their allegations
and ended their plea with a curious observation:

> Your excellency we hope will wisely consider, as
> the above mentioned abuses of the justices diverting
> from the fundamental laws and great ends of mag-
> istracy and government, so the qualities of the men,
> considered without the ornaments of their honor-
> able office to recommend 'em to your Excellencys
> good liking we believe those will be found to be but
> of a size with their neighbors.

The justices, stripped of their acquired office, were no different and no better than anyone else, and so deserved no more
respect than anyone else. Even worse, since they had no independent base, they could be tempted by petty gain and thereby
corrupted.[20]

Just how wealthy or poor Newtown's justices were is
hard to ascertain, but the scanty evidence suggests no wide
gulf between the justices and other officeholders. At least
eight townsmen served as justices between 1692 and 1723.
There are no tax lists for this period and none of the eight left
an inventory, but wills are some help. Richard Betts left cash
legacies totalling £350, and Thomas Betts left his daughters
£300. These bequests were to be paid by the male heirs who
inherited all of the lands. Six of the eight owned slaves,
whereas in 1698 only one of four townsmen and one of three
officeholders did. Perhaps more to the point were justices'
land trading patterns. Ninety-two other townsmen held at last
one town office and engaged in at least one land transaction,
for an average of 8.9 land transactions. The eight justices had
an average of 17.9 land transactions—double the average

for town officers, who were themselves among the better-off townsmen. John Hunt, who evoked the harshest criticism, was the most aggressive. He involved himself in forty-five land transactions. Justices might have been a shade or two wealthier than others, but if the land records mean anything, they were much more opportunistic.[21]

The contempt for those supposedly one's betters—the justices in reply noted that the petitioners "insinuate" that they are considerable persons in the parish—suggests that status and station were fluid but hardening. Those who failed to make it would remain where they were. The value of station and hierarchy remained. Further evidence of these social trends is the increased frequency of the term "Gentleman" in the inventories and land records.[22]

The 1719 petition complained that those with the status of justice were unworthy. It also noted the increased power of those who held that status. Redressing the wrongs articulated in the petition would "prevent the effects that abused power and authority threatens our persons and estates with." The language is biased, but the increased power and authority were real, both in law and in practice. Moreover, the increasing intrusion of the justice into town administration, as well as justice, illustrates the increasing need for go-betweens, or political brokers. Newtown's justices were the most important of the pivotal people linking town with province, thereby integrating the two into a functioning one, and the same was true in Massachusetts.[23]

Probably the most visible increase in the justices' power during this period were their roles as judges in petty civil cases. The abolition of the town court saw many of its powers transferred from the elected magistrates to the appointed justices, but the justices' power also increased in other ways. They were in charge of ordering tax collection for both the various war efforts and the minister's salary. In 1705 they were given the additional authority to collect for the minister if the vestry refused to do so, and in 1721 they were to administer the oath of office to the vestry. In 1701, justices examined the public charges of each town and county and issued the towns warrants for choosing assessors. They were to make available yearly funds for the poor. In 1714 fencing came under their purview, and in 1721 the town pound. Even the town meeting was under the scrutiny of the resident justice, towns being empowered to meet as directed "under the hands and seals of any two of his Majesty's Justices."[24]

In early Massachusetts the magistrates held powers exercised elsewhere by justices of the peace. After the reorganization of the colony in 1692, Massachusetts' justices looked even more like New York's. Called "justices," and appointed by the governor, they could settle civil disputes, punish various civil crimes, appoint town watchmen, issue warrants and writs, order vagrants and fortune-tellers punished, imprison Negroes and Indians, and fine negligent officials. They could also call town meetings, levy local taxes, and approve town bylaws. In theory, they could do a lot, but in fact, as in Newtown they did little.[25]

In keeping with the scale of society which favored face-to-face rather than hierarchical interaction, the justices' role in local affairs was more passive than active. The town continued to choose its assessors and fence viewers as it had before. Undoubtedly, the justice was at the election as a Newtown freeholder. But provincial access to local affairs went deeper than using the justice as a middleman between town and province. Given Newtown's dual localism, the Governor's Council and the law could always mediate within the town when called upon by Newtowners to do so.

In 1693, some townsmen, responding to the increased taxation of King William's War, or to a levy of one pence per pound on real and personal estates, petitioned the council to have their assessment examined. In May this was done, the report stating that "the assessors have rated by head or poll and have made some mistakes." The next year Newtown had its first major problem with its tax collector. The March 1693 minutes note John Berrien elected collector for the following year, but in March 1694 Joris Abramson petitioned Governor Benjamin Fletcher that, being "picked upon for collector of the country rate and not understanding English," he be relieved. Abramson further noted that he was not chosen by the town. Therefore, he must have been chosen by the justices. His petition was granted, the town minutes noting that Edward Hunt should be collector in Joris Abramson's stead, "by virtue of a [sic] order from the Council."[26]

In 1703 there were again difficulties with the tax collector. Thomas Wychingham, one of Newtown's more affluent inhabitants, complained to the council that John Parcell, the duly elected collector, was illiterate. The council then informed the Queens County justices that Parcell was dismissed. The justices in turn appointed Thomas Morrell, who never served either. In April 1704, the town elected Daniel Lawrence collector.[27]

Newtown's problems with tax collectors clarify a number of different issues. First, they show how important and highly charged an issue taxation continued to be. Townsmen were loath to part with their property and, if necessary, would protect it by going up the political hierarchy. Second, the choice of tax collectors by other than town vote reveals that the latent power of the justices and the county court could be utilized. Third, the petition of Joris Abramson and the complaint of Thomas Wychingham both demonstrate that the town considered tax collection an undesirable job to be fobbed off on its lesser members, and that this sleight of hand was unacceptable. Newtown was too well-integrated into the province to use officials who could neither read nor write English. Literacy was crucial in dealing with the complexity of the outside world.

Road building and maintenance also illustrate Newtown as a reactor to outside pressure. The growing population of Queens County and the need to move both people and goods from place to place resulted in a great deal of local road construction. The law prodded the town. In 1688 the province granted justices the power to lay out all highways between towns. In 1691 the assembly ordered the towns to yearly name three persons to supervise and regulate highways and fences—which Newtown did in 1691. Unfortunately, in following years Newtown and the neighboring towns, like their New England neighbors, neglected electing road supervisors. This local apathy led the assembly to take over highway supervision in 1703. Henceforth, Newtown would need outside permission to alter the public highways. As early as 1704, Newtown petitioned the General Assembly for a change in the road to the Brooklyn ferry with all the expenses and bother such a request entailed. Highway supervision remained outside local control until 1739.[28]

There are other examples of Newtown's reaction to provincial pressure and the growing complexity of society. In 1703, as part of the meadow dispute, the council ordered Newtown to get its books in order. Newtown then began choosing ad hoc committees to inventory and keep track of the town's records. In 1699 the law directed that the town elect trustees or other persons to decide on the building and repairing of meetinghouses. Newtown did so. These responses were undertaken through the town meeting, which served as the local political unit.[29]

Provincial oversight of town affairs and the spread of the justices' authority occurred as the town itself did less. Townsmen continued to meet around three times a year, as in the previous period. However, a downward trend was emerging. The early 1690s and 1700–1704 were the town's most active periods; both during the Ministry Act crisis. Moreover, in 1702, the meadow dispute with Richard Betts and Thomas Lawrence came before the council. After 1718 the town met only once or twice a year. This pattern would continue long past the Revolution.

The atrophy of the town meeting occurred elsewhere. Before 1700, Jamaica met 4.84 times per year, but from 1700 to 1776 the town averaged 1.34 meetings a year. In Connecticut, a sample of sixteen towns shows that "all of them, though varying slightly in time and degree, tended to show a declining frequency of meetings in the early eighteenth century." This decline ended after 1765. The case for Massachusetts is more problematic. Watertown held more meetings in the 1690s than at any time through 1740. Figures for Dedham show a slight increase, from two meetings per year from 1636 to 1689 to 3.5 per year from 1689 to 1736, but the breakdown in published sources is not fine enough to measure variation within that long time span.[30]

Town meetings continued to make rules although these regulations became fewer in number. In 1695 the town decided which months rams could roam the commons, and in 1714 the town meeting voted that all fences would be four feet high. This fence height was specified in provincial law. Newtown's dependence upon outside law and authority again shows clearly when, in 1695, the town, worried about its wood supply, ruled that anyone taking wood from the common and selling it outside Newtown would forfeit the lumber and pay a fine. It then notes "this vote to be confirmed [by] the Court of Sessions and to be put in execution." No other legislation as such passed through the meeting.[31]

The town and purchasers had decided on the strategy to defend town boundaries, and the town made some of its own rules. It provided land for the Presbyterian minister, and it rented the townhouse to schoolteachers, when, as in 1720, such were available. It let the town pound and exempted Widow Leverich, Widow Strickland, and John Smith from taxes. The town kept track of its own proceedings and expenditures. Finally, and most importantly, every year the town meeting met and elected officers to do the routine and ad hoc chores of Newtown.[32]

Just as government had expanded from 1665 to 1691, so town administration grew more specialized from 1692 to 1723. Added to the constable, town clerk, assessors, collector, and supervisor, were a pound keeper, trustees, highway survey-ors, and fence viewers. The trustees, institutionalized in 1717, were in charge of renting out the town property. They could also act as town delegates in the boundary disputes. Highway surveyors were to "warn the inhabitants to mend and repair the highways at such times and seasons as they shall think fit." They could not lay out highways or appropriate property for highways.[33]

Even with the creation of new offices, Newtown con-tinued to create ad hoc committees whenever new situations arose. The most ad hoc committees were created in 1694. Their major tasks were to fight the Ministry Act and to find Newtown a minister. In the years 1704 to 1707, committees rented out lands and buildings and straightened out town rec-ords and accounts. Eventually trustees would do this, subject to audit by those especially chosen for that task. Ad hoc tasks averaged 1.5 per year in this period. However, as with the number of town meetings, a trend was developing. In 1722 townsmen elected Peter Berrien, Silas Titus, and James Renne to exchange the town's insufficient land deed on the minister's lot for a legal one. This was the last ad hoc task until 1738 when the boundary dispute again required attention.[34]

Ad hoc responsibilities were quickly done and the com-mittees doing them dispersed. Elected town offices had fixed tenures of one year, but the occupants could be re-elected. Table 5 looks at office tenures. As in the earlier period, most offices had a fair amount of rotation. Town clerks stayed in office longest, supervisors were next, and trustees third.

Town clerks were the longest tenured officers in Con-necticut, and probably elsewhere. Their longevity clearly shows how knowledge was power. By virtue of their position, which assured them access to all town records and all land transactions, they became indispensible for the well-ordering of both town and property rights. The longer a clerk stayed in office the more valuable he became. Supervisors and trustees were men who should have had high status in town. Both con-

TABLE 5

Tenure in Town Office,
1665–1723 (average number of years)

OFFICE	1665–1691	1692–1723
Constable	1.7	1.6
Town clerk	5.4	5.2
Assessor	1.8	1.5
Collector*		1.0
Supervisor		3.8
Fence viewer†		1.8
Trustees†		2.8
Highway surveyor		1.2

*Merged with constable after 1717.
†Began in 1717.
SOURCE: The town minute books.

trolled property. The supervisors were Newtown's delegates to the county board, which taxed, and the trustees administered town land.[35]

During the thirty-one years from 1692 to 1723 inclusive for which information exists, Newtown chose 106 men to hold town office. There is enough data on 105 of these men to compare them with each other. Based on surnames, 80 per cent of the officeholders were English, 17 percent were Dutch, and 3 percent were probably Huguenot or German. The integration of the Dutch into Newtown's officeholders is a change from the previous period when only 5 percent were Dutch. Moreover, the Dutch held important offices, such as supervisor and trustee. As the case of Joris Abramson illustrates, however, Dutch officeholders had to be able to speak and write English. On the 1715 militia lists 16 percent of the names were non-English, so this group's 20 percent in town office was better than their number might indicate. Ethnicity played no role in excluding them from town responsibility.[36]

The ethnic minority held office, and so did the religious

minorities. Among those whose religion is known, twenty-three were Presbyterian, but seven were Church of England, six Quaker, and three Dutch Reformed. The sample is small, but the fact that Quakers and Anglicans held office at all suggests that personal religious preference played a diminished role in local sensibilities. The town polity would hold, unspoiled by allegiances arrayed along religious lines.

Officeholders could be Dutch and could be Quaker; they could not be impoverished. There are no tax lists between 1692 and 1723 so wealth must be assessed indirectly. Thirty-two percent owned slaves, about the same percentage as in the earlier period, but in 1698 only 25 per cent of Newtowners owned slaves.[37]

Wealth itself did not necessarily mean long tenure in office. The wills show that Thomas Wychingham was very well off. Yet he only held office for three years, and those three years were spent in three different offices. Those who held long years in office were prosperous since townsmen believed that economic independence forestalled manipulation. Probably implicit in this idea was the assumption that those who managed their own affairs well would competently manage town business. Competence should not be confused with deference. Even the most primitive cultures rank people in terms of their abilities. As society becomes more complex, its need for those with special skills increases. By 1723 those skills included literacy and facility with English as shown by townsmen refusing to accept tax collectors who possessed neither. Requiring English for town office broke down ethnic differences, since Dutchmen who wished to be part of the potential office-holding pool would have to speak English. This linguistic requirement is evidence for growing homogeneity.

Dutch incorporation into town leadership went beyond the town's bounds with the appointment of John and Nicholas Berrien as justices of the peace. The choice of the Berriens is clever since they intermarried more with the English than any other Newtown family. They were probably the most culturally assimilated of the Dutch, yet their names and religious preference showed them to think of themselves as Dutch. As justices they served as brokers, but not just as go-betweens for a minority ethnic constituency. When John Berrien died in 1711 he was probably in his thirties. Up until his death he had served five years in four offices. Indeed, almost all of the justices of the peace were elected to town office. They averaged 11.9 years in office, far above the group average of 6.2 years.[38]

The life of the man who served the town the longest shows many of the trends developing in Newtown. Joseph Sackett held seven offices for a total of forty-eight years. Sackett was born in Connecticut in 1656 and probably came to Newtown with his maternal grandfather, William Blomfield. By 1689, he had married Elizabeth Betts. She died in 1702, and he married a woman named Anne. By 1711, Sackett was married again, to the widow Mercy Whitehead Betts, his former sister-in-law. By his three wives he had at least eleven children, ten of whom survived childhood. He was first a congregationalist but became a Presbyterian when the Newtown church changed denominations. He died in 1719.[39]

Joseph Sackett also actively engaged in Newtown's domestic land market. He exchanged seven pieces of land to consolidate his holdings and engaged in a total of fifty-nine land transactions, the most of anybody in town. Some of these lands were also gifts from his childless uncle, Daniel Blomfield. He styled himself a yeoman or a planter. In 1710 he listed himself as a gentleman. Sackett's will shows him to be comfortably off, leaving legacies totalling more than £50 and the time due from an indentured servant. No slaves are mentioned. Sackett's trust in the future and his perception of the limitations of the present were revealed in the lands he bought beyond Newtown in New Jersey. These holdings were bequeathed to his eight married children and the daughter of his deceased daughter. Joseph Jr., as the oldest son, received a double share. The rest shared equally.[40]

Joseph Sackett began his office holding career in 1682

with an ad hoc position. He went on to serve twenty-three times in that capacity. In 1687 his fellow townsmen elected him assessor and collector. In 1700 he was a fence viewer, highway surveyor, and supervisor. In 1706 he was chosen a trustee. Sackett held many offices, sometimes concurrently, as befits a member of a small-scale society. He also represented Newtown to the outside through some of his ad hoc tasks such as settling a minister and agitating about the town bounds. As a supervisor he met with the other town supervisors on the Queens County board.[41]

By 1723 Newtown was firmly entrenched in New York's political structure. Townsmen knew first hand through the Church of England crisis how the English viewed the role of colonies. They also knew how rapacious governors could be. Townsmen seemed to lose control of their own affairs. Judicial reforms replaced the elected town court with appointed justices. These justices, in turn, were given a broad mandate to force towns to raise taxes and build fences and to supervise town meetings. What really happened belies first impressions. Newtowners in these years actively or passively resisted what they disliked, utilized what they needed, and accepted the growing complexity of town government without protest. When forced to build roads and fences they did. When forced to fill new kinds of town offices they did. And secure within the twin safeguards of country ideology and the sanctity of private property, they went about the business of their private lives.

CHAPTER 6

Life in the Years of Plenty

Newtown's increasingly complex institutions served a population which led increasingly complex lives. Townsmen were close enough to New York City to avail themselves of the goods and services that an Atlantic economy offered. Both economic and social change were slow but inexorable. The most immediate alteration, underway by 1692 but not complete until 1723, was the distribution of all town lands.

Townsmen's lives centered on land. In the earliest years this property was available in a number of ways, demonstrated clearly by the land acquisition patterns of the Hallett family. Founder William had had a number of options available to him. He could have bought from the Indians, petitioned the governor for a grant, or bought from private individuals. He did all three. He could also have become a purchaser in Newtown, and thereby gained access to town lands. He chose not to do this. The choices open to Captain William of the second generation were more limited. The Indians and the provincial government no longer controlled land in the Newtown vicinity. Captain William could still buy land or purchase right, both of which he did. He also bought land in Flushing. He also would buy land with, and inherit land from, his father. Indeed, fathers helping sons would be a Hallett pattern, and would give the Halletts a competitive edge over some of their neighbors.

The third generation of Halletts (see Figure 1) had the same options as their fathers, and they utilized them with the help of their fathers. In 1705, Captain William sold William Jr. lands and meadow right at Hell Gate, as well as property in Jamaica and Connecticut. It was on the Hell Gate plantation in 1708 that William Jr. was murdered by his slaves. Most of the Hallett family lived around Hell Gate and Halletts Cove, but in the third generation this residential clannishness began to break down. Joseph bought sixty acres at Maspeth Kill with his father, Captain William. The rest of his estate was a sixty-two-acre gift from his father which specified that the land belonged to Joseph and then to his male heirs. If Joseph died without heirs the property reverted to his father, as had the lands of the slain William Jr. William Jr.'s properties eventually went to the next in line, his brother Joseph. Joseph acknowledged his right to these holdings by buying lands previously surveyed for his older brother at Hell Gate. He lived at Hell Gate.[1]

Moses Hallett, Captain William's third son, also received land from his father that was to go next to his male heir and failing that, back to Captain William's estate. In the same year of this seventy-acre gift Moses died, leaving a pregnant widow. His lands, in trust for his posthumous son, William Moses, were rented out at £7 per year, the proceeds to help support his widow and child.[2]

Captain William had two more sons, George and Richard, but neither received gifts of land. George left Newtown altogether. Richard, a Quaker, bought 170 acres of land at Maspeth Kills. He lived there near the other Newtown Friends.[3]

Captain William Hallett hoped to keep his lands in the family by writing into the deed that real estate would descend from his sons to his grandsons. His brother, Samuel Sr., did the same. Samuel bought no land but inherited the home farm from his father. He had only one son, Samuel Jr., to whom he gave all of his estate. This deed of gift specified that at Samuel Jr.'s death the lands would fall to his son Samuel and his male

FIGURE 1

The First Three Generations of Halletts

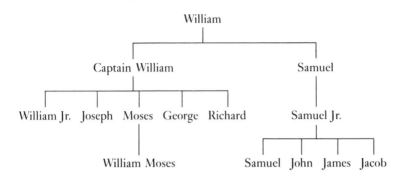

heirs, or, failing heirs, to Samuel's brother John, then to John's brother James and his male heirs, or James' brother Jacob and his male heirs.[4]

The attempts by Captain William and Samuel to pre-serve their holdings for their posterity through entail was un-usual in America. Neither Linda Auwers nor Philip Greven note it. These restrictions loosened by the time of Captain William's will in 1729. Perhaps bowing to the caprices of lon-gevity Captain William left land to his sons and in default of males and their male heirs to females. Most gifts to children were free and clear. The Halletts were also unusual in trans-acting most of their business with each other. Other New-towners not having large enough land holdings may not have had this luxury.[5]

Private land was exchanged, given away, or sold. The records contain 694 land transactions for this period. Of the 694, 4 percent were exchanges, 9 percent were gifts, and 86 percent were sales. As in the previous period exchanges were but a small percentage of the conveyances, but, if compared to all exchanges for the 110 years between 1665 and 1775, they made up 64 percent of all exchanges. Indeed, the exchanges between 1665 and 1723 comprise 95 percent of all exchanges. When the town gave out lands between 1665 and 1723, it did so in scattered bits and pieces. Townsmen consolidated their holdings by trading distant plots for closer ones. Gifts also made up a small 4 percent of the 694 conveyances, but this percentage is similar to the proportion for the earlier period. The same holds true for sales, which were 86 percent of the 694 transactions and 84 percent of the previous years' conveyances.[6]

There are differences in land transaction patterns between 1665–1691 and 1692–1723, but they do not lie in the kinds of conveyances. Instead, they exist in the kinds of lands conveyed. As in the earlier years, people were either buying whole farms or putting them together. A farm required upland and meadow, and these were the types of lands most frequently transferred. Meadow, the scarcest land in Newtown, changed hands less frequently in these years than in previous ones. The percentage of meadow sold declined from 26 percent to 15 percent. Upland, arable land needed for crops, which was often still wooded, shows greater availability. This increase was due to the town land divisions. It was upland that comprised the town commons, which the purchasers voted to divide or sell. The downward trend in meadow and the upward trend in upland suggest that townsmen were increasing the size of their farms, but that they were fashioning fewer new farms. A good farm required meadow. Upland could augment holdings, but in and of itself could not support the livestock a farm required. With the parcelling out of meadow one of the limits of the physical environment was reached, and with it ended an adaptation based solely on mixed farming.

There are other changes suggested by the kinds of land sold, though these are not as important as the decline in meadow. Lots, those small pieces of land which are usually in the town and would eventually be built upon, declined from 5 percent to .4 percent. This decrease shows the building up of the town center. Even by 1692, there were few house lots without houses in Newtown town. Purchase rights, however, changed hands more frequently. Trading these made sense only when they could be exchanged for land. The 1679 division did not produce a market for purchase rights, but the 1684 division rights sold in the 1690s. The last division of 1695 also led to buying and selling. Purchase right gave its owner land, but it also gave him a vote in the proprietors' meetings. Perhaps this vote enticed some, like the Halletts. After 1723, purchase rights would disappear along with the purchasers.[7]

Purchase right usually granted a fairly small plot and the land conveyances reflected this. Of 479 transactions that give land size, 46 percent, or almost one-half, were ten acres or less; 68 percent were twenty acres or less. This pattern differed little from the earlier period. What changed was the larger percentage of lands over fifty acres which were transferred. Twenty-nine percent of these conveyances were for lands over fifty acres compared to 12 percent of the 1665–1691 transactions. This increase results from the piecing together of whole farms and the breaking up of holdings like those of the Halletts. What remains striking throughout is the generally small size of the lots changing hands.[8]

The declining availability of land should have forced land prices up, and it did. While there were insufficient meadow sales to chart a trend, meadow averaged £3 17s. per acre in the years 1700–1714. The median price of upland climbed from £1 per acre in 1695–1699, to £3 in 1710–1714, to £4 in 1720–1723. Whole farms sold to non-kin also increased in price. In 1695–1699 the highest price per acre cost of a farm was £3. By 1705–1709 the per acre cost had risen to £7 15s., before levelling off at £6 10s. in the years 1715–1723.

Land shortages resulted in rising land prices elsewhere. Jean Peyer notes for Jamaica an increase in the cost of planting land, house and home lots, woods and upland. Greven found that land value rose "increasing every decade from 1710 to 1750." In Northampton, Massachusetts, a frontier area, the price of good arable rose from £6 to £9 per acre in 1706–1712, to £30 to £36 per acre in the 1730s.[9]

Kinsmen paid less. In 1708 Jacob Fine bought a fifty-six-acre farm from the heirs of John Fine for £160, or £2 17s. per acre. That same year John and Daniel Lawrence purchased from Jonathan and Mary Lawrence a forty-six-acre farm plus an unspecified share in his father Thomas's lot and the common right it contained for £200. The per acre price was a maximum of £4 10s. Both farms were considerably below the highest prices paid for farms. As James Henretta noted in a broader context, people's decisions reflect many non-economic considerations. Newtown's land sales show that kinship ties often outweighed monetary gain: family expectations tempered market values. And as lands became ever harder to acquire after 1723, family played an increasingly important role in land distribution.[10]

Most Newtown land was sold to and by townsmen, but the records also show some absentee ownership. Of the 694 land transactions, 689 give the residence of buyer and seller. Townsmen bought and sold with one another in 75 percent of the transactions. This figure is about the same as the 74 percent for the previous period. Townsmen took from outsiders in 9 percent of the transactions and conveyed to outsiders in 11 percent of the cases. These low figures seem higher than they really are, because in 65 percent of the transactions between 1690 and 1720, absentees selling lands in Newtown either once lived there or were related to those who did. They were not strangers. John Stevenson moved to Westchester, but he still owned lands in Newtown that he conveyed to his brother in 1710. Jeromus and Tryntie Remsen, and Joris and Angentie Rapelje, of Brookland, sold their interest in Cornelius Berrien's Newtown estate. Both Tryntie and Angentie were Cornelius' heirs who had married and moved a few miles away.[11]

The outsiders buying land were often men from neighboring towns. Dow Van Ditmus and Theodore Polhemus lived in Jamaica, while John Bennet resided in Flatbush. They might have purchased land adjoining the lands they already owned on Newtown's boundaries. Or they might have been buying land for their children. The Polhemuses would eventually be one of Newtown's wealthiest families, although they did not actually move to Newtown until 1764.[12]

Buying land in other towns so that heirs might inherit appealed to townmen, though the practice was never widespread. The Halletts owned land in Flushing and Jamaica, and the land records of Jamaica show that other townsmen held lands there. Similar conveyances from Flushing, Bushwick, and Brookland undoubtedly contain a few Newtown purchasers although the wills, a chief source of information on land, rarely mention lands in adjoining towns. None of the earlier wills discussed outside lands. Two wills in this period listed parcels of land in New Jersey, while one left property in Orange County, New York. Leaving Newtown for other areas with land meant choosing to maintain an agrarian lifestyle at the expense of family proximity. Other choices were possible such as combining skills with agriculture thereby adapting to less land but remaining in town.[13]

The period 1692–1723 saw the end of Newtown's public lands and the beginning of inheritance beyond the town. Newtown's thirty-nine wills also show other patterns. Daughters might be more apt to inherit land than previously. The percentage of cases in which all children shared rose from 25 to 31. The percentage of just sons receiving land declined from 28 to 13. Wives continued to do poorly, rarely receiving land to dispose of as they wished. Only 13 percent of wives were given real estate. Primogeniture was entirely absent from the wills, as was inheritance as a form of social control. No will demanded that an heir reconsider his or her lifestyle. Finally, 13 percent of the wills mentioned no land. Omitting reference to real estate did not mean that there was none. However, those with property who took the time to write a will, usually specified who got what.[14]

Males received land more often and women more often got personal property. Farming was man's work, and those who could hired or bought others to help them. The land records noted some who called themselves "laborer," but the act of acquiring land usually changed that status. In 1701, Jonathan Fish called himself a laborer when he received a house and land from his father; by 1715, he styled himself a vintner. The evidence is scant, but it seems that sons awaiting land might call themselves day laborers and work for others. John White, a newcomer, bought a fifty-acre farm through a mortgage from Samuel Moore Jr. Thereafter he called himself "yeoman." Other laborers might have worked in the few non-agricultural outlets in Newtown. There were some flour mills and a fulling mill. William Hallett, an entrepreneur, owned a sloop and a brickyard. By 1698 he sold bricks by the thousands, both in Newtown and neighboring villages. His records also note that in 1698 "Charles Sharp entered his time to serve the season for ten shillings a month." So did both Jacob Reder and Thomas Burd who worked for ten shillings a month. The next year Hannah Rescoe engaged to work for thirty-six shillings a quarter. Reder would later own land in Newtown. Other free labor was provided by fellow townsmen who owned farms but sought to augment their larders in the same way the part-time artisans would. They did cartwork, mowed hay, or drove cattle.[15]

Part-time artisans and day laborers suggest that individual townsmen were not self-sufficient but existed symbiotically with one another. William Hallett's accounts from 1696 to 1708 show a wide range of expenditures for what appear to be local goods. Manufactured items included slippers and shoes for the family and slaves. Hallett also purchased services. Hides were tanned and cloth woven. Among the commodities he bought were tallow, apples, turnips, oats, barley, hops, cider, cheese, and butter. He also bought lambs, shoats, and meat, such as turkey and beef. These purchases seem to be for Hallett's household, and almost all of these goods could have been produced on his lands if he had wanted to expend his resources that way. Rather than specialize in subsistence agriculture, however, Hallett preferred to diversify, buying his necessities from neighbors.[16]

Townsmen also bought from those outside of Newtown. William Hallett purchased hats for himself and his son Richard from William Whit. Several townsmen, including John Burroughs, John Denman, Daniel Lawrence, John Way, and John Leverich, utilized Captain George Woolsey's general store in Jamaica. They bought basins, locks, files, and nails. Daniel Lawrence also had Woolsey, who was a carpenter, mend a chair. In return for these goods and services townsmen paid Woolsey, either in cash, or flour, beef, cider, or wood.[17]

The surplus goods that farms provided utilized family, free, and unfree labor. Free labor was probably available in Newtown on a part-time basis. Unfree laborers were available when the owners wanted them. Only one will notes an indentured servant, a Hugh McCarty, whose time was left to John Sackett by his father Joseph. McCarty must have left town sometime later, because he does not appear again in the surviving records. In 1687 Newtown's labor force included forty-nine slaves and thirty-one servants. By 1698 the number of slaves had almost doubled, to ninety-three, while a 1711 census listed 164. White servants were not listed in the censuses or the inventories. Obviously, the shift from free to unfree labor was well underway. Such a change would close off opportunities for unskilled whites. Just as in the American South of a century or more later, black labor drove out free white labor and closed off a possible economic niche.[18]

Male slaves continued to serve mainly as farm workers and, as before, were usually left with the widow for her use. Richard Alsop left his Negro man, Jacob, to his wife, Hannah, but upon her death or remarriage he went to an Alsop daughter. Edward Hunt left his wife the use of his Negro man, but for only four years. After the four years were up, the slave was to be sold and the money divided among Hunt's wife and daughters. Thomas Betts gave "Negro Harry" to his son Richard outright, but Thomas Jr.'s man, Charles, had to serve the widow Betts for eight years. The Negro boy Peter was at her disposal for ten years, after which he went to son Daniel. None of Thomas Sr.'s daughters received slaves. There was only one Indian slave mentioned, in Moses Hallett's 1698 inventory.[19]

Presumably, female slaves worked in the house, but they also did field work when necessary. In 1692, "Black Mary" helped weed the Indian corn, harvested, and made hay when she could be spared from the garden, the orchard, and carding work.[20]

Slaves still formed a major part of people's estates, but they were no longer their most valuable pieces of property. William Post left behind five bondsmen worth £129, but he also held six bonds worth £500. Leaving aside the bonds, his slaves were 42 percent of his property. Thomas Wychingham owned a man and a woman worth £95, but he also left bonds worth £104.[21]

The twenty surviving inventories provide an economic silhouette of the town. They reveal a farming village that included livestock and part-time artisans. Wheat, corn, buckwheat, and barley were part of men's estates. People kept oxen, cattle, horses, sheep, and swine. Thomas Hughes also had turkeys, cocks, hens, and ducks. Among men's tools were grindstones, planes, and saws. As before, the inventories also include cloth and yarn.[22]

In 1708, Captain William Hallett tragically lost his oldest son, William Jr., when William's black and Indian slaves murdered the entire family. William Jr. was aged thirty-eight. That same year Captain William also lost his third son, Moses, aged twenty-seven. In both cases personal estates were inventoried. Taken together, these inventories clarify both Newtown's economy and its social order.

William Jr.'s estate was worth £233 excluding the value of his two murderers, which would have been about £90. It shows he had a number of skills and economic adaptations. He owned livestock worth £73, including horses, cows, and sheep. His tools included planes, axes, chisels, gouges, chains, two pairs of money scales, and shoemaker's tools. He owned scythes, shears, hoes, a plow, and a harrow. His household goods included tables, chairs, and beds. He kept both a sword and a gun. William Hallett also owned clothing, including britches, vest, waistcoat, hose, and gloves worth about £10. Ruth, his wife, wore a silk petticoat, damask gown, and black silk hood. They owned a regular saddle and a sidesaddle. He had pewter dishes, brass kettles worth £11, and nine knives and forks. The inventory contains yarn and various kinds of cloth. He also had a library of twenty-four English books. Finally, Hallett's estate included genuine luxury articles. A silver tankard was valued at £16; a gold ring at 15s. Moreover, his inventory calls him "Gentleman," a title appearing for the first time in the inventories.[23]

Moses Hallett's estate was more modest, and his tools show him to be less diversified than his brother. Worth £179, the estate's value was about one-half that of William's. He owned one Indian slave worth £40 and livestock worth £59. His farm equipment included a wagon, axes, augers, scythes, and wheels. There were no plows or harrows. Moses' house contained beds, bolsters, chests, and chairs. He kept a pair of pistols and a sword; his clothing was worth about £9. Moses Hallett's household had pewter tankards, porringers, plates, dishes, and basins, as well as £1 7s. worth of brass kettles. Spoons are noted, but no forks, and no silver. Like his brother, and most townsmen, he owned yarn and cloth. He also held three books. He was styled a yeoman in the inventory.[24]

Not everyone was as affluent as was William Hallett Jr. or his brother Moses. But even poorer men's wealth looked different from before. Jeremiah Burroughs left an estate of £79, but of that value over £56 were accounts due him: John Jousenbery owed him £1 10s., Samuel Edsall £5 5s. It seems that Burroughs was a small-scale trader, buying and selling local stock and country goods. He sold three cattle and a steer to Tunis Titus, a calf and a sheep to Joseph Sackett. Benjamin Cornish bought a barrel of cider and Joseph Firman some bees. All of these names but the first are familiar as Newtowners.[25]

Wills and inventories, while they remain agricultural, show a difference between the Newtown of 1723 and 1691. The economy was more diversified, and the inhabitants more economically stratified, both signs of growing heterogeneity. The most obvious signs of diversification are the varied part-time occupations people engaged in and the appearance of bonds and debts as major assets. The Halletts owned a sloop and the brickworks. Thomas Hughes and Johannis Fine were both listed as blacksmiths in their inventories, but Hughes also owned livestock and grain, as well as a fair assortment of textiles. Fine owned livestock, plows, and harrows, as well as winter crops in the ground. The land records list cordwainer, millwright, clerk, bricklayer, tailor, weaver, wheelwright, brewer, vintner, and cooper. Jesse Kip, upon first buying land in Newtown, called himself a goldsmith, but in subsequent transactions he referred to himself as a miller. Goldsmithing was too specialized and too urban for Newtown. The most common alternative occupation was weaving, which helps explain the yarns and cloths in the inventories.[26]

There were also bonds and monies out on loan recorded in the inventories and wills. These occurred after 1703, when William Post's estate showed £500 on bond. These monies represented 62 percent of his estate. Four years later Thomas Wychingham was owed £104 in bonds and debts. Even black-smith Thomas Hughes carried £76 of book debts, "error excepted," at the time of his death. This was his largest single asset, his slave, worth £40, being next. The wills show the same sort of diversification. Edward Hunt held a bond from his brother Ralph and Richard Alsop a £30 bond from a Mr. Crumline. William Case Jr. specified that his executors sell his estate and place the money out at interest "until my children are of age." He must have felt that their best interests were served through investment, not land.[27]

The reallocation of resources which bonds represent, says a number of things about Newtown's economy and townsmen's attitudes toward money. First, to loan money at interest requires having money available. By 1703, some inhabitants found they had surplus cash, credit, or goods that could, by themselves, generate more goods. Only a maturing economy, one past the subsistence stage, contains this surplus. Second, loaning money at interest requires seeing money as a commodity valued like any other. The medieval economy, or a Biblically-based economy—one following what Harry Stout calls Old Testament law—sees money-lending as evil and the pursuit of wealth through interest-bearing investment as usury. Bonds are unlikely to become part of an estate where they carry such negative moral connotations. Old ideas were changing, and not only in New York. Ronald Snell's analysis of the Hampshire County magistracy shows that the wealthy diversified and included among their investments loans, bonds, and mortgages.[28]

Newtown's inventories as a whole suggest a rising standard of living, as well as more diverse property. As in the earlier period, the inventories are problematic because they are so few. The twenty which survive represent only 23 percent of known decedents, consequently a lesser percentage of total decedents. Of the twenty who left behind inventories, the ages of sixteen can be estimated. Two were in their twenties, two in their thirties, five in their forties, five in their fifties, and two sixty or older. Wealth and age are unrelated in this small group. Both men in their twenties left behind estates between £100 and £200, while three of the five in their forties and three of the five in their fifties left estates valued at less than £100. William Post, whose estate of £806 was the largest, was probably in his forties. Unfortunately, there are no tax lists which would provide a base line.[29]

The value of Newtown's estates ranged from the £3 of James Way to the £806 of William Post. Comparing these inventories with those from 1665–1691 shows that an increase in wealth cannot be attributed solely to inflation. New York's rate of exchange before 1690 averaged between £125 and £130 New York currency to £100 sterling. Between 1690 and 1723 it averaged between £130 and £165. The prices of commodities show overall stability. Livestock was worth more in the 1670s and declined in value thereafter. Indian corn was worth 2s. 6d. a bushel in December 1670, 1702, November 1707, and January 1715. Estates were worth more because they contained both larger quantities of some goods and a broader variety of articles. Pewter utensils and books appear more often. Josias Robinson left goods valued at £89, but among his possessions were four pewter platters and eight pewter plates. Even John Fine, whose entire estate was worth £50, had pewter platters. Jacobus Bass had a Bible, while Daniel Blomfield had a Bible and three old sermon books. Money scales appear in various inventories. And then there were, for the first time, the luxuries, such as William Hallett Jr.'s gold ring and silver tankard. Thomas Wychingham owned a pair of gold buttons. Richard Betts had four silver spoons, while Thomas Hughes had two silver spoons and an ivory box, and Edward Hunt had two pairs of britches with silver buttons.[30]

This pattern was repeated elsewhere. According to Patricia J. Tracy, Northampton, Massachusetts, by 1700, was no longer a frontier society: "The inhabitants enjoyed more and better houses, even a few luxury items such as sugar, raisins, rum, and cloth, ribbons, and even furniture imported from Boston." Lois Green Carr and Lorena Walsh found that after 1716, Maryland decedents showed greater numbers of amenities, and the wealthy had real luxuries. In Tidewater, Virginia, the crucial years were 1700–1719. Only then did luxuries such as silver, china, mirrors, silks, and jewelry appear.[31]

Finally, there are changes in the titles that people used to describe themselves. The justices, by virtue of their office, were styled "Esquire." But some in Newtown were calling themselves "Gentlemen." William Hallett first used this designation in 1688, in a deed of gift to his son Samuel. In the following years Joseph Sackett Sr., Richard Betts Jr., Samuel Moore, John Hunt, Joris Brinkerhoff, and Richard and John Alsop would also identify themselves as gentlemen. The inventories accord this title to William Hallett Jr., and Edward Hunt.[32]

The rising prosperity of some townsmen reflected Newtown's access to the outside. In 1692 a weekly public market opened in Jamaica, where grain, cattle, provisions, and other merchandise could be sold or bartered from 8:00 A.M. to sunset. That same year Queens County was permitted one fair in May and another in October. Kings County was also granted an annual autumn fair. No longer would townsmen have to take their produce to New York City.[33]

Linking Newtown with Jamaica and Kings County were a series of new roads (see Map 1). In 1703 the Queens County road supervisors laid out the major highways between Newtown, Jamaica, and Flushing. The next year they laid out five highways, in 1708 four, in 1716 three, and in 1722 two. That year Newtown's commissioners also laid out a boat landing next to the highway that led to the New York ferry. Townsmen needed access to the city. All official business was carried on there, be it paying the quitrent or filing for probate. And some townsmen had even more extensive private business activities. Peter Chock, in 1696, represented the Boston creditors of the pirate Captain William Kidd. Their needs would link him to Boston as well as to New York.[34]

The increasing need for roads meant that townsmen were slowly but surely integrating into the larger provincial economy, polity, and society, a process which would accelerate after 1723. Moreover, this pattern also marked New England's evolution. The years 1710 to 1740 witnessed Connecticut's economic transformation. According to Bruce C. Daniels, the colony changed

> from a society of subsistence farmers who produced primarily for themselves and the local market to a

society of producers of commercial crops for export. Intertown transportation systems were developed, artisanal and manufacturing activities were accentuated, agricultural specialization by region and town developed, trade greatly increased, and large-scale merchants appeared, developing contact with much of the Atlantic world.[35]

Those who bought and sold beyond Newtown's bounds could care for themselves, but not everyone was self-sufficient. By law, the indigent were the responsibility of each town and parish. "Freeholders chosen in every town parish and precinct shall provide for the poor," noted the act passed in 1691, but what really happened is hard to say. The town tried to help in ways that involved no capital. In 1700, for example, the widow Gentrup was given the town house and land, as long as she lived there. When taxes were collected in 1718, three persons were exempted. Perhaps they were old or incapacitated. The law provided for these exigencies.[36]

The church and family tried to help those who needed it. Joseph Burroughs paid his arrears for both the minister's salary and the poor, which suggests that the congregation had a fund of some sort. The Quakers also used their budget to help needy Friends through loans or outright gifts. The Flushing quarterly meeting of September 1704 noted, "it was proposed to give something to Thomas Brishey [?] to buy him a warm coat."[37]

Families also tried to provide for their own. John Fine left something to all of his children, but he was especially concerned about Daniel. He left him £25 more than the rest "by reason of his distemper." Other fathers shared the same concern for their children. John Reeder Jr. named his wife and brother Isaac his executors. They were charged to to see that his children were "all brought up in learning if it be possible."[38]

Learning usually took place at home. Newtown had no public school, as such. Ministers served, at times, as school masters, just as the town house, as in 1720, occasionally served as a school. Private schooling was available to some. In 1698, Jeremiah Burroughs' sons, John and Joseph, both went to school, as did Elizabeth and Richard Hallett, the children of Captain William. Education cost the Burroughs 10s. In 1721 Joseph Hallett gave to Samuel Hallett, Samuel and Joseph Moore, Thomas Skillman, and Isaac Burgaw "equal share and right and title with myself" to a lot for a schoolhouse, "to be equally enjoyed by them and for them to send what number of children they think fit." This primary school served the northern side of Newtown and was open to both Dutch and English students.[39]

Joseph Hallett's gift is interesting for two reasons. First, it is the first of what will be four such bequests, all in different parts of the town. Joseph Hallett had school-age children in 1721, as did all of the other trustees. This schoolhouse met their own immediate needs, not some abstract ideal. Second, it includes a Huguenot turned Dutch Reformed trustee whose other behavior indicated strong Dutch identification. Isaac Burgaw married a Dutch woman, Hillietie, named his children Dutch names, and married them off to spouses surnamed Van Alst, Volkerson, Luyster, and Opdyke, as well as a Parcell which might be an English name. Burgaw belonged to the Dutch Reformed church, but the education that his children received would be English, not Dutch. Clearly, Burgaw valued both his non-English ethnic heritage and secular non-Dutch education. He personifies what Ronald Howard calls "cultural federalism." Ethnic identification was taught in the home, but English culture was transmitted through the schools, leading to a dualistic identity among New Yorkers.[40]

Apprenticeship was another way for children to receive an education, especially if their father were dead. In 1713 John Earhart, son of the deceased John Coonroes Earhart, with the "good liking" of his mother and her new husband, apprenticed himself to Woodhull Tourneur to learn the trade of weaver and also to read, write, and cypher. At the end of this time he would receive two good suits of clothes "for all parts of his body" and four good weaver's reeds. Thomas Strickland, son of Jonathan, deceased, apprenticed himself to John Berrien for six years. Berrien was to teach him weaving, reading, writing, and arithmetic. He also provided young Strickland with meat, drink, clothing, washing, and lodging, and would in the end give him a new Dutch loom, two reeds, and two new suits of clothes. Girls received less. Robert Seybolt found no apprenticeship indenture that called for teaching females arithmetic, although many provided for reading and writing. In 1716 Mary Linter bound herself to Woodhull Tourneur for three years, she to get sufficient meat, lodging, etc. "fitting for an apprentice," but the contract says nothing about weaving or schooling.[41]

Children might be bound out, but wives also needed protection. Husbands specified what their wives were entitled to, be it one-third of the moveable estate or a bed and hearth for life. All wills where there was a wife noted made some provision for her. Richard Alsop's will is fairly typical. He left his wife Hannah one-half of his dwelling house, one-third of his orchard, and one and one-half buildings during her widowhood. She also received one-third of his moveable estate and the use of a Negro man. Jacobus Boss, less well-off than Alsop, left his wife Catherine sole dispersal of his estate to pay debts and use for her lifetime. Their children would get whatever remained after her death.[42]

This system could break down, though it seemed to function well most of the time. In January 1704, the widow Mary Lawrence petitioned the governor for her one-third left by the will of her husband. Indeed, Major Thomas Lawrence's will left her one-third of the moveable estate indoors and out, all homespun cloth, yarns and lambswool, and the privilege of their dwelling house during her widowhood. Her petition noted that her sons refused to pay her her share and were undervaluing the goods involved. Perhaps Mary chose this form of redress because her son William was a member of the Governor's Council and she hoped to shame him into a settlement. An inquiry was held, but the results went unrecorded. Mary Lawrence was not poor and downtrodden. She knew how to obtain redress of her grievances, even if the accused parties were her own powerful children.[43]

Mary Lawrence was probably an old woman in 1704. Her husband, Major Thomas, had been listed in the Indian purchase of 1656; her son William had married in 1676; and she had numerous grandchildren. How typical she was is difficult to say given Newtown's poor demographic data. The death dates of 42 men and 17 women born between 1670 and 1699 who reached age twenty-one, i.e. matured in these years, suggest long life. Ninety-five percent of the men and 94 percent of the women lived until age forty and over 70 percent of the men and 55 percent of the women reached age sixty. These figures are somewhat higher than Philip Greven found for Andover and might be biased upward, at least for the twenty and thirty-year-olds. The calculated ages for those inventoried lends them some support, however.[44]

What did death mean to this society? Only one record survives:

> Edmund Titus one that received the truth many year since and lived and died in it in his latter days his eyes grew dim that he could not see and thick of hearing all of which he bore very patiently in the time of his last sickness his daughter Pheby Field standing by him he said my life is in Christ my God with more comfortable words his last were these I have put away all filthiness and superfluity of naughtiness. I have received with meekness the engrafted word that is able to save the soul and so after departed this life in a quiet frame of spirit sensible to the last.

Edmund Titus was a Quaker. Years before he had presided over his daughter's marriage. He died an old man.[45]

Death, whenever it came, could be expensive. In 1698

Jeremiah Burroughs swam after his loose canoe, got caught in the current, and drowned. His death required someone to go to New York City, and someone to take an inventory of his estate. Burial required a coffin. These expenses totalled £1 1s. In 1700, Benjamin Field probated his father's will. Costs included filing for probate, witnesses, certificates, fees, bonds, letters of administration, and, finally 2s. 6d. for a crier and drum. In all, it cost the estate £2 11s., of which 10s. went to the judge and 13s. 6d. for entering and copying the will. The deceased, Robert Field, was a Quaker. His funeral would have been simple.[46]

Funerals could be elaborate. The deceased could have a coffin, and his body would move to its final resting place amid the beating of drums and the tolling of bells, all of which cost money. If the funeral were large enough, the family would give mourning gifts, a custom that first surfaced around 1700, although it might have been practiced earlier. William Urquhart, the Anglican minister, specifically noted in his will of 1709 that his desire was that "there may be no great pomp or formality used at my funeral; and that none except my wife be put in mourning, that no rings, gloves, or scarfs be given." Indeed, his wealth was incommensurate with his position. Of relatively high status as a minister, his estate shows him poor. Mourning gifts would have left nothing for his wife and young family.[47]

Urquhart died a young man, but most town folk lived longer than he. Longer life meant later distribution of property, and less chance of a son inheriting a farm as a young man. With land becoming scarcer and lives continuing long, sons would remain at home and dependent, perhaps leave the natal home and pursue a trade in Newtown, or leave Newtown altogether. Staying at home and under one's father's roof would probably mean delaying marriage, since most households contained a nuclear or, in some instances, a stem family. The 1698 census of households shows an average of 5.7 white persons per household. Given this number, it seems that sons did not bring their brides home to live with their parents.

Marriage still linked families as it would continue to do throughout the colonial period. Captain William Hallett's ten children all married. Four of their first marriages were to townspeople, and two of these four were to one family, the Blackwells. Intermarriage between a few families suggests that networks were kept intensive rather than extensive. The available resources were shared with fewer people but fewer outside sources were tapped. In Massachusetts familial inter-marriage usually occurred among the more wealthy. The Hal-letts were among Newtown's elite, as were the Blackwells. Other Hallett marriages reinforced their social position. Cap-tain William's brother had only one son, Samuel, who married Bridget Blackwell, further cementing the ties between Hal-letts and Blackwells. Of Samuel's five daughters, one married a townsman, Justice James Hazard. The four Newtown fami-lies into which the Halletts intermarried were all prosperous, and all were English.[48]

With land availability declining, but longevity, residence patterns, marriage, and household size remaining the same, some individuals faced with the limits of the physical environ-ment chose to leave Newtown. The 1698 census listed 145 householders. Two militia lists in 1715 contained 123 names. Correlating the census with the militia lists, genealogical ma-terials, and land records shows a low crude persistence rate of 41 percent and a refined rate, which takes into account known deaths, of between 57 and 59 percent. This percentage is about the same as the earlier period. Surnames show about the same rate of mobility. The 1698 census, which lists New-town's population as 783 whites and 93 slaves, has 48 old, and 42 new, surnames. Twenty-seven names have disappeared. The militia lists have 39 names that appeared in 1698, but 29 that did not. Fifty-one are gone from the record. The Mas-sachusetts and Connecticut towns for which roughly com-parable calculations exist show greater persistence rates. Ded-ham in the 1690s had a crude rate of 83 percent and a refined rate of 96 percent. However, by 1723–1733 the crude rate had fallen to 55 percent. Windsor, Connecticut, between 1676 and

1686 had a crude rate of 57 percent and a refined rate of 71 percent. Eighteenth-century figures are lacking.[49]

By 1790 there were twenty-seven families in Newtown that had been there since 1698. Twenty-four left sufficient records behind to find and trace sons. Within these twenty-four obviously stable families few adults with grown children left Newtown. Those who did were most likely to leave between 1700 and 1725. Perhaps they recognized the growing lack of opportunity, or perhaps they were just restless: their numbers are too small to conclude anything. Those who had the greatest movement of sons were born in 1640–1659. Their sons would come of age in the 1690s through the 1720s—the years when Newtown first experienced land shortages. Thirty-one percent of these sons left, and another 29 percent disappeared from the record. Parents born after 1659 saw more of their children remain in town.[50]

Those who chose to leave would find it difficult to move close by. Of those born before 1725, forty left Newtown. Eighteen, or 45 percent, went south to New Jersey. Five, or 12.5 percent, went across the East River to Westchester. Another five went to New York City. Only two remained in Queens County, while another two went next door to Kings County. By the time those born between 1700 and 1725 came of age, which would be roughly 1725 to 1750, townsmen were going further afield. Jonathan Hazard moved to Orange County, New York, while Cornelius Luyster moved to Dutchess County. Gilbert Woodward went all the way to the West Indies. Such migration patterns broke down Newtown's isolation even further.[51]

Moving meant leaving behind family. It also meant leaving behind institutions, like the church. The Anglican controversy undoubtedly brought all the religious groups to a finer sense of their own identity. Townsmen were still predominantly dissenters who opposed the Church of England. Part of their struggle was political and fought in the assembly. At home, they tried to provide a decent house and hire an independent minister to occupy it.

The ministerial search was an ongoing project in Newtown. In 1694 the town voted to both repair the meeting house and search in New England for an appropriate minister. An ad hoc committee asked John Morse to come to Newtown, and in 1695 monies were raised for his salary, "them that pay to the minister will pay to fetching him." To sweeten the offer, the town, in the midst of fighting the Ministry Act, voted to build a parsonage that they never constructed. Instead, in 1697 the town decided to buy a house and land, selling town land to pay for them, which they delivered to Mr. Morse for his use while he preached the Gospel. That same year, in good congregational fashion, the town voted to ordain him.[52]

In 1700 the town again agreed to build a two-story townhouse, completely furnished, on the town lot next to the minister's house. This largesse was probably in response to the 1699 "Bill to Enable the Respective Towns . . . to Build and Repair their Meeting Houses and Other Public Buildings." Townsmen also chose collectors to collect Morse's salary, a free will offering not so freely given. By 1700 an ad hoc committee was trying to pry the rates from those delinquent and talk the minister into staying. His death in 1700 at the age of twenty-six made the latter unnecessary, and once again Newtown looked for a clergyman.[53]

In 1701 the town lot and parsonage were offered to Mr. Robert Breck. He stayed for three years but then resigned, perhaps in response to Governor Cornbury's campaign against dissenting clergymen. From 1704 to 1709 Newtown had no minister, although itinerants, like Francis MacKemie, were welcomed. MacKemie, preaching in Newtown without warrant from the governor, was arrested for his Newtown sermon. The minister's house was rented out and the monies put into the town treasury.[54]

Newtown finally found someone to stay in Samuel Pumroy. Pumroy had excellent credentials, but he was in some ways a peculiar, hence a revealing, choice. Born in Northampton, Massachusetts, he graduated from Yale at the age of eighteen. He then studied under Solomon Stoddard, one of New England's most famous and controversial ministers, and Pumroy's own minister while he was a child.[55]

Solomon Stoddard was a pivotal figure in the religious history of New England. He began his ministry in Northampton, Massachusetts, in 1669. By 1687 the Massachusetts clergy knew about his heterodox position on salvation and the visible church. Stoddard saw God as inscrutable and His selection of the saved unalterable. Men could neither save themselves nor outguess God. All were potentially of the elect and all should partake of communion. Since no visible church existed, the whole community formed the church. This church, in turn, existed within a "national church," run by authoritative synods of ministers and lay representatives. In other words, Stoddard's view of church organization was presbyterian, not congregational.[56]

The tension between congregational and presbyterian organization had long troubled the New England churches, and they had tried various ways of maintaining a presbyterian discipline within a congregational structure. Foremost among these were clerical consociations. By the early eighteenth century these informal ways had become more routinized. Boston and Cambridge's ministers, spearheaded by the Mathers, formed the Cambridge Association in 1690. In 1708, Connecticut's ministers went further and endorsed the Saybrook Platform. This document, according to Perry Miller, "institutionalized the ecclesiastical theories of Solomon Stoddard." Stoddard himself organized the Hampshire Association in western Massachusetts in 1714.[57]

Newtown, long fertile ground for those with presbyterian leanings, must have been well-informed about New England theology and controversy. Indeed, if Newtown's behavior was at all typical, New Yorkers were far better versed in the larger theological issues of the time than has been sus-

pected. Newtowners, in selecting a student of Solomon Stoddard, went to the heart of presbyterianism in New England.
Called by Newtown, Reverend Samuel Pumroy was ordained
in Massachusetts by Stoddard and two of his followers, John
and William Williams, not by Newtown.[58]

Pumroy made changes in the church of Newtown. Most
important to his congregation, he took them officially into the
Presbyterian church, applying in 1715 for membership in the
Philadelphia Presbytery. Two years later, he helped to orga-
nize the Presbytery of Long Island. Given Newtown's history, it is not surprising that townsmen welcomed this change.
As in New England, the fight against the Church of England
made the weakness of individual congregations manifest. Newtown was strengthening its religious base and extending the
range of its networks beyond town bounds by formally joining a presbytery. In 1723, the purchasers and proprietors of
Newtown, to stifle "slender dark and doubtful expressions"
regranted the seventy-four acres laid out and surveyed to Mr.
Samuel Pumroy, "minister of the Presbyterian congregation
of Newtown . . . and to all succeeding ministers of the Presbyterian persuasion." In true ecumenical spirit the signers included those, like Casper Springsteen and Abraham Boss,
who were not Presbyterians. Pumroy remained in Newtown
until his death in 1744.[59]

Newtowners' search for ministers and their willingness
to concede town lands show that they valued religion, though
not necessarily conformity. While ministers might, in fact,
have trouble collecting salaries, the town, in theory, recognized their right to recompense. This right was based on a voluntary offering by townsmen that was collected by men
chosen at town meeting to collect it. The seventy-four-acre
parsonage, which would be all that remained of Newtown's
common lands, was specifically granted to a Presbyterian minister. No other kind would do. When Newtown was without
one, the town rented out the parsonage, and the town's Presbyterians heard the gospel preached in Jamaica.

The majority of Newtown's English inhabitants were Presbyterians. The Dutch remained Dutch Reformed. Many Dutch lived in Kings County, and, until 1715, all Queens County's Dutch Reformed had to go there to worship. In that year the congregation of the Reformed Low Church in Queens County purchased land in Jamaica and built a church. Here would sit the county's Dutch Reformed, each in his assigned pew according to his rank in the community. The church had no minister but was visited by one of the dominies from New York or Kings County. The Jamaica church was probably part of a circuit. On those Sundays when the minister was absent, the congregation could either go where he was, or conduct services under lay leadership. Only the minister could administer communion, and those wanting to partake would have to travel elsewhere. This pattern continued until the nineteenth century and helped weld the Dutch Reformed from different towns together, just as the presbytery bound Presbyterians from different towns together.[60]

Marriage choice also united the Dutch Reformed. As in both earlier and later periods, few married outside of the Dutch community. Of 111 marriages between 1692 and 1723, 12 (11 percent) were mixed, while an additional 6 (5 percent) were unclear. Of the 12 who married across ethnic lines, 3 were part of the Berrien-Edsall connection, and 4 were Pettits. Thus 7, or over one-half of those who married out, belonged to only two families. Most townsmen preferred to marry within their own ethnic group.[61]

The Presbyterian and Dutch Reformed churches found their congregations naturally. The Church of England had governmental help, which in these years kept some from supporting it. The controversy over the establishment of the Church of England began with the Ministry Act of 1693 which created parishes and assigned responsibility for ministers' salaries. While the act did not specify any denomination, the governors felt that they should appoint the ministers and that those ministers should be Anglican. In 1702 the Society for the Propogation of the Gospel (SPG) took over responsibility for sending over clergymen and teachers, and in 1705 the General Assembly clarified the governor's role in appointing clergymen. With at least some trained personnel and political support the Anglican church was ready to minister to its western Queens County congregation. Jamaica was the parish seat.[62]

Queens County's first minister, the Reverend Gordon, arrived in June 1702 and died in July. He was paid by the SPG. His successor, William Urquahart, settled by Governor Cornbury against the wishes of Jamaica Parish, arrived in 1704 at the peak of the church controversy. At Jamaica he found "a tolerably good church, built of stone, a parsonage house, orchard and two-hundred acres of land . . . and £60 per annum, settled by Act of Assembly . . . . There is in the Church a common prayer book and a cushion but no vestments, nor vessels for the communion table." The churchwardens and vestry were dissenters who refused to provide bread and wine. Newtown also had a church, but it is unclear what building that was. Governor Cornbury gave it to Urquahart. Flushing, the other town in the parish, did not even have a building, much less any of the other necessities for Anglican worship.[63]

First reports to the SPG were bleak. Mr. Urquahart recorded that Jamaica Parish had 2,000 souls but only twenty communicants. Newtown Anglicans rode to Jamaica, even though, Urquahart felt, they could afford and wished their own church. Flushing was beyond the pale, "most of the inhabitants thereof are Quakers, who rove through the country from one village to another, talk blasphemy, corrupt the youth, and do much mischief." Urquahart's labors ended with his death in 1707.[64]

Thomas Poyer became the parish's next minister. He was responsible for services and religious education, noting to the SPG that he gave lectures on week-days, "many twelve miles distant." In Newtown and Flushing "there is no convenience of private houses, so I have to use public ones," a rather damning statement about the strength of the church. He also catechized all sent to him twice a week in the church and once every two weeks at his home. Communion was held four or five times a year.[65]

In 1712, the Anglican church took a major step toward respectability when Joseph Hallett, one of the town elite, had Thomas Poyer baptize his infant son William. The next year Reverend Poyer baptized Joseph, his wife Lydia, their four other children, and Joseph's brother George. George was married in the Protestant Episcopal Church in 1718. Eventually, all of the Halletts but Quaker Richard and his family would accept the Church of England.[66]

By 1717, Thomas Poyer estimated, his parish of three towns contained 409 families of which 80 came to church. There were 400 hearers and 60 communicants. In 1724 he noted 40 communicants so the earlier figure was probably a generous guess. He died in 1732, worn down with the feuding and lawsuits over his salary and other perquisites. He never lived in Newtown.[67]

The Anglican clergy had its problems with the Presbyterians who controlled the vestry, but it reserved its worst epithets for the Quakers. This is ironic because the Quakers had calmed down. No longer would a Mary Case disrupt the meeting house of Newtown. Indeed, witness in public had ceased altogether. Instead, the Friends minded their own affairs and used institutional channels to redress grievances. In doing so, they not only acknowledged the legitimacy of the state but also their own rights as part of the larger polity. They were by now integrated into New York Province.

The Quakers were the closest knit of Newtown's religious groups. Oppression and their keen sense of being both different and purer bonded them together. The smallest unit among the Friends was the weekly meeting, which could meet twice a week at some private house. In the early 1680s, Newtown Friends were joined to the Flushing Weekly Meeting, and those living at Maspeth Kills were united with the Gravesend Meeting of Kings County. Weekly meetings were united by a monthly meeting. In 1684, Gravesend, Flushing, and Westchester organized together. This monthly meeting rotated from place to place. Monthly meetings elected representatives to a quarterly meeting, and the quarterly meeting sent people to a yearly meeting of all New York Quakers. Friends also visited other meetings and entertained visiting Friends. In these ways Quakers knew each other and could maintain discipline without benefit of clergy.[68]

Maintaining conformity was a major concern of the Quaker brethren. The monthly meeting appointed inspectors to look at the weekly meetings and make sure that they acted appropriately. Individual behavior was scrutinized even more closely. Families were visited, and a board was appointed to admonish and instruct those who strayed in dress, words, or absence from meetings. Those who drank too much, who danced and sang, or who otherwise behaved in excessive ways were spoken to. The guilty publicly renounced their ill behavior or were declared out of unity. Friends were not allowed to strike each other or to sue one another in court. All disputes were to stay within the meeting and be resolved there. When people moved they were given certificates of clearance which would admit them to the Society of their new residence.[69]

Quakers were forbidden to marry out; however, a spouse could become a Friend. Richard Hallett married Amy Bowne, a daughter of Flushing's leading Quaker family. For whatever reason, Richard became a Quaker. Once inside, his behavior, like anyone else's, was the concern of all, for a breach of discipline was a break in the whole. The very phrase "out of unity" points out that Friends were distinct and separate. Conformity with the mass culture would mean an end to the Society.[70]

Quakers had special bonds to one another that governed their private lives, but, within a larger context, they were also at odds with their society. By the 1690s, their conflicts with the majority culture were aired through appropriate channels, thereby bringing their behavior within the norms of the larger society, not through individual witness. When Friends were prevented from voting, in 1702, they sent a petition to the governor setting forth their grievances. They also included "their suffering by the pretense of a law to build a house for a nonconformist minister . . . at Newtown," by which Thomas Stevenson and his son, refusing to pay the tax, had their horses seized by the Newtown collector. When the petition went unanswered, the quarterly meeting met with Governor Cornbury. Whether Thomas Stevenson Sr. or Jr., retrieved their horses remains unknown.[71]

The collectors sent to levy the tax on the Stevensons were probably met with a polite refusal since neither Stevenson was cited for abusive behavior. Not everyone was so gentle. The most important breach of justice in Newtown, and the only one of its kind to occur within town bounds, was the murder of William Hallett Jr. and his family by their slaves.

Governor Cornbury called it "that most barbarous murder," when on January 24, 1708, William Hallett Jr., his pregnant wife Ruth, and five children were slain in their sleep by their Indian and black bondsmen. William was thirty-eight and in the prime of his life. The Hallett murders raise many issues. One, the act may be considered political, a signal for a general uprising of slaves against their masters. Certainly the New York authorities considered this a possibility as they discovered two "accomplices." They also tightened up the slave laws by ordering sheriffs to flog any slave who disturbed the peace. The murders may also be seen as personal acts of rebellion. The murderers were a male Indian and a female black. He, at least, must have known freedom at one time since Indians could be enslaved but were not born slaves. Both refused to accept their bondage and committed that act most likely to bring their discontent into public view. Third, the incident shows interracial cooperation, a fearsome prospect in all of the colonies. Indian and black in this case identified themselves as slaves, not as Indians or blacks, and they united against their masters.[72]

Provincial response to the Hallett murders was brutal in the extreme. No white murderer would ever have been treated as these slaves were. Their trial was speedy and included torture, perhaps to make them reveal a conspiracy. Two other blacks were named and condemned. The two murderers were publicly and painfully executed. The Indian was hanged alive in chains and partially impaled so that his death was prolonged. The woman was burned alive. As one witness recalled, they "were put to all manner of torment possible."[73]

In any society, punishment helps set the bounds of the social order. Under the town court, those lower in status who offended those higher up also offended the town's sense of hierarchy. They were publicly humiliated to remind them of their place and the community of its commitment to maintain the status quo. The inhumane and overpoweringly cruel treatment of the slave murderers also carried a message. At least partially underpinned by fear, these sentences were a warning that those who violently crossed racial lines would be quickly and agonizingly disposed of. They were beyond the social order, and no mercy would be shown them. It also, of course, showed where power lay and what societal values were. Blacks and Indians were inferior to even the lowest whites.

The Hallett murders were unusual in another respect because violence of any sort seems rare. Without records from the justices of the peace it is hard to know what happened at the lowest level, but fragmentary evidence suggests that the kinds of problems heard by the town court were now presented before a justice of the peace or a justice and a freeholder. In 1723, Joseph Sackett prosecuted Hannah Strickland for slandering his wife. Justice James Hazard and freeholder Jacob Reeder heard the case. Hannah acknowledged her guilt, but whether in public or privately to Justice Hazard and Jacob Reeder is unclear. It is unlikely that the cases themselves were heard before a potentially large and critical audience, as would have been the case previously. The shame of public exposure was part of Newtown's past; privacy before the law a harbinger of a more individualistic, less communal future. The presence of a freeholder as a co-judge must have tempered the powers of the justice of the peace, who was now and would remain the petty court of first instance, the resident symbol of higher authority.[74]

By 1723 Newtown had long been a settled community. It was visibly tied to surrounding towns and the metropolis by roads, ferries, and the East River. Less visible, but equally strong, were political, economic, and religious networks. County government and the increasing importance of the justice of the peace insured that Newtown was linked horizontally with other towns and vertically with the provincial power structure. An increasing standard of living allowed townsmen to enjoy imported and local goods purchased in neighboring towns and New York City. Religious pluralism broke down parochial religious concerns. All congregations except the Presbyterians transcended town boundaries, thereby throwing townsmen into close contact with co-religionists from other communities. Presbyterian church organization, by its very nature, did the same. The model of a rural enclave wallowing in its provincial isolation never fit Newtown. The years after 1723 would see even greater integration of the town into the province and the empire.

PART FOUR

1724–1775:

Integration
into
New York Province

CHAPTER 7

Authority, Taxation, and the Coming of the Revolution

Between 1724 and 1744 the processes already underway by 1723 continued with little outside interference. County and provincial authority in the person of the justice of the peace eroded the town meeting, but neither county nor province asked for very much, and little was demanded in return. By 1724 the British Empire had been at peace for a good ten years, as Robert Walpole's policies of isolationism in Europe protected both the mother country and her children. This peace continued until the 1740s, when new blood and new ambition saw new glory in old-fashioned warfare. The outbreak of King George's War required provincial taxes that continued almost unabated until 1767. This war effort and its successor, the Seven Years' War, forced the towns to provide men, goods, and services in concert with one another. The agitation surrounding the Association and the Intolerable Acts thus occurred within the context of long-standing cooperation among county folk.

Few issues forced the town to enter into provincial politics. The Church of England controversies had subsided, and the only long-standing problem was the boundary with Bushwick. Newtown never gave up. In 1738 the issue resurfaced, and in 1741 townsmen ordered the trustees to hire the provincial surveyor, or anyone else thought proper, to run the lines again. In 1764, an October town meeting warned the town to defend itself against the "unreasonable pretenses of the people of Bushwick." In 1768, the General Assembly authorized commissioners to settle the boundary between Kings and Queens Counties, thereby drawing the boundary between Bushwick and Newtown. Ironically, this 1769 line was the same as the one drawn in 1672. For ninety-seven years the townsmen had agitated and spent scarce funds in vain.[1]

The settlement of Newtown bounds through the same kind of process that had failed so many times before reflected a changed perception of authority, and a shift in scale, though the manner in which the problem was handled might have changed the outcome. Previously, the governor, governor and council, or the court had tried to settle things. These bodies were appointed. This time, however, the General Assembly, containing Newtown's and Bushwick's elected representatives, passed a law saying the line would be drawn. But maybe more was at issue. Robert Gross has pointed out that the inhabitants of Concord, Massachusetts, settled old scores with one another when faced with an outside threat. By 1769, both Newtowners and their Bushwick neighbors had supported the British in the Seven Years' War with their bodies and their shillings, but they had fought as New Yorkers under one identification. Heterogeneous in the context of town identity, they were homogeneous when viewed at a higher level.[2]

In the boundary dispute Newtown sought out provincial help, but the town, like New England towns, also reacted to provincial prodding. Most of these directives were in the form of laws regulating such mundane matters as town buildings, fence heights, and swine. Newtown usually went along with whatever laws were passed, but not always. In 1752 Newtown revised its swine law, allowing any hogs suitably yoked and ringed to run upon the highways. This relaxed ruling ignored the 1739 provincial swine code, and Justice Van Dyne dissented, declaring "he would stand to the act of assembly concerning swine and desired the same to be entered." Justice Van Dyne, in arguing against the town, was asserting his identity as a representative of the province. This changing angle of vision was probably a slow, perhaps unconscious, process, but the record shows that Van Dyne placed his role of justice before his role of townsman. Few of Newtown's inhabitants and justices felt that way, and the pigs ran free. Local convenience could still outweigh provincial authority.[3]

Scrupulous adherence to the law was easiest when the law's requirements were minimal. Few issues stood out during the long years of peace, but this harmony was shattered in the 1740s with the coming of the war. The first to feel the effects of wartime measures were the pacifist Quakers, who refused to bear arms. By 1755 the colonial assembly was raising troops in New York, but Quakers were exempted. Instead of military service, each male of militia age had to register with the county clerk and pay a fine. During times of alarm, those refusing to carry weapons had to turn out anyway, with "one good spade, iron shod shovel, and pick ax and six empty bags, each bag sufficient to contain two bushels, and shall serve as pioneers or laborers." The fines mounted up. At least £194 10s. were levied, but the true total was undoubtedly higher, since Queens County Friends paid £102 in 1756 alone.[4]

The outbreak of warfare in the 1740s affected not just the Quakers but all townsmen. The first and most obvious impact that Newtowners faced was increased taxes; the second and more subtle change was their active participation with each other and with strangers as war brought troops and refugees to the town.

When Lord Loudoun, commander-in-chief of the British forces in America, wrote to William Pitt in 1757 "the taxes which the people pay in this country, are really so trifling, that they do not deserve the name," he was speaking of a time already past. During peacetime the province made few demands. Indeed, the only taxes levied upon Newtown were in the 1720s, when Newtown was assessed £155 for cancelling bills of credit, securing trade with the Indians, repairing barracks in New York City, and paying a lobbyist in England. All of these expenses were either war-related or peace-keeping expenditures. Regular governmental revenues were raised through the quitrent, various taxes on nonessentials, such as wigs and slaves, and the liquor excise.[5]

The county required more, but not much more, from townsmen. Fixed expenditures were the salaries of Queens County's representatives to the New York General Assembly, and the per diem of the county board of supervisors. Other county responsibilities included bounties on predators, but these ended in 1730, as wildcats and foxes retreated before a growing human population. The county transported vagrants and vagabonds, fed and tended prisoners in jail, prosecuted slaves and felons, and paid coroner's fees. None of these tasks was especially costly, and the record suggests that Queens County, and by implication Newtown, had little trouble with either the wandering poor or the resident miscreant. Newtown's share of county expenses ranged from £2 to £40 10s. Its average assessment was £13 10s.[6]

The town also needed money, but town levies were even lower than county ones. Newtown's quitrent remained fixed at £3 4s. The town paid fees to the town clerk, assessors, collectors, and the like, which averaged around £4 5s. It also collected for the various town houses built and the Bushwick boundary dispute. These town expenses averaged another £15 per year. County and town levies together usually cost Newtown less than £30 per year. With a minimal taxpaying population of 210 persons, the per taxpayer cost would average about three shillings a year, hardly a large sum and only about one-sixth of the rate paid between 1692 and 1723. This tax would cost less than one bushel of wheat at 3s. 6d. per bushel, or one day's wages at 3s. per day.[7]

The onset of King George's War in 1744 saw the beginning of provincial tax levies designed to pay for troops and supplies. Newtown's quota was £26 7s. The provincial assembly levied no taxes in 1745, but from 1746 until 1767—

FIGURE 2

Newtown's Share of Provincial Taxes

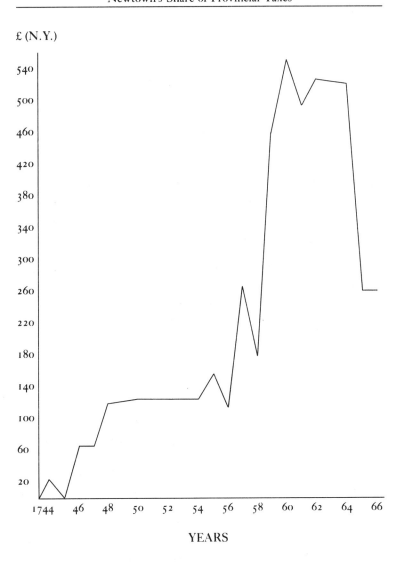

£ (N.Y.)

YEARS

twenty–one years, a whole generation—New Yorkers paid for war. King George's conflict ended in 1748, but the taxes raised to finance it expired in 1755. That year a new and larger confrontation between France and England began. Called the Seven Years' War, it would be much more costly. In 1746, Newtown paid £64 16s. toward King George's War. Two years later, this assessment almost doubled, to £128 10s (see Figure 2). These taxes were low, however, compared to those brought by the new war. In 1755, Newtown's bill was £155 6s., which in 1757 increased to £268 16s., and by 1760 was £530 6s. Taxes continued to hover around £500 until 1765, when Parliament's reimbursements to the colony were applied to wartime levies. At that point, Newtown's taxes almost halved to £261 2s. The total bill for the two wars was £5,355 11s., all of which was paid.[8]

Five thousand pounds seems like a lot of money, but a better measure of its impact on the population would be the cost per taxpayer. The 1744 levy of £26 7s. cost the average taxpayer about 2s. The most expensive year of 1760 cost him 41s. The average tax bill for the whole period was 18s. Given that a taxpayer's normal debt was 3s. per year (which he continued to pay in addition to everything else), the new demands were a large increase. On the average, taxes were seven times higher than normal, and, during the worst year, taxes were fourteen times more than their peacetime rates.[9]

A fourteen-fold, or even a seven-fold tax increase looks extreme, but wars often bring prosperity by creating new markets for produce. If local farmers did find new demands for their goods then the prices of goods should have risen. Inflation would erode real profits but would also ease the tax burdens as taxes were paid in inflated currencies. This economic spiral lagged in New York. The first real price rise in wholesale domestic prices came in 1759. These prices continued to rise until 1762 when they declined. In 1764 prices began to climb again, reaching a peak in 1772, from which they then dropped (see Figure 3), but never to the lows pre-

FIGURE 3

Domestic Price Index

INDEX (in N.Y. £)

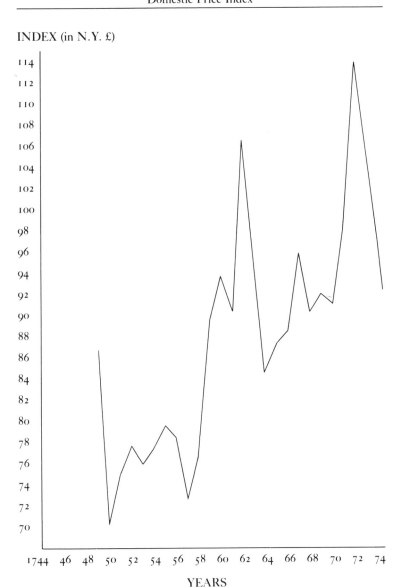

YEARS

ceding 1758. While taxes doubled, then doubled again, wholesale prices never even doubled. To make enough profit to
cover the new demands, Newtown's yeomen would have had
to place more acreage into crops. But the limits had been
reached, no more land was available, and the less desirable
plots were already coming under cultivation. Finally, inflation
shows up in the rates of exchange which governed the value
of New York's money. Between 1744 and 1766, the ratio of
New York currency to sterling averaged between 167.20 and
191.46. This fluctuation was very narrow and meant that
taxes were not being paid in greatly devalued local currency.[10]

Direct provincial taxes were only one cost of the colonial
wars. The county also levied war-related expenses, including
lookouts on the coast, the buildings, bedding, food, and can-
dles for barracks, and a field hospital. These costs added another £29 to the tax bill and added another two shillings to
each taxpayer's total expense. From an average tax bill of three
shillings in 1743, taxes had risen to forty-six shillings in 1760.
To pay forty-six shilllings, each townsman would have needed
nine bushels of wheat at 5s. per bushel, or fifteen days' wages
at 3s. per day. Neither free lands on which to grow more crops
or high demands for unskilled labor characterized Newtown[11]

The cost of the colonial wars to America's taxpayers has
yet to be systematically studied, but scattered evidence suggests that the price of British ambition, taken in its broadest
sense, was high. Gary Nash, in his recent exhaustive study of
the northern urban centers, found that wars required high
taxes. The renewal of hostilities in the 1740s raised Boston's
taxes from an average of twelve shillings around 1730, to fifty
shillings around 1748, "a fourfold increase in fifteen years."
Between 1750 and 1754, each taxable poll paid an average of
fifty-five shillings for provincial taxes alone, "the highest in
history." Total taxes averaged eighty-eight shillings, which
came out to a real and personal property tax of 66 percent of
assessed value. This rate was levied for the three years of
1758, 1759, and 1760. For the next five years Bostonians faced

an annual tax bill of eighty-nine shillings, which apparently broke the back of local resources and went partially unpaid. Nash's thesis is that wages could not begin to keep pace with fiscal demand and Boston faced the ensuing peace with higher poverty rates than the city could handle.[12]

The countryside also paid for war. David Grayson Allen, looking at Massachusetts' town petitions for the abatement of provincial taxes, found that these pleas usually came "in times of economic distress (almost exclusively during one of the colonial wars)."[13]

The power to tax is the power to control. Townsmen, by meeting their financial obligations, were saying, as they had said before, that they accepted the province's right to tax. New York, however, came through the experience of the Seven Years' War with two other perceptions of taxation. The first was that the war had strained local resources. New York's General Assembly reminded both king and Parliament of this sacrifice in 1764. Addressing King George III, the assembly noted that "we flatter ourselves, that this People has given your Majesty, the most recent Proofs of their Zeal for the Glory of their Sovereign, of their Readiness to bleed at every Vein in his Service, and of that uncommon Alacrity with which they have in the late war, so glorious to your Majesty, and your royal Grandfather, even out of their Poverty so liberally contributed to the Common Cause." Their message to Parliament, while less striking in its imagery of a people ready to lay down their life's blood for a "common cause," concentrated more on the costs of the war: "our taxes have been equal to our Abilities, [and] . . . our Contribution surpassed our Strength." Moreover, this condition was acknowledged by Parliament. This was the "reality," using Gordon Wood's terminology, of taxation.[14]

The second perception that New York gained from its experience with taxation was a heightened sense of autonomy expressed through "rhetoric." The same petitions that reminded Britain that New York would, could, and did give freely of scarce resources also jealously maintained that *only* New York could expend those resources. The petition to George III identified New York's interest with Great Britain's, but insisted that "in exercising the Power of Taxing ourselves, your Majesty's Service, and the public Welfare were our invariable objects." This petition, in response to the Revenue Act by which Great Britain would tax sugars for the purpose of raising a revenue, began the province's opposition to, indeed denial of, Parliament's right to tax Americans. In so doing, New Yorkers were denying the assumption that Parliament's interest and New York's interest were one—that they belonged to a homogeneous body with a common interest. These petitions, written not only by New York, but by the other colonies as well, were the opening wedge of a self-conscious difference, a heterogeneity, which would eventually split the empire. This theme will reappear in the 1770s.[15]

The high taxes and increasing self-consciousness resulting from them were not the only legacies or dislocations brought by the war. The barracking of troops, the establishment of a field hospital, and the resettlement of French Canadian refugees and other prisoners of war brought new and unwanted people to Newtown. Newtown's social boundaries were fixed by 1750. They were wide enough to cover the Dutchmen, Englishmen, Anglicans, and Quakers who shared local values, Protestantism, and world views, but they did not cover those who fell outside of these constraints. On May 6, 1756, a town meeting to "search into the rights of the town . . . the people being much in contention this meeting was dismissed by Thomas Betts Justice." Never before had a town meeting been peremptorily adjourned. Possibly the issue was housing the French Canadians whom the British had removed from Nova Scotia and relocated throughout the colonies. In any case, on that same May 6, 1756, the New York Council ordered Seres Etben, his wife, and eight children to Newtown. By 1758, the town had voted to build them a house, but that is the last that is heard of them. They bought no land and appeared in none of the church records. Perhaps at the end of the war they resettled in Canada, as did Massachusetts' "neutral French." [16]

Prisoners of war also lived in Newtown. Captured officers lodged in private homes until they could be exchanged. The General Assembly paid for their board. At least six townsmen hosted these men from 1756 to 1759. Captured French officers were probably preferable to an impoverished yeoman family of ten. Least desirable were soldiers and the sick. When Newtown's justices called a special meeting in February of 1757 to discuss how to billet soldiers alloted to the town, the people again disagreed so violently that the justices dismissed the meeting. Eventually, the General Assembly empowered the county supervisors to raise taxes "for relieving such parts of said county as are burdened with quartering troops," thus spreading these costs, but again, as with taxation, an issue was raised that had larger implications. They would be articulated later. [17]

By 1756, the appointed justices of the peace, not the elected town officers, seemed in control of the town meeting. The increased power of the justice accompanied the decreasing importance of the town meeting itself. Before 1724, the town met an average of three times a year, but between 1724 and 1775 the town met an average of 1.2 times per year. Only in 1747 did the town meet more than twice, and then it decided to rent the town house and elected a new assessor, the old one refusing to serve. The few rules and regulations passed concerned swine and fencing and gave the highway masters power to fine and prosecute those refusing to clear the roadways. Only five regulations passed during these fifty-one years. [18]

By 1724 town life in Newtown, as in other towns, had settled into a routine. In Jamaica the average number of town meetings declined after 1700, from 4.84 per year to 1.34 per year. Connecticut's oldest towns averaged between 1.7 and 2.3 meetings yearly between 1720 and 1770. Newer villages began with more activity but then slacked off. Towns, when they did meet, did little. Neither York nor Hampshire County towns in Massachusetts passed a single law between 1692 and 1750. Instead, towns met, held elections, and dispersed.[19]

Each year Newtown met to elect officers, and this choice of people remained the meeting's primary purpose. The number of offices continued to expand with the addition of overseers of highways and appraisers of intestate estates. Both of those were responsible positions with duties that went beyond the town. Highway overseers were elected in response to new laws from the province, not local need. They actually laid out highways and could confiscate property to facilitate this. Appraisers of intestate estates evaluated the property of those who died without wills. Both helped integrate town and province.[20]

Appraisers of intestate estates were the last new officers that the New York provincial assembly created. Local government had increased from three offices under the Dutch to ten in 1740. The process was one of increased specialization and institutionalization. Moreover it was also one of integration, since a number of eighteenth-century offices, such as supervisor, highway surveyor, and appraiser of intestate estates, required contact with men from other towns or provincial officials. And this process happened elsewhere. On the county level in Massachusetts, Hendrik Hartog notes, "the conception of undifferentiated judicial government that underwrote the power of a sessions court over county life gradually unravelled and was replaced by a modern conception of county government as an administrative agency." In Dedham between 1700 and 1775, according to Edward Cook, "a set of tightly meshed and essentially undifferentiated institutions gave way to several sets of distinct institutions serving clearly defined functions." Speaking for Connecticut, but also for other places, Bruce Daniels sums this up by noting that institutionalization began with the first generation and was an inexorable process: "Growth and differentiation in governments was the political response to the modernization process."[21]

Institutionalizing tasks meant less need for ad hoc structures. While new situations still called for the creation of ad hoc offices, these were much fewer than before. Between 1724 and 1775 the town elected only eight ad hoc committees. Whereas from 1692 to 1723 the town had averaged 1.5 committees per year, now it averaged one every six years. These committees rented the town house, oversaw the town books, and met with the county supervisors in 1753. The last ad hoc task the town assigned, ironically, was akin to the first. In 1764 six townsmen were chosen to oversee the boundary dispute with Bushwick. No further committees were elected to discuss British taxes or any other concern of the 1760s or 1770s.[22]

The decline in town meetings and ad hoc committees was accompainied by longer tenure in the yearly-elected town offices; hence there were fewer participants (see Table 6).

TABLE 6

Tenure in Town Office,
1665–1775 (average number of years)

OFFICE	1665–1691	1692–1723	1724–1775
Constable	1.7	1.6	2.7
Town clerk	5.4	5.2	12.8
Assessor	1.8	1.5	1.3
Collector*		1.0	
Supervisor		3.8	12.8
Fence viewer †		1.8	5.8
Trustees †		2.8	5.1
Highway surveyor		1.2	1.0
Appraiser of intestate estates ‡			7.6
Highway overseer §			3.0

*Merged with constable after 1717.
† Began in 1717.
‡ Began in 1740.
§ Began in 1734.
SOURCE: The town minute books.

Again, as in New England, only the least desirable jobs of assessor and highway surveyor rotated freely. Other positions,
like supervisor, trustee, and appraiser of intestate estates, became frozen. Some, like the town clerkship, were almost pro-
prietaries. Jacob Reeder held this position for thirty-three
years, his successor for only three, and then Samuel Moore
and Samuel Moore III kept it between them for another
twenty-four.[23]

From 1724 to 1775, Newtown chose 157 men to fill town
offices. Using the 156 men who held normal tenures, they
averaged 5.7 years in 2.1 offices during their lifetimes. Most
people held very few positions during their lives. Twenty-
seven percent of Newtown's officers only held office for one
year, and another 33 percent served two or three years. The
large number who held an office only for a short time reflected
the crucial importance of roads and the ever-increasing number of people who served as highway surveyors. This task was
performed by three men, until 1741, when their number increased to four. By 1750, ten men filled this slot each year, and
by 1775 eighteen. Indeed, by 1775 eighty-four, or a full 53
percent of those holding office, had helped clear Newtown's
roads. No other elected office had so many persons pass
through it.

Most men gave little service to the town; therefore, the
few who really were town leaders stand out. The 157th man
to hold office was Samuel Fish Jr., who served for ninety-
three years in five different offices. His life illustrates many of
the ongoing processes in Newtown.

Samuel Fish Jr. was born in 1704, the son of Jonathan
Fish, town clerk and a major officeholder of the preceding generation. In 1727 he married Angenettie Berrien, daughter of
John Berrien and Ruth Rapalje Edsall. He was one of the few
Englishmen to marry into a Dutch family, albeit his mother-
in-law was the stepdaughter of the Englishman Samuel Edsall. Others in the Fish family also intermarried with the Berriens. Samuel's uncle Samuel had married his wife's mother,

the widow Ruth Berrien. Therefore, Samuel had married his step-cousin. How much Dutch culture was left to his bride is difficult to ascertain. They belonged to the Presbyterian church. These marriages tied the Fish family to the Berriens and the Rapaljes, two of the more prominent Dutch families. In 1747, Angenettie Fish died in childbirth, and the next year Samuel married Abigail Howard. She died in 1750, perhaps also in childbirth, and two years later he married the widow Ann Betts. He died in 1767 at about the age of sixty-three. By his three wives Samuel had at least fifteen children. Three sons and five daughters were noted in his 1767 will.[24]

Samuel Fish's economic career shows him to be an entrepreneur who owned land but did not farm it. In 1724 he and his siblings inherited land from their father. He also bought and inherited land through his first wife's people, the Berriens. Some of these latter pieces he sold to his wife's uncle Nathaniel. In 1748, calling himself a vintner, he sold thirty-three acres to Samuel Moore, the Younger. Most of his land he kept for his sons.[25]

By 1767, the year that Samuel died, he was one of Newtown's two innkeepers. His will shows him to be a wealthy man, well-tied to the provincial economy and conspicuous consumption patterns. He had slaves and silver and a riding chair. Each of his three married daughters was to receive £500 over what was already given them. His two underage daughters would get £500 each when of age. These monies were to go toward their education and two feather beds and furniture. His widow, Ann, and two youngest children moved their abode to a house, land, garden, and orchard that were currently rented out. Samuel's executors were to buy out the four years remaining on the lease. His sons were given land that appears to have been bought with them in mind. Jonathan received at least sixty-four acres for which he paid the estate £400. Richard received at least forty-five acres. In a codicil to his will Samuel gave his homestead to son Samuel for only his lifetime. Upon his death the estate was to be sold at public vendue, or given to whichever remaining son paid £1,200. Finally, Samuel left bequests to the Presbyterian church.[26]

Well off, Samuel Fish Jr. was centrally located at the one place in town sure to be on a main thoroughfare, and sure to be patronized by traveller and local alike. Indeed, taverns were probably the major political and communication centers for most towns. Fish also had other duties that brought him into contact with others. Although probably not a justice of the peace, he did serve on the court bench. His militia company elected him lieutenant and then captain. He bears this title in the records. Given wealth, occupation, and contacts, Samuel Fish Jr. was an ideal broker. He began his political career in 1725 with the office of fence viewer. He held that post for twenty-four years. In 1734 he was elected appraiser of intestate estates, a position that he held for thirty years. In 1740 he was elected trustee and in 1743 pound keeper. He also held one ad hoc post. Adding to his connections were the numerous positions held by other family members. His grandfather, father, uncles, and in-laws all were town officers.[27]

Both the English and the Dutch held town office. Of the 157 men in the group, 60.5 percent had English last names, and 33.8 percent had Dutch surnames. The Dutch had gained since 1724, almost doubling the percentage of Dutchmen elected to town positions. This gain outstripped their place in the larger population. In 1771 the Dutch were about 21 percent of Newtown's households. The Dutch, therefore, held more offices proportionately than the English. Moreover, many of these offices were important, such as trustee or highway commissioner.

Members of the minority religious groups also held office. The religious affiliations of ninety-five men can be identified, and, of these, one-third were Presbyterian and one–half Dutch Reformed. Only ten men were Anglican, and eight were Quakers.[28]

Minority religious groups held office in Newtown, but, perhaps more surprisingly, by the mid-eighteenth century they also did in New England. Bruce E. Steiner found that Connecticut Anglicans began to hold elected positions by the 1730s. Divisive church politics and the dispersion of settlement from town centers led townsmen to choose known and trusted men less caught up in religious factionalism. Steiner calls the trend a "local politics of diversity," and he stresses that it succeeded because of kinship and friendship bonds at the local level. The General Assembly never appointed churchmen; their neighbors elected them. Edward M. Cook also found both toleration and inclusion. Presbyterians in congregational towns; Anglicans, Baptists, and Quakers all were chosen selectmen although Quakers averaged shorter terms. Cook concludes: "Dissenters could take their place in town affairs once they stopped threatening the community and symbolically became loyal members of it, and local peace then demanded that the town accomodate their personal ambitions and policy preferences immediately."[29]

The wealth of officeholders is harder to assess than ethnicity or religion. About 40 percent of them held slaves, but this figure might reflect the percentage of slaveholders in the larger population. Some people were undoubtedly wealthy. Both Joseph Lawrence and William Hazard engaged in single land transactions worth £2,750, and Daniel Betts left a considerable fortune behind him. The poor were probably excluded from everything but clearing the highways.[30]

Wealth had not necessarily meant great town service in the past, and it did not now. As Edward Cook noted for his New England towns, no town ever gave its leadership positions to the top five or six men on a tax list. Twelve Newtown officeholders bought or sold a single piece of land valued at £900 or more. Among the twelve was the active officer Samuel Fish Jr., but, leaving him aside, the others served a mean number of 6.6 years in 3.1 different offices. This record was only slightly better than for the officeholders as a whole.[31]

Two of the wealthier twelve were justices of the peace, as were sixteen other officeholders. These eighteen men represented 11.5 percent of the sample. They held an average of 13.2 years in 4.5 offices, much higher than the total, and correlating with the pattern found for the earlier period. Justices not only held more offices for longer tenures, they were also more likely to be appointed to ad hoc committees and to serve as appraisers of intestate estates. They were especially important to the everyday political life of the town.[32]

The increasing role of the justices, along with the decreasing number of town meetings, ad hoc committees, and access to the more important offices, meant that discussions about issues that concerned Newtown as a whole were less frequently held. But no other meetings replaced them. While townsmen had extensive ties to Jamaica, the county seat, and to New York City, the provincial capitol, these contacts only functioned when the environment remained stable. When the political and economic climate began to change during the 1750s due to the demands of the Seven Years' War, linkages broke down. These claims bypassed the local consensus in two important ways. First, the whole notion of housing strangers and troops went against the sanctity of private property as embodied in one's own home. Moreover, these requirements, while articulated through the General Assembly, originated outside of that body and were military decisions. Newtown had no representatives in the British army and neither did New York. In New York City, feelings ran high against billeting officers in private homes. Memories of these feelings would lead the province to oppose the Quartering Act of 1765. Second, these new people were strangers. Their world view was alien to that of the townsmen.[33]

The 1770s proved even harder to come to terms with, as townsmen were asked to take stands on issues that polarized long-standing values. On the one hand, there was pride in and identification with British nationality. On the other hand, their rights of property and representation were being violated, even as the king's representatives assured colonists that these rights were being protected. The middlemen, who should have mediated the conflict, never existed. When the political crises of the 1770s came to Newtown, neither county nor town seemed willing to act in a corporate capacity. This vacuum left individuals to gather in extraordinary bodies and pass resolutions without the imprimatur of either town or county.

The Stamp Act Congress, the Non-importation agreements, the Boston Massacre, and the Boston Tea Party made no traceable impact on Newtown or the other Queens County towns. By 1774, however, the New York Committee of Correspondence brought grievances to the attention of the county's inhabitants, as well as the towns' and, demanded that people take sides. The first issue was whether to send delegates to the First Continental Congress meeting in Philadelphia. The New York committee decided to send representatives but wanted the counties to do so also. Queens County refused, Lieutenant Governor Cadwallader Colden noting in October that "six persons have not been got to meet for the purpose."[34]

By December, people were more divided. Perhaps spurred on by Jamaica, which had passed a series of anti-Parliamentary resolves, Newtowners met on December 10th, "pursuant to advertisement of the supervisor," and created their own committee of correspondence composed of seventeen freeholders. The seventeen were headed by Colonel Jacob Blackwell. The others included justices Daniel Rapalje and Richard Alsop, as well as other substantial townsmen, both Dutch and English. The committee members were in no way rabble-rousers or malcontents, and their very moderation would split the committee almost immediately. Nineteen days later, Jacob Blackwell published a list of resolves much like Jamaica's, and eleven of the committee resigned. Blackwell went on to more important duties, and Newtown's Committee of Correspondence, still ethnically mixed, lost the town justices which had given it so much legitimacy.[35]

The December 10th meeting was never recorded in Newtown's town minutes and neither was the committee's report of December 19th. Maybe townsmen were being prudent, for the resolutions set out the problem in irresolvable terms. Having listed the late acts of Parliament, that were intended to raise revenue, "bind the people of these colonies by statute in all cases whatsoever," and extend Vice-Admiralty court and customs jurisdictions, and the various so-called Intolerable Acts, the committee then concluded that these acts "absolutely intended to deprive His Majesty's most dutiful and loyal subjects of the American Colonies of their most inestimable rights and privileges by subjecting them to the British Parliament." But if these were His Majesty's dutiful and loyal subjects then were not they also subject to Parliament, and if not Parliament then who was it that could "take their property?" The five resolves which followed tried to answer that question.[36]

The first three resolutions said little that had not been said before in Newtown's long history. The first declared allegiance to King George III and the "illustrious House of Hanover." It also asserted the right, under royal protection, "to enjoy the privileges of the Constitution of Great Britain." The second resolve argued, as had the Remonstrance of 1653, "that man ought to have the disposition of his property either by himself or his representatives," and the third declared that it was "our indispensible duty" to hand posterity the same rights and privileges townsmen had inherited from their ancestors, "particularly that of disposing of our own property."[37]

The next two resolutions were trickier. Instead of appealing to loyalty to the crown and Britain's ancient constitution—to an identification with England—resolves four and five declared obedience to the congress meeting in Philadelphia. Resolve four stated that opposition was required to acts of Parliament imposing taxes in America and that opposition would be coordinated, not in Newtown or Queens County or New York, but in Philadelphia, and by "Delegates sent by each Colony . . . . As we are willing to establish harmony and union, we will, as far as our influence extends, endeavor that the measures of Congress be strictly adhered to in this town." This resolution claimed both a change in scale and a homogeneity of interest which was new and disturbing. In effect, Newtown's interest lay with all other colonists in America, not just with those whom one knew first- or second-hand. The brokers linking the town to the congress were the delegates to the congress, and, even more important, they were also the revolutionary committees which would take upon themselves much more power than any town had given its elected officials. As Resolve four states, their concern would be "to observe the conduct of all persons touching said association." The committees were erecting new social limits not too different from those attempted by the more pious and self-conscious seventeenth-century New England ideologues. All who could not conform would be penalized. To a people who jealously withheld power from their own town officials, and who had no guidelines for excluding others from the community of the village, this innovation must have smacked of mob rule or worse.[38]

Resolution five is the most interesting of the resolves. It states the essential contradiction between the perception of the problem and its resolution. The problem was how to oppose "the several late tyrannical and oppressive acts of the British Parliament," while still bearing "true allegiance" to the king, and how to secure "liberty and privileges as freeborn Englishmen and again restore harmony and confidence throughout the British Empire." The solution was to act through "our worthy Delegates in the General Congress," a body with no authority or charter from the king and one which lay outside the institutional structures of the British empire. The Committee of Correspondence acted as middlemen linking Newtowners to the townsmen of other colonies. In terms of a homogeneous interest, the Continental Congress united the heterogeneous colonies. No structure united the colonies to Great Britain, and by the time that Joseph Galloway proposed his 1774 Plan of Union it was too little too late.[39]

The ease with which some townsmen could join with others, not only from distant towns but from other provinces, suggests both common values and a shared vocabulary. By 1774, Newtown had voiced its commitment to the sanctity of private property protected by representative government for over one hundred and twenty years. Recent work on other towns shows these same long-held values articulated in much the same way. Indeed, when Samuel Adams sent out his anti-Parliamentary "The Votes and Proceedings of the Town of Boston" to 260 towns and districts, he knew his audience would understand him. They had a whole history of doing so. Ipswich, Massachusetts, began its opposition to taxation with-out representation in 1655, two years after Newtown's Re-monstrance. In 1687, faced with Governor Edmund Andros' call for a tax, Ipswich voted no. Styling themselves "freeborn English subjects of his Majesty," they stated that their liberty as freeborn subjects was protected by "the statutory laws of the land," which gave only elected assemblies the authority to tax. In 1717 the issue rose again, and this time was answered in terms of natural law. Power, according to Minister John Wise, resides with the people.[40]

Ipswich used the rhetoric of natural law and English freedom to protect local concerns. The protection of these in-terests from those who wished gain for themselves constituted the basic tenet of country ideology, which saw economic in-dependence as the cornerstone of liberty. Richard Bushman noted how pervasive its tenets were in Massachusetts, even by 1713. And the arguments used by Daniel Bull et al. against the Queens County justices establish its roots in New York by about the same time.[41]

Before men had to actually choose which side to take in the 1770s, the people of Ipswich and Hubbardston, Massa-chusetts, and Newtown, New York, accepted that Parliament could not tax, and that Great Britain's assuming the salaries of court justices made those judges less independent. Robert E. Brown's conclusion that the American Revolution was fought to preserve democracy was half right. Democracy was not the issue, but the sanctity of local authority was. In a sense, the Revolution preserved a consensus, approved of and shared at the town level, concerning the locus of power and the channels through which that power flowed.[42]

The question in Newtown was not about abstractions, such as "the rights of Englishmen," but about whether those agreed-upon liberties were actually in danger. The reaction to Newtown's resolves came swiftly. On January 12, 1775, a letter disowning both resolves and Continental Congress appeared in Rivington's *Gazette*. In full, it declared that:

> We, the subscribers were in no way concerned in certain resolves signed by Jacob Blackwell, Chairman, entered into by some inhabitants of Newtown, approving the proceedings of the Continental Congress; neither do we acknowledge any other representatives but the General Assembly of the Province.

This statement, addressing only the fourth and fifth resolves, denied the change in social scale which the resolves implied. For the fifty-six townsmen who entered their protest, identification stopped at New York's boundaries.[43]

The dissenters from Newtown's set of resolves were a mixed lot. The fifty-six signatures included James, Richard, and William Hallett Jr., relatives of Jacob Blackwell, as well as Justices Rapalje and Alsop, who were members of Newtown's original Committee of Correspondence. These protests demonstrated that family loyalty was secondary to political conviction. Not only the Halletts, but the Moores, Rikers, and Morrells disagreed among themselves on which course to take.

In April of 1775, the question of electing representatives to the Second Continental Congress again required action. New York's provincial convention needed to elect delegates and again asked Queens County, not the towns, to attend the meeting. Perhaps Newtown was motivated by the "Queens County Freeholder," who asked his "Friends and Fellow-

Townsmen" in the language now current in all the colonies, to "adopt such constitutional measures as they shall judge most efficacious to frustrate the tyrannical and wicked designs of a corrupt and arbitrary ministry" and warned that "if we join those hirelings and tools of state, who aim at preventing the choice of delegates to the congress, our conduct may rivet the chains, not only upon ourselves, but on our posterity." At the poll, one hundred freeholders voted, among them Samuel and Jacob Hallett Jr., but conspicuously absent were most of the fifty-six who wrote to the *Gazette*. Only five names appear on both lists, Dow Van Dyne's being the most curious. He was the only Newtown Tory whose estate was confiscated at the end of the Revolutionary War. Newtown elected Jacob Black-well, but the rest of the county declined to send delegates. One town's vote was insufficient, and Queens lost its voice in the convention.[44]

Events quickly moved beyond the town. Americans shed blood at Lexington and Concord and positions hardened. New York's Provincial Congress met and decided that Queens County was represented, irrespective that "a great number of inhabitants of the said county are not disposed to a representa-tion at this board, and have dissented therefrom." This state-ment seems peculiar if not seen in a larger context. In essence, the Provincial Congress was arguing for virtual representation. Queens County was represented because Queens County shared the rights and duties of the rest of the province and was an indistinguishable part of the whole body politic. Parlia-ment used the same argument, one that was rejected by the congress. Locally, committees formed to carry out the orders of the Continental Congress. Those who met in December of 1774 composed Newtown's subcommittee. These were New-town's hard-core Whigs. Newtown's supposed hard-core To-ries, including Captain Samuel, James, Richard, and Thomas Hallett were singled out later, when the Provincial Congress, responding to rumors that the British were arming their sup-porters, requested the disaffected to come before them. When these "delinquents" refused to appear, they were put outside the law's protection and their names published. Worse was in store. In January, the congress disarmed those opposed to it and arrested Captain Samuel and other leaders.[45]

As Newtown became part of the county and province it lost sight of the whole picture of itself, which it would have had as a semiautonomous town before 1692. Without this holistic sense of its own best interest, it became harder for the town to act. More parts would have to be geared up and enmeshed; more specialized interests convinced that a course of action was reasonable. By the 1750s, townsmen had trouble doing this. For the first time a justice disbanded a town meeting. In the 1770s, the town refused to act in its corporate capacity at all and for much the same reasons. Instead, the town fragmented, some choosing one side, some the other, and some neither. Specialization had broken down town consensus, making it hard for the town to react to the new political situation it faced. Newtowners belonged to different ethnic and religious groups, had different claims to town office and varied economic needs, some of which went far beyond the town. They needed brokers to tie people together within the new political context, but these roles had not yet evolved to mediate the problem, by 1775, and then, with the British about to disembark their army, it was too late. Civilians had disagreed in 1774, but by December of 1775 disagreement was no longer possible. The next move was to arm and disarm, the last would be the British occupation of Newtown.

The outwardly peaceful life of townsmen would be shattered in 1776. No one foresaw those events and no one anticipated the hardships they would cause. On August 9, 1775, Robert Hallett, living in St. Croix, wrote to his brother Thomas:

I hear you have very troublesome times among you, for these times must be disagreeable to you, and all reasonable people to hear of so much blood shed among you, God grant that there may be a reconciliation among you before there is a fusion of more blood.

But there was no reconciliation, even among reasonable people, like the good yeomen and artisans of Newtown.[46]

CHAPTER 8

The Diversification of Newtown's Economy

The town that British troops occupied in 1776 was basically agricultural. Their barracks lay in meadows; their marches took them past fields ripe with barley and wheat. Newtown was a farming village and the base of its economy was the land.

By 1723 the population had reached the limits of town land. Adaptation took a number of forms: people could remain on the land but farm smaller farms; they could, as some had always done, combine artisan skills with farming; they could go into trades but keep orchards and gardens; they could work as skilled or unskilled laborers; they could invest money, as well as farm and craft; or they could leave town. As Darrett Rutman has pointed out, economic opportunity and population density both trigger migration. If people can find work where they are they will stay. Newtowners' major strategy seemed to be a shift to part-time agriculture, as men combined skills and investments with smaller farms. They themselves recognized this change, calling themselves tailors or cordwainers even though they owned farms.[1]

As in the earlier period, the Hallett family illustrates the economic processes underway. Some twenty-one Halletts recorded land transactions between 1724 and 1775. Most of these were sales, but a few were gifts. As in the earlier period an overwhelming number of these transactions were kept within the family. Of forty-one land acquisitions, only one was from an outsider. Of fifty-five transactions disposing of land, only eighteen, or 32 percent, were to non-Halletts, and even then many of these people were related to the Halletts through marriage or blood. Ten persons with different sur-names bought land, but Edmund Penfold, Nathaniel Provost, and John Greenoak married Hallett women. Ludlam Hare married a Hallett grandchild, and William Leverich became Robert Hallett's father-in-law. There are a number of William Lawrences in Newtown, but the one mentioned in the land records could have been the son of Elizabeth Hallett Law-rence. Of the ten names only four have no discernible connec-tion with the family. In the distribution of increasingly scarce resources the family fell back upon itself, and in its land sales, at least, bounded the world according to kinship ties.

In the third generation, Justice Joseph Hallett was the major heir of Captain William (see Figure 4). By his two wives he had nine sons and no daughters. This large number of sons to provide for meant that land holdings would be fragmented and some sons would do without. Nathaniel, the youngest, lived at home with his mother. He died in 1752 leaving no real estate. Jacob lived at various times in New York City. He dis-posed of his land to his brothers. Thomas moved to Flushing.[2]

For the fourth generation, options for acquiring land were considerably narrowed. Land within Newtown could be inherited or purchased. There were no other choices. Given that the physical limits were set, Hallett males in the fourth generation, the sons of Justice Joseph, would receive sharply reduced farmsteads, most often from a relative. Joseph's two older sons died young. His eldest, Joseph, was his chief heir. When Joseph, died his patrimony descended to his infant son. This son, upon reaching maturity, sold most of his land to his uncles and moved to New York City. Moses, second son of Joseph, died in his mid-twenties, also leaving a young son. His executors sold his estate, which contained only 14 acres.

FIGURE 4

Genealogy of Second-, Third-, and Fourth-Generation
Male Halletts and Their Acreage

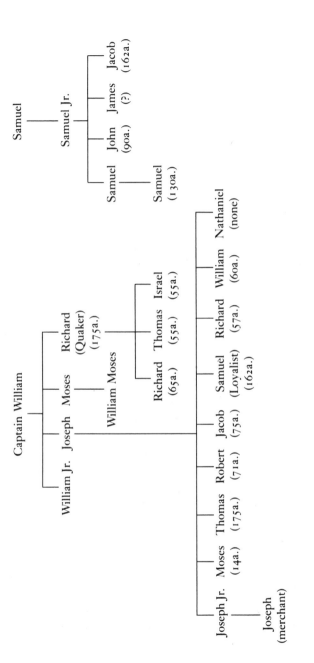

Thomas acquired 13 acres from his father and another 15 acres from outsider Daniel Rapalje. His major purchase was 147 acres from his nephew Joseph, who was named in the sale as "the only son and heir of Joseph Jr." Joseph also sold him some land in Jamaica. At some point he left Newtown to live in Flushing. Robert acquired 12 acres from his father, 13 from his brother Thomas, 46 from his brother Jacob, and one-half a patent right in Greenwich, Connecticut. His total holdings seem to have been around 71 acres. Jacob bought 75 acres and one-half a patent right in Greenwich from nephew Joseph. The loyalist Samuel bought 162 acres from his brothers and one-half a purchase right in Greenwich. Richard bought 57 acres from his brothers. William, the youngest surviving son, acquired at least 60 acres. He often sold lands jointly with his widowed mother.

Joseph Hallett Sr. acquired about 350 acres of land. His sons would own fractions of that. His chief heir, his grandson Joseph, equalized the family holdings by selling 280 acres to his four landless uncles. These sales, all at values below market price, might have been in response to Joseph Sr.'s will, now lost, for they took place a year after his death; or they might have provided Joseph with the capital to become a merchant in New York City. What these sales did, however, was irrevocably break up the large original farm.[3]

Captain William had two other sons of the third generation, Moses and Richard. Moses died young, leaving a son, William Moses, who sold 45 acres to non-Halletts. His father's executors had sold his father's farm. Moses' brother Richard left three sons Richard, Thomas, and Israel. Richard bought 65 acres from his father, but died aged thirty. Thomas inherited his father Richard's farmhouse and the northern one-half of the farm. Israel inherited the southern half of the farm. Each half was probably 55 acres.[4]

Founder William's second son, Samuel, had tried to keep his estate intact by specifying that it would descend through only one of the male line. His only son, Samuel, the third generation, inherited the whole farm. Samuel Jr. had four sons, Samuel, John, James, and Jacob. Contrary to the intent of his grandfather, he divided up his land among three of this fourth generation. Samuel got unspecified land. At his death in 1750 it probably reverted back to his father, who then gave 130 acres to Samuel's son, his grandson. John received 128 acres as a gift from his father. He sold part of this to his brother Jacob and at his death owned 90 acres. James does not appear in the record. Jacob acquired 117 acres from his father and 45 from his brother John. This branch of the family had larger farms than Captain William's branch, but they had fewer sons.

Hallett transactions made up a part of the 455 conveyances that remain for the years 1724 to 1775. This number of transactions represents a drastic decline in the rate of conveyances per year, a pattern also seen in the neighboring town of Jamaica. From 1665 to 1691 there were 13 conveyances per year, from 1692 to 1723, 21.7 per year; from 1724 to 1775, 8.9 per year. Over 50 percent of all conveyances took place by 1710, and over 70 percent by 1735. In 1784, admittedly after a debilitating war and occupation, 23 percent of Newtown residents on the tax list were landless. Of these 49 people, 27 had personal property worth less than £50, which ranked them from 96 to 108 on the tax list of 108 names. Thirteen townsmen, of whom five were women, owned no land, but £100 or more of personal property. At £100, a person would rank 88 on the list. Land still seems important for economic wellbeing.[5]

The earlier transactions included exchanges, gifts, and sales. The later ones contained few exchanges, because scattered properties had already been consolidated. Gifts increased slightly, but not enough to matter. Sales rose, from 86 percent of the total number, to 91 percent. There were no longer any town land grants, which meant that townsmen must either buy or inherit land. Buying land, however, was becoming increasingly more difficult, especially if there were no kinsmen with lands to sell.

The decreasing number of transactions was only one of the changes in the town's land structure. Both meadow and upland became harder to acquire, upland falling from 39 percent of the 1692–1723 transactions to 20 percent of this period's transactions. Whole farms make up a larger percentage of transactions, rising from 20 percent to 32 percent. Whole farms were more costly than pieces of land, and it took more capital to buy one. Yet, without upland and even more important, meadow, which now comprises only 7 percent of the conveyances, a townsman could not put together a farm. Additional evidence of land shortages comes from the increasing sales of marginal and uncleared land. Both swamp and woodland changed hands more frequently. Finally, there were a larger number of houses, lots, and small farms being sold.

The increasing number of houses with small lots suggests physical and economic changes in Newtown. First, this increase indicates a growing population density, as lands along the roads near the town center were taken out of crop or orchard and sold as house lots. Secondly, it bespeaks a growing class of artisans, who might do some farming on the side but were forced to rely on their skills for the majority of their income. A house lot, usually meaning a parcel under six acres, was not large enough to farm. Its owner would have to do something else. Perhaps he could open a shop, as did the weaver Peter Renne.[6]

The Halletts were trading small pieces of land by 1770, as were most townsmen. Twenty-five percent of the 413 conveyances that list land size were 5 acres or less, too small to qualify as a farm; 78 percent were under 50 acres. The trend over time is for pieces from 6 to 20 acres to become less available and for lands from 21 to 75 acres to become more available. These lands sound as if they would make nice additions to a farm, but by the first third of the eighteenth century these lands were whole farms. In 1726 William and Martha Leverich sold about 30 acres to John Culvert. Included were the houses, barns, orchard, and lot of 6 acres, and the rest was land by the fresh pond. Culvert would later buy another 6.5 acres and a third small piece of land. In 1748 Elnathan Field Sr. sold David Springsteen 50 acres of land, houses, and orchard, with an additional 4 acres of meadow. Springsteen eventually left this farm to his son, Casparus, who already lived there.[7]

Farms were becoming smaller and small parcels were changing hands. However, these years also show an increasing percentage, although still a small number, of larger parcels changing hands. These lands were the most expensive and the most desirable, but they were often a way of settlng an estate and would be sold by a man's heirs to one of his sons. As the Hallett transactions show, many never reached the open market.

Given what seem to be land scarcities, prices should have risen as they did. The price of upland doubled between 1720 and 1755 and tripled between 1720 and 1775, selling for £13 1s. per acre by then. Meadow went from £3 17s. per acre in 1720 to £12 10s. by 1764. Woodland, now appearing on the market, also tripled, from £5 in 1720 to £15 1s. by 1760. Newtown's woods were important and irreplaceable. They would be depleted during the Revolution, leaving the inhabitants to dig peat from the bogs for fuel. Farm prices were also rising. The highest price paid per acre to non-kin climbed from £2 17s. in 1695 to £33 7s. by 1769. Lowest prices per acre also rose, although not as steadily, from £1 17s. in 1700 to £13 5s. in 1775. Kinsmen might pay less. In 1749 Joseph Hallett sold his son Jacob fifteen acres of upland and meadow but only charged him £5, obviously a token amount. Such cases aside, the direction of land prices was decidedly up. And as noted in assessing taxation, inflation in no way kept pace and made up the difference.[8]

Land shortages occurred throughout the older settled areas of colonial America. Massachusetts' local studies show the declining size of farms, be it in Northampton in the Connecticut Valley, Andover and Dedham further east, or Ipswich on the coast. Connecticut showed a similar pattern, as did parts of New Jersey. Because of the land shortage, land prices in most places rose, and the family became more important.[9]

Whole farms and large parcels of land were the economic backbone of an agricultural village. However, townsmen, even when selling land, often preferred to keep it within the family. Some transactions mentioned kin ties; in others identical surnames suggested a relationship. Over the whole 1665–1775 period, 21 percent of all transactions were among kin, measuring kin only by surname or direct information. But 40 percent of the whole farms and 47 percent of the parcels over one hundred acres went to family. It was easier for a purchaser to acquire a farm or a large tract if he were related to a Newtown landowner. Hallett conveyances are an obvious example, but there are others. In 1739, Carel Debevoise of Brookland sold an 85.5-acre farm on the Newtown border to his son John for £600. John, listed as living in Newtown, actually lived on his father's farmstead. The increasing importance of family in providing for children once town sources of farmland disappeared was another example of a widespread adaptive pattern. Indeed, it provides further evidence for what James Henretta calls the *mentalité* of colonial America—a world view where "rights and responsibilities stretched across generations."[10]

Given these strong family patterns, and the decreasing availability of farms and large parcels of farmland, it became increasingly more difficult for those outside these networks to acquire land. Eighty-two percent of all transactions, an increase of 7 percent, are between townsmen. Thirteen percent of all conveyances were townsmen buying land from outsiders, but, as in the previous period, most of the outsiders were once townsmen themselves, were related to townsmen, or lived in the adjoining towns. Carel Debevoise was an example of the latter. He probably bought the land that he owned in Newtown for his son. He himself lived just a few miles away. Only 4 percent of the conveyances, down from 11 percent, represent newcomers buying land. Four, or 1 percent of the transactions, are between outsiders or else refer to land outside of Newtown. If Newtown attracted strangers they would have had to work for others or pursue trades while renting their quarters in town. There was no land available for them to purchase.

With less land available, townsmen needed to diversify in order to make a living. The Hallett sons are good examples. Few listed themselves as yeomen, although most were part-time farmers. William was a tailor and his cousin William a cordwainer. Richard was a cordwainer, Joseph a mariner, Thomas a carpenter, Jacob a brickmaker, and Samuel Jr. a boatman. For a few years Joseph Hallett, who called himself a Gentleman, owned one-half of a flour mill, but he was not a miller and he must have hired others to work for him. Being on the East River, the Halletts used the water. Some were boatmen, and Samuel owned a sloop of twenty tons. Many of the land conveyances note landing places from which boats and canoes bearing produce and other commodities could leave for New York City.[11]

Other Newtowners also carried on trades. There were masons, joiners, and blacksmiths. Wools, yarns, and leathers remained important, with townsmen having a choice of weavers, tailors and shoemakers. Joseph Cary was a woolcomber. By 1729 both Samuel Fish Jr. and John Morse listed themselves as vintners. John Morrell was a butcher. Samuel and Richard Berrien were mariners.[12]

Economic diversification was a common response to the shared problem of land shortages. In 1771 only 16 percent of Ipswich's adult males owned the sixty acres necessary for a self-sufficient farm. The remaining townsmen, many with some land, worked at least part-time at other things. Andover's sons faced a similar problem. Philip Greven found that about one-quarter of the third generation followed a trade or craft at some point in their lives. In Connecticut percentages were about the same. By 1775, 25 percent of townsmen were

either part-time or full-time artisans. The same was true in
eastern New Jersey and other parts of New York.[13]

Skilled country folk plying their trades competed with
urban craftsmen once decent roads connected city to town.
New York City artisans recognized this threat in 1753, when
an anonymous letter to the *New-York Post Boy* complained:

> It should not be permitted for one man to carry on
> the business of tanning, currying and shoemaking;
> much less ought a farmer to do one, or all three oc-
> cupations within himself; . . . a farmer also ought
> to employ himself in his proper occupation without
> meddling with smiths, masons, carpenters, coopers
> or any other mechanical arts, except making and
> mending his plow, harrow, or any other utensil for
> farming.[14]

During the years 1724 to 1775 Newtowners finally attracted and held shopkeepers and merchants. As early as
1679, Thomas Barker listed himself in the land records as a
merchant but what he traded in or for remains unknown. He
died in 1684. No other merchant appeared until 1714, when
Robert Wilson bought a house and nine acres of land. He apparently gave up his commercial activities and, by 1722, when
he sold a house, barn, orchard, and shop to Nathaniel Hazard,
called himself a yeoman. The implication was that Newtown
could not yet support a merchant. Hazard, from an old Newtown family, remained a merchant but bought and sold bits
and pieces of land through the 1720s. In 1728, living in New
York City where he died a wealthy and respected member of
the commercial community, he sold out to Nathaniel Lawrence, yeoman. In 1757, and again in 1769, another shopkeeper appeared in the land record. Some shopkeepers were
also merchants. In 1757 Daniel Betts Jr. called himself a shopkeeper, but his will of 1762, which left considerable property,
accorded him the more prestigious title merchant. Oliver Wa-

ters, with whom the Halletts traded and to whom they might have been related through marriage, was probably a merchant since he delivered money and goods both in Newtown and New York City.[15]

The growing importance of merchants, as both purveyors of goods and cultural middlemen breaking down the isolation of the countryside, was one of the most important and widespread social phenomena of the eighteenth century. In Dedham "a more dispersed, commercial, and interdependent economy had developed between urban and rural, and within rural areas of [Middlesex] county" well before 1750. James Henretta notes the increasing importance of middlemen as the market economy expanded, as does Bruce Daniels. Robert E. Mutch, speaking for eighteenth-century Massachusetts, summed up this relationship:

> The merchant, constantly seeking to increase his opportunities, created markets by finding new buyers (and, so, over the long run broke down the very isolation and backwardness that were the basis for his preeminence). The merchant provided a very valuable service, that of exchange: he made available to the American villager the products of West Indian slaves and British cottagers.[16]

Newer opportunities made more goods and services available, yet older values persisted. At the same time that townsmen bought exotic merchandise, they chose to do it in the old-fashioned way of the small-scale society that relies on coreligionists, kinfolk, or those who are known first-hand through friendship or proximity. The New York merchant Joshua Delaplain had a number of Newtown customers, including Richard Hallett, Jonathan Fish, Wiliam Palmer, John Berrien, and William Field. Delaplain, a Quaker and joiner as well as a merchant, apparently appealed to many of Queens County's Friends, who gave him their business.[17]

The Hallett receipt book shows a decided preference for family. At some point, Joseph Hallett of the fifth generation became a New York City merchant. He married the daughter of Nathanial Hazard. The Halletts also bought from the firm of Alsop and Hazard. The kinds of goods townsmen purchased from the outside were varied. In 1757 Thomas Hallett purchased serge, buckram, silk, buttons, mohair, thread, linen, binding, and other cloths. In 1764 he bought silk, buttons, buckram, shoes, stockings, handkerchiefs, gloves, and cinnamon.[18]

Some Newtowners had other outside economic activities. These included loans and land speculations. In 1735 John Burroughs received £5 for his part in the New Cornwall mines. Closer to home were loans and mortgages. Bonds first appeared in the 1692–1723 inventories, and they continued in wills and family papers. Wealthy John Sackett left behind bonds of £34 and £100, while William Gilmore, styled a laborer in his will, left an estate of "goods, bonds, or money."[19]

When bonds were secured by land they became mortgages. Townsmen had always made some use of mortgages to finance farms and to raise capital. There seem to be few mortgages in the years before 1692, when lands were readily available. These few suggest that the poor were borrowing from the rich, or that townsmen were borrowing from outsiders. In 1680, Ralph Doxey mortgaged his house and ten acres to William Hallett Sr. for £5. He agreed to pay one-half of this loan in labor and the rest in wheat within a year. Doxey was not listed in the 1683 tax list but Hallett was third. Two years later Thomas Etherington bound his land to Thomas Stevenson. Etherington was the third poorest man on the 1683 tax list. Thomas Stevenson was seventh wealthiest. Outside lenders included Charles Bridges of Manhattan, then Flushing, and Hare Kirsted and Hartman Wessels of New York City.[20]

From 1692 to 1723 there were still only eighteen mortgages. Some poorer men were buying land from those more wealthy by mortgaging these farms. John White, one of Newtown's more successful inhabitants, began in 1713 by buying a fifty-acre farm from Samuel Moore Jr. The next year, calling himself a yeoman, not a laborer, he bought four more acres. By his death in 1760, he had purchased sixteen times and sold four times. Townsmen were still occasionally borrowing from outsiders, but most transactions were from fellow townsmen.[21]

By 1754, New York's first law requiring a separate record for mortgages had gone into effect. Recorded by the county clerk, these mortgage "libers" kept track of who borrowed from whom. These transactions show a decided pattern. Instead of being in the hands of a few, they were spread out among the many. Most, but not all, seemed to be townsmen. Some 86 of the 137 persons in the mortgages were identified as townsmen in the land records, and another 12 were residents on the 1784 tax list. At least 72 percent were townsmen. The same pattern held true for Jamaica and Ipswich. By spreading credit among a large number of townsmen, people were building up both economic and social networks. Each transaction, still with somebody known and trusted, established a relationship.[22]

Mortgages show decided loan preferences. The Dutch preferred to borrow from fellow Dutchmen. Indeed, only Sarah Bayaner borrowed from a creditor with an English name. Dutchmen did lend to non-Dutchmen. At least thirteen non-English creditors held mortgages from English debtors. Mortgages, unlike land transactions, were seldom between relatives, except when the creditor was a woman. Families did loan one another money. In 1770 James Hallett borrowed £27 9s. from Joseph, but the bond had no land backing it, just trust. In small scale societies, as Burton Benedict has pointed out, business and family can become confused. "Where one is doing business with one's relatives, friends, and neighbours, it is difficult to apply impersonal standards. A shopkeeper with close personal ties with his clientele will find it very difficult to be an impersonal creditor and this may well lead him into bankruptcy." It would have been hard to foreclose on a fellow

Dutchman or a brother or a son. It would have been easier, although still unpleasant, to foreclose on a neighbor.[23]

Fifty persons borrowed, 42 lent, and 9 did both. Creditors were rarely borrowers and borrowers rarely loaned money. Those who did borrow did so infrequently. Of the 50 debtors, 38, or 76 percent, borrowed only once or twice. Of the 12 who borrowed more often, no one did so more than five times. Moreover, these heavier debtors were concentrated. There were 17 Halletts in the mortgage record, and 6 of them were among the heavier borrowers. One-half of those borrowing more than twice were Halletts.

Both men and women mortgaged land in their own names, but men did so far more frequently and for larger sums. Of the fifty debtors three were women. In 1768 Sarah Bayaner mortgaged a house and six acres to William Mills for £50. The next year Abigail Hazard borrowed £46 on housing and one–half acre, and Hannah Sloan raised £20 on one acre of land and an orchard. She borrowed again in 1771 this time mortgaging a house and eighteen acres. She was the only woman with two mortgages. Women owned little land and so had little to enter as collateral. They appear far more frequently as cosigners with their husbands. By signing a mortgage, the woman was protected from having her husband sign away her dower rights to land without her knowledge, but whether her signature was required, as in land sales, is unclear. If her husband died, the mortgage became one of his estate's debts and one that, by 1761, preceded her dower right.[24]

Women could be debtors, and they also appear, albeit infrequently, as creditors. Four women were named among the forty-two creditors. One was a widow in Brookland, two were widows in Newtown, and one cannot be positively identified. Since women rarely transacted business in the marketplace their mortgages might have reflected an older, non-market orientation that involved kindred. At least one of the widows, Ann Fish, who granted a £200 mortgage to William Sackett Jr. was relict of one of the wealthiest men in Newtown. Possibly, monies were invested, not by her, but in her name. Moreover, William Sackett Jr. was most likely her son-in-law. Sarah Betts, who was either a widow or a spinster—there are two Sarah Bettses—was involved in quite a complicated land transaction. While Richard Fish and his wife, Sarah, nee Betts, borrowed from her, she in turn loaned the money against a bond that she stood bound in against a bond Richard Betts stood bound in with Richard Fish to Daniel Rapalje's widow. Again, the transaction sounds like a family affair.[25]

The majority of creditors were men whose patterns of investments appear identical to the patterns of debt. Of the forty-two mortgage-holders, 79 percent owned only one or two mortgages. Eight people owned three to five, and one, James Way, held eight. No single family was as prominent among the creditors as were the Halletts among the debtors. Mortgages were a means of raising capital, not a way of avoiding otherwise inevitable economic collapse. The Newtown mortgages ranged between the £12 borrowed by Joseph and Helena Morrell to the £1,000 loaned to Samuel and Elizabeth Hallett. Other large sums loaned were £959 10s. to Morris Hazard on the basis of a gristmill and lot, and £871 3s. to Joseph Woodard. Both Hazard and Woodard repaid their loans. Samuel Hallett, exiled in Canada, still owed his debt as of 1786 when it was sold by his creditor to others.[26]

Both £12 and £1,000 are extremes. Most mortgages fell between £100 and £500. Interest rates were fairly low, fluctuating between 5 and 7 percent—the rates set by law. These low interest rates, as well as constraints based on friendship and kinship, might have discouraged heavy investment and help to explain why there were so few large mortgage holders.

New York law kept interest rates low thereby regulating profit. Moreover, the province also made available another source of capital through the provincial loan office. Established in 1737, this office loaned provincial funds to individuals at a 5 percent interest rate. These loans were administered by the counties and secured by mortgages on land. The profits would go into the provincial treasury. Queens County was originally granted £6,000, and in 1738 it began to advertise that this money was available. Notices were posted in conspicuous places, such as Samuel Fish Jr.'s inn and Justice Fish's mill.[27]

The loan office was a prime example of shifting scale in Newtown's economic sphere in two ways. First, where townsmen once were limited to the private capital or credit of family, friends, or acquaintances, now townsmen had access to the larger resources of the province. This access was not completely impersonal, but it was moving in that direction. Second, loans were secured by the value of property, not by personal reputation. Who one was became less important than what one owned.

The loan office made available credit, but the responsibility for default lay with the county. A bad loan meant that the taxpayer would have to reimburse the province. Queens County was well aware of its liabilities. The county supervisors in their charge to the loan officers said that they expected them "to be very exact in the perusing of deeds and papers etc. relating to the title of those lands . . . and strict in their examination of witnesses concerning the value of the lands." Owners of wooded lands of little intrinsic value were required to agree not to cut the timber. The property itself, not the reputation of the owner, secured the loan.[28]

Queens County's loan office worked smoothly and was a popular institution. Most people repaid their loans, and those who defaulted had their lands sold at public vendue. The first foreclosure, and the only one to cost the taxpayers anything, was in 1746. Problems with mortgages appear in 1755 and run on until 1769. During these years the loan officers rechecked some mortgages for sufficient security and foreclosed on those few who could not repay. These were also the years of the heaviest provincial taxation. The increased difficulties men had repaying loans suggest growing, although not necessarily debilitating, hardship.[29]

Townsmen took advantage of the loan office. Unfortunately, only Liber D (1754–1760) survives, but it lists names, occupations, and the amount of money borrowed. The thirty-two mortgages held by twenty-four townsmen ranged between £21 and £494 15s. Seventeen of these borrowers were also private debtors, and, again, the Halletts held the most mortgages. Six of the thirty-two loan office grants were in their hands. Other families also borrowed heavily, the Ketchams having four loan office transactions and the Culvers, Firmans, Robert Field, and James Way three each. Twenty-two, or 69 percent, of the mortgages went to six families. James Way was the largest debtor having borrowed £889 10s. He was also, however, the largest single private creditor, holding eight mortgages from his fellow townsmen. He borrowed from the county at 5 percent and loaned at 7 percent, making himself a fast and presumably secure 2 percent. The twenty-four townsmen securing loan office monies must have been the better credit risks. James Way, the Halletts, and the rest in Liber D all repaid their loans without incident.[30]

Detailed information from Jamaica shows that the major county town and Newtown shared equal access to resources. Indeed, Newtowners borrowed more. Between 1756[?] and 1760 the loan office accepted twenty-four mortgages from twenty-one Jamaica residents. Loans ranged from £10 to £174. Eleven of the debtors called themselves yeomen, two were justices, and the rest were craftsmen and a shopkeeper. All paid back their loans.[31]

Townsmen continued to buy land outside Newtown for their children. For example, Captain William Hallett acquired six hundred square miles from the Indians. This land, lying on the New York-Connecticut border along the north shore of Long Island Sound, was probably the purchase right noted among various younger Halletts' land acquisitions. Unlike many such speculative purchases, this one never brought its owners anything since the Halletts were unable to make their tenants pay rent. Others did better. In 1724, Thomas Stevenson, one of the wealthier men in Newtown, left over one thousand acres in West New Jersey to sons and grandsons.

Hendrick Lodt, William Parcell, John Burroughs Sr., John Burroughs Jr., and Joseph Sackett also left lands in New Jersey. William Case had lands in Delaware and what is now Martha's Vineyard. Other areas in which Newtowners invested were Westchester and Orange Counties. At his death in 1755, Joseph Sackett, another wealthy Newtowner, left lands in Goshen and the Wayawanda Patent in Orange County, as well as in New Jersey. Nathaniel Fish, who died in 1769, gave his executors permission to sell lands and meadows that included property in Wayawanda and Minisink in Orange and Ulster Counties. Sackett, Fish, and perhaps a few others were in the forefront of New York's speculative land market if they were buying Orange and Ulster County tracts. As entrepreneurs, they had extended their credit and their connections beyond the town's boundaries and into the heart of provincial politics.[32]

Men in Jamaica and Dedham, Massachusetts, did the same. Jamaica settlers speculated in the large New York land grants, although, like Newtowners, they were not original grantees. As investors they turned to lands in Wayawanda, Minisink, and the Great Nine Partners. Massachusetts did not grant principality-sized patents but did award holdings ever further from settled areas. By 1765 Dedham wills left land in more remote places, not just in adjoining towns.[33]

Some townsmen left lands closer to home. Hendrick Lodt, who left land in New Jersey, owned some acreage in Kings County. Two John Coes, members of one of Newtown's first families, left lands in Jamaica and Hempstead. But the implication in the wills is that the lands in nearby towns were just as difficult to acquire as was land in Newtown. The economically astute were going farther afield, reacting to what Douglas Lamar Jones calls the "double safety valve" of the frontier and the seaports. To keep a family's wealth intact some sons would have to leave Newtown.[34]

The Hallett clan, including founder William, contained forty-one males who were born before 1740 and reached twenty-one. They were by far the largest among the oldest families. One Hallett adult left Newtown with his family; ten others left as young men. Of these ten, three were born before 1700 and seven between 1700 and 1740. Most went to New York City, but at least one, Joseph, son of Thomas, went to the island of St. Croix. Seven disappeared from the record. Three had no sons, but the other nineteen carved up old William's land and remained in Newtown with their own sons.

The 1784 tax rate lists eight Halletts. Highest on the list is Stephen, son and heir of James through the line of Samuel. Stephen was fifth on the list with an estate of £1,600. Seventh on the list was the estate of Samuel Hallett, rated at £1,500. This was the exiled loyalist Samuel. After these two large estates, Hallett fortunes drop precipitously to the bottom of the tax list. There are 108 slots on the list; Jacob is 59 with an estate of £310 and the rest are lower. Phoebe, widow of Thomas, is 67; the estate of Israel is 69; William Sr. is 78; Richard is 87; and William Jr., still perhaps a young man, is 105, with an estate of £12. These poorer Halletts are from the line of Captain William—the line having the most sons.[35]

The Indian purchase giving William Hallett hundreds of acres made the Halletts unique. Others had no such legacy upon which to fall back. The Leverichs and the Alsops were also among Newtown's oldest families. William Leverich was one of the town's earliest settlers and first ministers. Educated at Emanual College, Cambridge, he came to America in 1633. Reverend Leverich followed the typical restless patterns of the founding generation. He went first to Dover, New Hampshire, and then to Boston, Duxbury, and Sandwich, Massachusetts. Leaving Massachusetts, he settled in Oyster Bay and then Huntington, Long Island, finally appearing in Newtown by 1666. He died in 1677, leaving sons Caleb and Eleazer (see Figure 5). Eleazer, divorced for impotence, died without issue, but Caleb had one son, John, who predeceased him when he died in 1703. Caleb lived to give his grandsons, William, Benjamin, and John, land in both Newtown and Oyster Bay.[36]

William Leverich became a carpenter, but in 1732 he

FIGURE 5

Genealogy of the Leverich Family

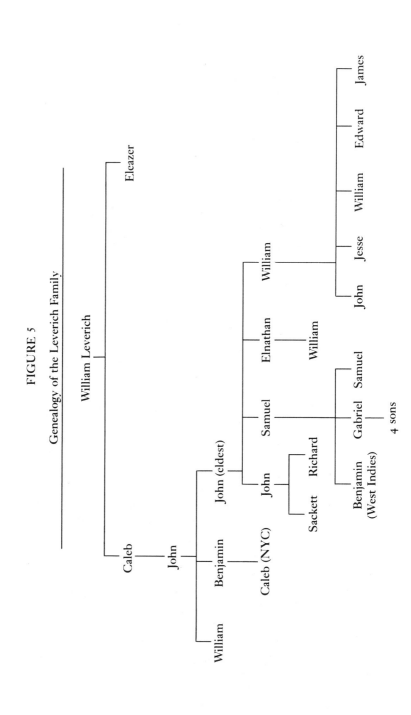

bought a 110-acre farm to add to his other small pieces of land. He died intestate in 1754, leaving no sons. His brother Benjamin did not do as well and left few traces in the land records. He died around 1732, having produced a son, Caleb, who worked as a painter in New York City. None of Caleb's children returned to Newtown. John, oldest son of John, was born in 1696. He married three times and all times well by Newtown's standards. He died in 1780. John had four sons who reached maturity: John, Samuel, Elnathan, and William. A mason by trade, he bought bits and pieces of land, but he also inherited from his grandfather and perhaps through his wives.

John, son of John, also became a mason and married his step-sister Elizabeth Sackett. He moved to Fishkill, Dutchess County, for a short time but then returned to Newtown, where he died in 1780, the same year as his elderly father. He shows only one small land purchase. John had two sons, Sackett and Richard, of whom Sackett never married. Richard, born around 1757, died in Newtown in 1836. John's brother Samuel remained in Newtown, where he died in a winter accident in 1759. He left behind three young children, Benjamin, Gabriel, and Samuel. Benjamin died in the West Indies; Gabriel died in 1825, leaving four sons. The third son, Samuel, became a weaver. Elnathan also died relatively young in 1784. He left one son, William. William, last son of John, died in 1787. He married twice and fathered John, Jesse, William, Edward, James, and numerous daughters. He was a blacksmith.

According to the 1784 tax list, there were five Leverich households paying taxes. Of the 108 rankings on the list, young Edward and William Jr. rated 107, being just about the poorest taxpayers in Newtown. Sarah, widow of John, was 82, William Sr. was 52, and Sackett, heir perhaps to Sackett monies, was 49. This was hardly a remarkable showing. One hundred years previously Caleb had almost ranked in the top third of the town. His assessment of £98 was also about one-third of top-ranked John Smith's £300. Sackett Leverich's £450 in 1784 was not even one-fifth of top-ranked Abraham Polhemus's £2,500. From rather propitious beginnings, the Leverichs had slid to middling and lower.

The 1784 tax list shows Richard Alsop to be the fourth wealthiest man in Newtown, with an assessed estate of £1,750. He is the only Alsop listed on the tax roll. In 1683 Thomas Wandall, the foundation stone of the Alsop fortune, was fifth in town. His nephew Richard was not listed. Between the first Richard and 1740 only nine Alsop males reached the age of twenty-one. Of that nine only two lived their entire lives in Newtown, and one of those two apparently sired no children. The Alsops branched out. They became merchants and land speculators. Most important, they had few sons who achieved maturity and even fewer who stayed in Newtown.

The Leverichs and the Alsops are examples of a wider phenomenon. Twenty-four of Newtown's twenty-seven most stable families left behind enough information to follow sons. Of the 496 males born before 1740, about 3 percent left town as adults with children, 19 percent moved as young men, 15 percent had no sons of their own, and 35 percent stayed in Newtown and produced sons who reached their majority. Sixty percent of the Leverich males stayed and produced adult sons; only 10 percent left. The Alsops did just the opposite. Eleven percent of their sons stayed and reared their own sons to adulthood, while 56 percent of the sons left. Most of the older wealthier families in Newtown had more than the average number of sons leave town. On the 1784 tax list, eight of the oldest families appear in the top 10 percent. Six of these eight have an emigration rate above the 19 percent of the sample. The Halletts and the Burroughses appear among both the highest and the lowest 10 percent of the tax list, showing that, within a family, some branches did better than others. The Halletts exported 25 percent of their young men and kept 59 percent. The Burroughses had a zero emigration rate. Nobody left. Fifty percent of the Burroughses had sons who stayed and begot their own sons.

Family size and wealth were related in Newtown, and, undoubtedly, they were elsewhere. When land was plentiful, more sons might have been an asset, but when fertility outpaced acreage something had to give. John Waters found that those families that did best in Guilford had only one heir; next were those with two sons; and then those with three and four sons. Where land was unavailable sons left. Daniel Scott Smith found a similar pattern in Hingham. Those with fewer adult siblings were wealthier than those with many siblings.[37]

Land shortages forced some sons from Newtown, but they also changed inheritances for those who stayed. In the fifty years before the Revolution, women lost most ground. Whereas, in 1692–1723, daughters as well as sons, in 31 percent of the wills, and wives in 13 percent, inherited land, in the latter years all children inherited land in only 11 percent of the cases, and wives fell below 1 percent. With less property at her disposal, a woman became more vulnerable. In Northampton, wills that expressed the hope that children and their mother would live in peace and harmony were written after 1730—that is, after land became a problem. In Newtown, leaving all land to one son increased to 6 percent, but this still included only eight cases. Andover's pattern of significantly increased primogeniture did not take place in Newtown.[38]

The most interesting pattern to emerge shows all of a man's land being sold. During the earlier period this posthumous sale of land occurred in three wills, or 8 percent of the cases. Now twenty-six wills, or 20 percent, stipulate that the land be sold. Sometimes an estate was disposed of because the children were underage and the widow would be better able to provide for them if she had funds. This would be true if the holdings were small or if other investments brought a good and safe rate of return. Burgoon Burga ordered both his real and personal estate disposed of, and from those monies his son Isaac would get £15 as his birthright, "when of age." In other cases, the estate was sold to one of the sons and he then paid off the legacies. In this way all children got their share but the property was held intact so that at least one heir would end up with a farm large enough to sustain himself. Samuel Fish Jr.'s will specified that this happen. John Lawrence's will of 1765 required that his farm "go to any of my sons who are the highest bidder and all children to share equally in my estate except daughter Anna who is to have £60 less." No longer might sons expect to inherit free and clear. If they had no capital from other sources they would lose the land. The "other sources" were probably trades.[39]

The decreasing availability of land caused more men to sell their holdings. It also resulted in an increased number of estates that mention no land at all, though here again the lack of land in a will does not guarantee that there was none. From 1692 to 1723 13 percent of the wills noted no land. From 1724 to 1775, 29 percent, more than double the earlier percentage, noted no land. Sometimes these wills read like Johannes Van Zandt's, which stated that his executors were to sell all of his estate except some personal property and some slaves. Van Zandt was fairly well-off, if the silver mugs and gold chains mean anything. There is no record of a land sale. The impression that most of the wills leave is that less able townsmen were trying to maximize the little that they had. In 1731, cordwainer Moses Hallett ordered his executors to "sell my small tenement, or house, barn, land and swamp and proceeds to be put out at interest for support of my child." The property consisted of about fourteen acres and sold for £132.[40]

Men's wills listed land; women's wills listed other kinds of property. Only four women of eleven who left wills bequeathed land, and of those at least one was childless and another a spinster. Elizabeth Clock, widow of shopkeeper Martin Clock, left a house and lot in New York City. Women's disposable wealth lay in personal goods and, most importantly, slaves. Spinster Hannah Titus, already infirm at the time of her father Content's death in 1730, was left bondsmen, which she bequeathed the next year to her sister, female cousin, and nephew. Widow Elizabeth Hunt gave her daughter a Negro girl, while Dinah Brinkerhoff left slaves to her daughters and son. Of the eleven women who left wills, seven, or 63 percent, held slaves. This large percentage illustrates the greater-than-average wealth of these women and throws into even sharper relief their lack of real property. Married women dying before their husbands made no will at all. Each woman who left a will is identified as a spinster or widow, with one exception. Rebecca Furman was a schoolmistress. She left behind land, a Negro girl, and a cow. The lack of women identified as anything other than widow or spinster does not mean that all women stayed within the household. Women could have tended shops or worked in the inn at Newtown. They could have bought and sold produce, spun and woven cloth, or tended the households of others. But these statuses were unrecognized by their society and left behind few and indirect traces.[41]

The large number of slaves left by women reflects the increased number of slaves in Newtown. Whereas in 1698 there were 93 blacks, in 1755 there were 163 over the age of fourteen. Given Queens County's slave population ratios, these adults were probably one-half of the total slave population, which would have been around 326. These 326 bondsmen were a threefold increase in the slave population over fifty-nine years—an increase unmatched by the white population. The rate of black population growth relative to white population growth suggests that black labor made Newtown a less attractive place for free white unattached labor. This impression is reinforced by the widespread distribution of the slaves. The 163 adults lived in eighty households, and, while Samuel Fish Sr. and Richard Alsop owned six Negroes each, most people held only one or two. Where there were slaves whites need not apply for work. Local unskilled labor would find itself redundant. Outsiders would find even fewer opportunities. Without work or land they did just as well if they stayed out of Newtown.[42]

The life of blacks in Newtown was probably one of relative isolation from other slaves given how few bondsmen any one household owned and, therefore, the lack of a slave quarters. Some undoubtedly lived in families with at least one parent, but life together was at the whim of the master, and families could be separated. When William Parcell died in 1728, he distributed his Negroes among his children. He further specified that if his Negro woman had another child that child would go to Parcell's son. The mother would remain with Parcell's daughter. Spinster Hannah Titus made it very clear that the Negro boy Jacob would go to her nephew, but her sister Abigail would tend him until he reached the age of two. Possibly, however, Jacob's mother had died.[43]

Some slaves were allowed to participate in various sacraments. They could be baptized, as was Dorcas, "a Negro girl." Michael Cromwell and Margaret Francis, and Sambo and Rose married. Most were probably left alone, "their masters considering them the worse for being taught and more apt to rebel," according to Westchester's Anglican minister. A few masters specified that upon their deaths their slaves could choose new masters. And a very few masters gave slaves freedom, either outright or if they could post the sureties required by New York law. John White allowed his Negro boy and girl to choose new masters, but Caesar was freed if he could find the security "and not be a charge on my estate." Whether slave or free Caesar was also given a horse.[44]

Most male slaves were probably all-purpose agricultural hands. Female slaves probably stayed in the home. White male children more often got male slaves and white female children female slaves. In 1728 William Parcell's daughter received a Negro woman, his sons Negro men. He also left behind an Indian woman and boy, the last Indians mentioned in Newtown. No white servants appeared in either wills or inventories of this period. Some indentureships undoubtedly existed in order to teach children skills, but the era of white contract labor seems over, both in Newtown and elsewhere in the province. Ronald W. Howard found that by the 1730s formal apprenticeship of a contractual nature was less important.

He suggests that skilled slaves and free artisans hired for wages filled New York's labor needs.[45]

Slaves were often the major asset of a woman's estate, but whether they resumed that position in men's estate is doubtful. The inventories for this period are even less representative of the living population than formerly. Of 211 known male decedents, only eleven inventories survive, and these fail to include the wealthiest of Newtown. Nine of the inventories are valued. They range from £20 to £397. Four are under £50. In 1733 Joseph Hallett's Negro boy was about one-quarter of his whole estate, which was worth £112. The largest inventory was Content Titus's 1730 estate of £397 6s., but he was not the wealthiest man in town, and 1730 is still early. Moreover, he was in his eighties and by his own admission no longer able to attend to business. His six slaves represent 49 percent of his estate. Other estates worth less show the same pattern. In 1728, 76 percent of William Parcell's inventory worth was in bondsmen, while William Lawrence, in 1732, left £276, of which 36 percent was valued in slaves.[46]

In 1731 Joseph Hallett died, aged about twenty-eight. His inventory, worth £111 14s., shows what a middling farmer owned. Aside from his Negro boy, Tom, his most valuable possessions were his beds and bed furniture. Next were his two oxen and a cart. He also owned five cattle, three horses, six pigs, and twelve sheep, besides wheat, rye, oats, flax, hay, Indian corn, peas, and tobacco. Hallett owned various farm tools including plows, axes, and a grindstone. Household furniture included a table, cupboard, looking glass, chairs, and chests. He owned pots, pans, bottles, tubs, sheets, towels, and table cloths. Other goods included a gun, some spoons, and ivory-hafted forks and knives. His wearing apparel, worth £7 5s., boasted four coats, one vest, two pairs of linsey breaches, a hat, a wig, and two pairs of footwear. Except for the forks and the wig, none of these belongings seem extravagant. Twenty-three years previous, Moses Hallett had died at approximately the same age. His estate was worth £60 more. He owned more livestock and a wagon, besides yarn, cloth, and three books. These goods were absent from Joseph's holding.[47]

Joseph Hallet was solely a farmer and Newtown was an agricultural village, but agriculture was not enough. The most economically successful had always diversified—founder William Hallett was a farmer, brickmaker, boatman, and carpenter—but by the 1730s, and even more by 1775, other skills were a necessity. Newtown's limited land resources required that townsmen make other adaptations. Some became artisans, others traders. Some invested in securities, others in lands beyond Newtown. Some left Newtown altogether and went to New York City. Sons without prospect, or otherwise lured by outside lands purchased by their far-sighted fathers, went to upper New York or New Jersey. And those with a taste for real adventure went as far as the West Indies. Whatever the choice, it meant greater participation in a larger, more complex economy. That participation would involve people in more far-ranging networks and further break down whatever provincial isolation divided them.

CHAPTER 9

Continuity and Change in the Social Order

Newtown's declining agricultural resources and its increasing interaction with the county and province led to changes in the social order. Wealth, educational opportunities, and ethnic and religious identification differentiated people vertically from one another. At the same time, however, wealth, consumption patterns, education, and religion united people horizontally with one another. These cross-cutting allegiances brought townsmen into contact with others from outside, augmenting the process of social integration to which shared political values and migration had already contributed.

The wealth accumulated by even the most fortunate of Newtown's farmers and artisans was comfortable but not overwhelming. The inventories show little new, and yet the distance between the wealthy and the not-so-wealthy was increasing and people were becoming economically distinct. Lands outside of Newtown have already been discussed, as have slaves. Other indications of wealth include the increasing number of wills that mention luxury goods.

Johannes Van Zandt left a great silver cup, silver mug, and silver spoon to his wife. His daughters were to get gold chains. Joris Brinkerhoff gave his eldest son a silver beaker; William Hallett left his silver tankard. Spinster Mary Scudder left her cousins satin, a small gilded trunk, silver buckles, satin stays, and a gold ring. There were the occasional larger bequests, like that of merchant Daniel Betts, who left his wife £800, some good furnishings, and a horse and riding chair. And there was, for the first time, the explicit desire to be *au courant*, to be part of the larger world, as wealthy innkeeper Samuel Fish Jr. demonstrated when he left his two unmarried daughters not just any feather beds and furniture but bedding to be "good and fashionable." Finally, there were the charitable bequests.[1]

Before 1724 few people bequeathed anything to anyone other than family or friends. After 1724 wills suggest a social conscience that saw beyond the family to the church. Twelve townspeople left money to religious bodies. Robert Field and later his widow, Phoebe, gave £35 to their Quaker brethren. Philip De Vivier gave £40 to the French church of New York, and the rest of his estate to the Presbyterian church of Newtown, the interest to support the minister and poor. Margaret Burroughs left the Presbyterians £100 for the ministry and society. The Fieldses, De Vivier, and Margaret Burroughs had no small or dependent children. Those who had families usually donated less, but that there were donations at all show that some could afford to give, and the wills that mentioned the poor noted that there were those who needed to receive.[2]

It is very difficult to judge how much poverty existed in Newtown, but bits and pieces of evidence suggest growing hardship. Land was less available and more expensive. Black slaves competed for the unskilled jobs. The Seven Years' War escalated taxation, and after the war prices rose. The county foreclosed on mortgages and took greater care to examine properties put up as collateral. There are no tax lists before 1784, after the Revolution, but the 1784 rate shows the same trend of increasing wealth polarization that Gary B. Nash and James T. Lemon found in Pennsylvania and Edward M. Cook and others found in New England. Cook's figures show that by 1775 the top 10 percent controlled 25 to 35 percent of taxable wealth. In the Newtown of 1784, the top 10 percent controlled 37 percent. The poorest 30 percent controlled 2.5 percent, a decline from 13.2 percent in 1683. These figures measure relative wealth, not absolute wealth. Those on the bottom could be better-off than the percentages suggest; however, those seventy-seven individuals in the bottom 30 percent each held £70 or less of real and personal property. Fifty-nine of them held £50 or less, the point at which the law dispensed with an estate inventory.[3]

In 1764 "several freeholders and inhabitants" of Queens County petitioned the General Assembly against the vagrancy laws, which they felt were insufficient. They stated "that several indigent persons in the said county, have erected small huts in the highways, or on small pieces of vacant land, in which vagrant persons are concealed, contrary to, and longer than the law allows." They wished to inflict corporal punishment upon these hospitable but impoverished hosts. The General Assembly voted down their request, evidently feeling that the laws on the books were strict enough. What is especially interesting about the petition is that evidence on vagrancy and vagabondage for the county shows no increase. If there were more indigents who harbored vagrants, they were of the home-grown variety.[4]

Real or perceived increases in the number of poor also plagued other places. Gary Nash has shown how Boston, with a small poor hinterland, felt the effects of population, war, and poverty before the other colonial cities. By the early 1740s, 25 percent of the population was too poor to be taxed. Urban migration by landless rural laborers led to an increased number of warnings out, Boston's way of denying responsibility for these people if they failed. Between 1721 and 1742 warnings out averaged 25 per year. These rose to 65 per year between 1745 and 1752, 200 per year between 1753 and 1764, the war years, and 450 in 1770. What was true for Boston was also true for the countryside. Essex County warnings out increased from 257 for the five years 1739 to 1743, to 400 betwen 1750 and 1754, to 862 between 1760 and 1764. They then dropped precipitously to 58 between 1770 and 1774. Western Hampshire County showed the same trend in these years. Warnings out rose from 50 to 88 to 306 and then dropped to 122. Not all people warned out were poor. What these figures show is a perception of potential poverty with its concomitant expense. As in Queens County, the threat and fear of indigency, not indigency itself, spurred action.[5]

In Massachusetts, the poor laws responded to the threat of a growing poor population by shifting responsibility for searching out the poor from the towns to the poor themselves. In New York, the law was less responsive, and the laws concerning the poor changed little between 1691 and 1775. The parish probably took ultimate responsibility if the family and church proved unable. The family always assumed first responsibility if it could. Husbands continued to specify in their wills that their wives would live in their houses and have ample food and shelter. When Joseph Hallett died in 1750 he left his widow £19 a year, plus the privilege of keeping two cows, a horse, two pigs, part of the garden, the great room of the house, the lean-to and one-half of the cellar window, apples, other fruit, wood, and one-quarter acre to plant, "for her dowry." This bequest was futher sealed by an agreement Mary made with Joseph's sons Thomas, Robert, Jacob, and Samuel. They continued to provide for her for the rest of her life.[6]

Parents also recognized the needs of their disabled children. In 1748 John Coe ordered that his lands be sold and his wife given his moveable estate, but his chief concern was his daughter Abigail, who was subject to "fits." He charged her brothers to maintain her if she could not provide for herself. Twenty years later the blacksmith John Morrell left his wife the east room of the house, furniture, goods, and milk and apples. He also singled out £100 for his blind grandson John Alburtis.[7]

Families provided for their own, but they also provided for other classes of dependents who had not previously appeared in wills. In 1735 John Coe died childless leaving lands to his brothers and nephews. He also left £5 to Rebecca Furman, "who now lives with me." William Van Dyne provided for sons and grandsons, but also for "old John Murphy" for his lifetime, if he chose to remain on Van Dyne's property. Even slaves were cared for. Johannes Van Alst, while disposing of his younger slaves, charged his children to maintain his Negro man Hector among them. More to the point were Richard Hallett's instructions. A Quaker, he ordered his old Negro man, James, be free and "supported by my sons if he is unable to support himself."[8]

Old Negro James became the responsiblity of the younger Halletts, but how far down the family lineage this care extended is unclear. Longer life spans meant that the aged might become the responsibility not only of children but of grandchildren as well. In 1739 the "poor impotent old widow" Mary Martin was a current and future charge to Hempstead Parish. In response, the churchwardens sued Mary Martin's four grandchildren, claiming that they could and should support her. The Court of General Sessions ordered them to appear at the next session "to show cause (if any they have) why they should not be assessed for the relief of their Grandmother according to law." Massachusetts also ordered families to pay if they could and used the courts to enforce these poor laws.[9]

Those who had no family might find help from the churches. When the Tiley family of the Flushing Monthly Meeting needed help, the meeting appointed two Friends to relieve their distress with "food and raiment as they think proper." They spent at least £4 15s. Elizabeth Tiley continued to be a problem, and six years later she still received aid. The June 1768 monthly meeting recognized her continuous necessity when it recorded, "whereas Elizabeth Tiley is often in want of divers necessaries and sometimes when application cannot be immediately made to the monthly meeting this meeting appoints Abigail Bowne and Eleanor Moode to supply her between the meetings with what they judge necessary."[10]

When neither family nor church would help the parish assumed responsibiliy. Supported by tax money raised in each town, the role of the parish was one of last resort. Local justices investigated each case, and they in turn could be sued if the parish felt itself abused. In 1725 the widow Elizabeth Semisse of Jamaica lost her home in a fire. She was officially and without incident declared an "object of charity" by two Queens County justices. In 1769, however, when justices Philip Edsall and Daniel Rapalje ordered John Johnson removed from Newtown to Hempstead, that parish appealed to the Court of Sessions. They won and spared themselves his maintenance. Caretakers elsewhere also contested their responsibility. In Massachusetts, towns, like New York's parishes, went to court to avoid paying for non-residents. By the 1760s they even used lawyers to present their cases. After the Revolution, the New York towns took charge of their poor. In 1784 each town elected poor officers, and in 1790 Newtown voted for its first poor house. The dislocations of the war apparently overwhelmed the older, more generalized institutions.[11]

Those unable to help themselves were often young. Families, of course, were the logical source of support, and the wills show time after time how fathers tried to provide. Children were still put out to trades. In 1732 William Lawrence died, leaving underage children and a pregnant wife. He asked that his children be brought up with the fear of God and put out to good trades when they were fit for the same. Eight years later, Samuel Wainwright ordered his father-in-law to bind his son, Samuel, to learn a trade. No other wills mention trades, as such, but others do note schooling. In 1750 Jonathan Coe left money for the education of his grandchildren, as did Sarah Titus the next year. Mariner Richard Langdon requested that his son be maintained and educated until he was twenty, and Nathaniel Fish ordered that his legacies to his daughters be put out at interest for their maintenance, education, and upbringing.[12]

Education in Newtown remained private. Some, like John Burroughs, sent their sons and daughters away. Others, like the Woodwards, kept their children nearby. Interest in education resulted in a growing number of schools and in the donation of lands upon which these schools stood. Joseph Hallett, John Lawrence, and Jacob Springsteen all gave small lots near their homes, and by 1740 there were at least four of these local schools in different parts of town. Their trustees were both Dutch and English and so, presumably, were their students. Classes were probably in English, given the names of town schoolteachers. During the years 1724–1775, Jacob Reeder, William Moore, James Harper, and Edward Smith listed themselves as schoolmasters in the records. Rebecca Furman was listed as a schoolmistress in her will. While it is impossible to determine what Reeder and the others taught, it was probably basic reading, writing, and perhaps arithmetic. William Moore was also a surveyor and thus might have known more practical mathematics than the others.[13]

The increasing importance of a basic education was felt elsewhere. In Connecticut, public money was used for schools after 1700. These funds were augmented by revenues raised through the sales of public lands in the 1730s, 1740s, and 1750s. At first, schools rotated within towns, but as population increased so did the number of schools, so that by mid-century schools were stationary, and most towns had more than one. Massachusetts was apparently more laggard, though the law recognized the need for schools and upgraded educational requirements. In 1710 males were to be taught reading and writing, females just reading. In 1741 males were also to learn arithmetic. Not until 1771 were females to be taught writing, and the laws never provided them with arithmetic. That schools often failed to keep up with good intentions shows up in the court records. Before 1750 towns were frequently presented for lack of schools, although they were seldom fined. After 1750 schools kept better pace with population.[14]

Not only were basic schools important, but after mid-century more specialized education became available. New-town's higher educational needs were first met in 1762, when William Rudge advertised his boarding school at Hallett's Cove in the *New York Mercury*. Late of Gloucester, England, he offered both practical and academic training that included "writing in the different hands, arithmetic in its different branches, the Italian method of bookkeeping by way of double entry, Latin and Greek." Lest parents fear that Newtown was too remote, he assured them that it was healthy, pleasant, and "from whence there is an opportunity of sending letters and parcels, and of having remittances almost every day by the pettiaugers." His advertisement ended with the names of his ethnically mixed Newtown endorsers: Jacob Blackwell, John Greenoak, Richard Berrien, Richard Penfold, Jacob Rapelje, John McDonnaugh, and seven Halletts.[15]

Three years later James McCarrell advertised much the same variety of courses as had William Rudge. "Encouraged by the universal approbation he had met with from the Gentlemen that has employed him, this year past," he noted reading, writing, arithmetic, bookkeeping, plain and spheric trigonometry, surveying, gauging, navigation, "etc. etc." He took both day students and boarders, teaching them "at the schoolhouse near Benjamin Waters."[16]

Rudge's academy and McCarrell's day school offered sophisticated curricula far broader than farmers or local artisans would need to know. This trend toward specialized training was evident in 1723, when New York City's first private school to teach these advanced subjects opened. In Connecticut, the urban towns did the same, establishing Latin grammar schools to prepare both urban and surrounding-area youth for college. According to Ronald Howard, private schools "reflected both the growing economic complexity of [New York] and the intellectual trends of the European Enlightenment." Both the curriculum and the schoolmaster linked townsmen to each other, to the province, and to other educated colonial Americans.[17]

Parents were responsible for their children, but in some cases children had no parents. Families could step in, as did Gabriel Furman, who brought up his cousin Mary Thompson. If an orphan were over fourteen the courts allowed him or her to choose a guardian. That person could be a relative or a stranger. In 1723 William Moses Hallett asked that his uncles William and Joseph be his guardians. Joseph Burroughs chose Philip Edsall. Edsall does not seem to be related. Younger children leave no trace in the records.[18]

The incompetent also needed protection. The Court of Chancery was responsible for guardianships, and it was often up to them to decide who was capable of what. In April 1760, James Renne of Newtown petitioned the court that his youngest brother, John, had been "deprived of reason" for twelve months. The court ordered an inquiry by prominent, though perhaps not disinterested, townsmen. They, in turn, found that John, aged forty-one, nine months, and single with no children, was indeed a lunatic, and the court gave Renne's uncle, William Hazard, custody of his person and James and Samuel Renne, his brother and nephew, custody of his property. Two years later John petitioned the court, asking that the inquisition by which he was found mentally incompetent be quashed. Unfortunately, few records note what became of those without family or of those considered dangerous. In 1760 "Mad Thomson" was brought to the Queens County jail, but why and for how long remains unknown.[19]

Diseases of the mind were little understood in the colonial period, but disease of any sort was problematic given contemporary medical knowledge. Newtown often had someone in town who was a medical specialist. During the Dutch period, a James Clerk, surgeon, lived in Maspeth Kills, and James Riker found three other "doctors" in the seventeenth century and five in the eighteenth. Drs. Jacob Ogden of Jamaica and David Conklin of Flushing were also called in by townsmen.[20]

The remedies available to doctors were limited by modern standards. During the smallpox epidemics that swept New York in 1731, 1738, 1745, 1752, and 1756, the first response was usually a day of prayer and fasting. Inoculation was known, but feared as a transmitter of the disease. In a way it was, since those newly inoculated were infectious, yet freely wandered around. A proclamation of June 9, 1747, recognized the danger and prohibited all doctors and surgeons from inoculating people.[21]

Queens County physicians knew about inoculation against smallpox as early as the 1730s. Other remedies against disease included bleeding, emetics, and cathartics. In 1770, the Woodward family paid Dr. David Conklin for cathartics, a mercury pill, and a blistering plaster.[22]

Primitive medicine and an increasingly severe disease environment that proved resistant to eighteenth-century medical techniques made life spans shorter and mortality rates higher in Newtown. The Hallett family, for whom there is good demographic information, is a case in point. Between 1670 and 1699, five Hallett males were born who reached adulthood. Three, or 60 percent, died in their seventies, two in their twenties. There were sixteen Hallett men born between 1700 and 1729 who survived childhood. Of the twelve for whom age of death is available, only three, or 25 percent, reached sixty, while five died before reaching forty. In the next generation, born between 1730 and 1759, of nine men, three, or 33 percent, lived to age sixty and four died before forty.[23]

Hallett deaths reflect a more general, declining longevity in a larger demographic pattern that includes both Newtown and New England. In Andover, fewer adults born between 1700 and 1729 reached their sixties. In Newtown, of 68 males born between 1700 and 1729, 44 percent died before age sixty. In the previous birth cohort of 42 males, only 28 percent failed to reach sixty. In Andover, of 198 males, 51 percent died before sixty. In the previous birth cohort of 192 males, only 19 percent failed to reach sixty. Other towns in Massachusetts experienced similar problems.[24]

The year 1750 saw a change in Newtown's mortality rates. The Presbyterian church's records of town deaths, which began in 1728, reached a devastating high of fifty-six deaths in 1750. In the following years, mortality decreased, but never to former levels. In 1732 the calculated death rate was 19.8 per thousand. Ten years later, this rate had declined to 14.2 per thousand. In 1752 the mortality rate more than doubled, to 34.4 per thousand. It was still climbing, reaching 39.9 per thousand, in 1762. By the decade of the Revolution, mortality was easing, and in 1771 the death rate was 28.2, the lowest it had been since the 1740s.[25]

The 1750s were a bad decade for the Halletts. Eight males died. Joseph and Samuel succumbed to old age, dying in their seventies. John and William Moses died of smallpox, and Richard was killed by a tree he was cutting down. It seems that old age, epidemic disease, and accident were what carried off most townsmen. Of 173 deaths that listed cause of death, 51, or 29 percent, were from old age; 46, or 27 percent, were from smallpox; and 34, or 30 percent, were accidental. All other causes of death, including childbirth, were part of the 25 percent remaining.[26]

The age of death for those born between 1730 and 1759 who reached the age of twenty-one rose, but not everyone reached twenty-one. Epidemic diseases carried off both young and old, but epidemic diseases could settle in, becoming endemic diseases. Always present in the population, they carried off children, who had the least resistance. If a rising death rate, especially among children, was caused by endemic disease, then those sharing Newtown's disease environment should have had similar mortality patterns. The Queens County census divides the white population into children and adults. In 1703, the first census differentiated by age, children under sixteen comprised 57 percent of the population. In 1756, they were 45 percent of the population. Children's deaths also increased in Massachusetts. In Andover fewer children born to the third generation survived. More generally, child mortality waxed and waned. Harry S. Stout found that the Great Awakening coincided with the peak years of diphtheria, or "throat distemper," when children's deaths soared.[27]

Deaths continued to be costly. In 1730 the Halletts spent £1 16s. for funeral gloves and another £3 for proving Captain William Hallett's will. Other expenses included renting a pall, ringing the church bells, laying out the corpse, and digging the grave. Families might also pay for refreshments furnished to the mourners.[28]

Birth was another human event that befell everybody. Perhaps as a response to the higher mortality rates, family size continued to decline in Newtown, as it did in New England. John Hallett had ten children, but three died of diphtheria. Jacob had six children, but three died in the early 1750s, probably of smallpox. Of the nine Hallett males born between 1700 and 1729 for whom evidence exists, only Captain Samuel, who married twice, had as many as ten surviving children. Five of the Halletts had four offspring or less. In the community, 63 percent of the thirty-four completed families of men born between 1700 and 1729 contained four children or more. The sixty-one born between 1730 and 1759 had even smaller families, with 52 percent having more than four children. Of those having fewer than eight children, the percentage rises from 59 percent for the first group, to 70 percent for the middle, and then down to 67 percent for those born between 1730 and 1759.[29]

Marriage continued to link families and unite resources. In the fourth generation there are seventeen Hallett males and twelve Hallett females. In Captain William's line, William Jr., was murdered and left no offspring, and Moses had only one son, William Moses, whose spouse is unrecorded. Quaker Richard left three sons and three daughters. Four of these children married Shotwells, members of a New Jersey Quaker family; Richard Jr. married Mary Way; and Sarah married William Webster. The extensive ties between the Halletts and the Shotwells was partially due to the small size of the Quaker community.

Joseph, son of William, had nine sons and one daughter by his two wives, Lydia Blackwell and the widow Mary Lawrence Greenoak. Five of his sons' first spouses can be identified. They included a Hallett, a Blackwell, a Moore, and two daughters of Captain Daniel Betts. All were women from better-off households, and at least two were related to the Halletts.

Samuel's line expanded in the fourth generation to include four sons and eight daughters who married. Eleven spouses' names survive. They are Millicum, Welling, Wright, Pettit, Lawrence, Berrien, Greenoak, Hallett, Betts, and two Blackwells. Cornelius Berrien was the first person with a non-English name to marry into the family, but his mother was Ruth Rapalje Edsall and his stepfather was Samuel Fish. His children were baptized in the Presbyterian Church. All the other names are probably English.

The fourth generation of Halletts cemented ties with a limited number of families that included their own relatives. While this pattern served to concentrate wealth, it also narrowed the range of persons to whom one could go for land or for help of other kinds. Perhaps the Halletts felt that their own resources were spreading too thin to support a large kinship network. Or perhaps it was easier to marry those they knew, like their cousins, or their sisters or brothers-in-law.

The fifth generation of Halletts felt the brunt of emigration and land shortages. At least twenty-three male and twenty-two female fifth-generation Halletts survived childhood. However, there were probably more. The fourth generation had begun moving away and as they did their children disappeared from the records. Of the forty-five, no information exists for thirteen males and four females. The reason is probably that males left the area. Those whose mates can be found followed the same pattern as their parents. They married into the Hazard, Blackwell, Burroughs, Penfold, Greenoak, Roach, Haire, Bragaw, Moore, and Hallett families. Three of the loyalist Samuel Hallett's children married

Moores. Two of Jacob Hallett's children married other Halletts. Isaac Bragaw was the only spouse of non-English descent and the only one of his siblings to marry into an English family. By the Revolution, endogamy, always the last barrier to assimilation, still remained.

Emigration, higher mortality rates, and smaller families slowed Newtown's overall population growth. Between 1656 and 1698 the white population more than doubled. But it never doubled again. In 1711 there were 839 white townsmen, in 1771 1,096, and in 1790 1,526 (see Table 7). The black population grew much faster. Perhaps wealthier townsmen were buying more slaves. But the wills and the Queens County censuses imply that the slave population was reproducing itself. Disease and accidents would kill blacks as well as whites, but the larger percentage of black children than white children in the 1756 Queens County census suggests that blacks had higher resistance to some diseases than did whites. And slaves could not emigrate, at least of their own free will. The bequests occasionally give slaves to children who lived outside of Newtown, but far more frequently slaves remained in town. By 1790 Newtown's slave population was five times what it had been in 1698. The white population had not even doubled.[30]

Black slaves arrived in Newtown at the convenience of their masters, but whites could choose to move there. Three groups did this: those who already owned land in Newtown, older New York City dwellers, and the poor, who might not have lived in town. The first group included families like the Polhemuses. Abraham Polhemus was a resident of Jamaica, but he owned an eighty-acre farm in Newtown. His son Abraham Jr. first bought a farm in 1764, but six years later he also purchased the Newtown properties of his father. If the land records are accurate, Abraham Polhemus spent over £2,000 on lands. By the 1784 tax list he was the wealthiest man in Newtown, while Abraham Jr. ranked fourteenth.[31]

The second group of newcomers can be found in the

TABLE 7

Newtown Population

YEAR	WHITES	SLAVES	FREE BLACKS
1656	347*		
1698	883†	93†	
1711	839‡	164‡	
1756		326§	
1771	1096#		
1790	1526‖	533‖	52‖

*Calculated from the Indian rate (*Town Minutes*, II, 218–219).
†Census of 1698 (Riker Collection, Memoria, Box 16, vol. 5, 147–150).
‡Calculated from the Census of 1711 (Riker Collection, Memoria, Box 18, vol. 14, 28).
§Calculated from the 1755 survey of adult slaves (*DHNY* III, 517).
#Calculated from the Census of 1771 (Memoria, Riker Collection, Box 16, vol. 5, 150–152).
‖First Federal Census of 1790.

wills. It looks as though they retired to Newtown after their productive lives were spent in New York City. Philip De Vivier died in 1745, listing himself as a Gentleman. He never appeared in any other extant Newtown record, and he never held a town office. His will bequeathed money to the French Church of New York, suggesting that he once attended worship there. Elizabeth Clock, the widow of Martin, left behind a house and lot in New York City. Neither she nor her husband seem to have participated in any town activity.[32]

The last of those who might have moved to town left little evidence behind. There are no surviving militia or tax lists, or censuses between 1715 and 1771, and there are fewer and fewer land transactions. James Riker, Newtown's foremost chronicler, said that these men were mainly foreign-born, from England, Ireland, and Germany, and "that they were residents appears from the fact of their being named as 'of

Captain Blackwell's company, etc.'" Possibly the county hired them to round out the provincial levies and for convenience listed them as part of the regular militia. They might also have been among those so-called indigents who set up shacks on the Jamaica Road and took in others like themselves.[33]

Those who were born, married, or died in Newtown often appeared at some point in the church records. These records are better by the mid-eighteenth century because the churches themselves were better organized. The Presbyterian church remained Newtown's largest throughout the colonial period. At first it was run entirely by the minister, but in 1724 Reverend Samuel Pumroy nominated Content Titus, James Renne, and Samuel Coe as elders. Initially, their task was to speak to those who were lax about attending worship services. As the record notes,

> Upon observation by Mr. Pumroy of the delin-
> quency of several members of this Church—as to
> attending upon the Public worship of God—and
> complaint being made thereof by him, it is ordered
> that Content Titus discourse with Widow Sever-
> ance touching her sons neglect, and with Ephraim
> Morse for his neglect also that James Renne dis-
> course with Joseph Morrell for his neglect in that
> Point. Also that Samuel Coe discourse with
> Thomas Pettit for his neglect, and that James Renne
> do discourse with Joseph Sackett, Esq. for his rare
> attending.

Neither age nor station preserved the laggard from the eye and comment of the religious community as embodied by the elders. In time, they probably took on other chores which freed the minister to pursue his more specialized ministerial functions. They also served as the thread preserving continuity when the church was leaderless.[34]

In 1744, Newtown's minister of eleven years died. This time the ministerial search was a church, not a town responsibility. The separation of church and town was one more example of increasing specialization, but it was also an example of secularization. In Connecticut, the same process occurred, as town and church ceased to be coterminous. The General Assembly created the first church societies in 1669, but the widespread division of towns into two or more church societies began after 1700. The society, not the town, taxed, elected officers, built meeting houses, regulated schools, and chose a minister. These functions, performed first by custom, were codified in 1728. Massachusetts towns could also divide into precincts with their own ministers. For example, in 1736 the Massachusetts General Assembly split Clapboardtrees from Dedham. And the same happened elsewhere.[35]

Newtown's Presbyterians filled in for two years with George MacNish, son of the former pastor of Jamaica, but he left in 1746 for Orange County. The same year Newtown's Presbyterians found Simon Horton, the minister who would serve them almost to the Revolution. Probably born on eastern Long Island, Horton graduated from Yale in 1731 and took his first congregation in New Jersey. In 1746 he moved to Newtown, where he remained until he resigned his ministry, apparently under pressure, in 1773.[36]

Simon Horton's successor lived only a few years in Newtown. A Scotsman by birth, Andrew Bay came to town in 1773 but ran afoul of local sensibilities. In 1775 the New York Presbytery met at Newtown after the Newtown congregation petitioned the New York Presbytery to remove him. Reverend Bay agreed to abide by a congregational vote instead of submitting to an inquiry, and was removed by a two to one margin.[37]

The Presbyterian church had stabilized during the eighteenth century. During its earlier years the town had struggled to first find and then keep a minister. With the ministries of Samuel Pumroy and Simon Horton, Newtown's Presbyterians could attend to their religious concerns without the fear of losing their religious and moral leaders.

The church's concerns were manifold. It provided a place where townspeople could meet socially, could hear a message of spiritual uplift or admonition, and could receive the sacraments that marked the boundaries of life and set them inside the community. Marriage was, of course, one of these, but baptism and communion were probably more important. Of special concern was the baptism of those who might die. In 1730, "John Smith being very sick professing faith in Christ[,] repentence for sin, and promising subjection to Christ in his Church was baptized." Twenty years later Samuel Hallett Jr. sent for Reverend Horton "and desired baptism for one of his being very sick. After I had discoursed with him and his wife they renewed the Covenant with God and promised subjection to Christ's Church and had that son Benjamin baptized." Samuel Hallett's call was especially gratifying to the Presbyterian minister because the other Hallett children had been baptized in the Church of England. Once the crisis was past, however, the Halletts continued to support the Protestant Episcopal Church. Their anxious and frightened call showed that they considered the act of baptism more important than the denomination of the minister performing the ceremony.[38]

Communion also symbolized the return of the ungodly to the communal fold. In 1739 Jonathan Hunt "acknowledging himself a sinner by nature and a great sinner by practice: declaring his sorrow and grief of heart for his wicked life[,] his hearty desire to fear and serve the Lord: his accepting of the Lord for his God and righteousness and covenanting with God to serve him. Giving himself up wholly to the Lord, was admitted to full communion."[39]

Almost any sin, including drunkenness, quarrelling, fighting, fornication, and adultery, could be forgiven if publicly acknowledged and sincerely repented. People were precious and their presence was necessary for the health of the whole body. In 1739 Anne Cowpesson[?], after admission and full communion, pleaded guilty of "conceiving by a man not her husband" and was barred from communion, but only until she declared her fault and her sorrow. Once she did, "her offence was forgiven her: Publication was made of this in general upon Friday March 30: before the Sacrament to the Church members also a propose [sic] that if any had anything to object against her being admitted to Communion they would signify it: no objection was made which was declared openly to her. So that she joined in Communion upon the Lords Day April 1, 1739."[40]

Public confession in church looked like public confession before the seventeenth-century town court. As Page Smith noted, the courtroom was a theater upon whose stage the reprobate acted out a morality play. In both court and church a person reaffirmed cultural norms by admitting in public that he or she had transgressed them. The offender was an example to the rest of the community and acquired a reputation that he or she could live down but that was also on public record. However, there are also differences. The town court embraced the whole town; the church only enfolded part of it. Communicants publicly bared their behavior to a part of society, and the sanctions imposed represented not the community's judgment but the congregation's. Community had broken down into specialized subsets, each with its own parochial norms. With church disapproval less important for maintaining social control, behavior should have become more tightly regulated by the courts. As will be discussed in detail later, the courts refused to fill this gap and took even less interest in private acts.[41]

The separation of church and town, and the more general secularization of society, broke the back of church discipline. This trend was especially significant in those places in New England where the minister felt his authority should go unchallenged. Patricia Tracy, in an excellent study of the ministry of Jonathan Edwards, traces this process through Timothy and Jonathan Edwards. Timothy, father of Jonathan and son-in-law of the great Solomon Stoddard, waged a ceaseless and futile battle with his East Windsor, Connecticut, congregation. He demanded authority but got little, and when he embraced the Saybrook Platform in 1708 his congregation refused to follow him. For the next fifty years minister and congregation fought over respect and salary: "Timothy's demands exacerbated the anti-clerical prejudices of his congregation, and their assertiveness only fueled his obstinacy." Jonathan Edwards grew up with two conflicting models of the pastor-flock relationship. The ideal, supposedly embodied in his grandfather, saw the minister supreme; the real, observed at home, saw the minister bitter and frustrated, a lonely moral voice crying in the wilderness.[42]

Those to whom the ministry reached out realized they could reject help. In Newtown, elder Samuel Coe went to see Thomas Pettit about his neglecting church but was told that Thomas had nothing to say and, more importantly, that nobody "had any power over him . . . [and] that he would not be obliged to attend upon the public worship any oftener than he pleased." Uncowed, the church decided to send a committee to talk with him further, but that committee could bring little but moral pressure to bear. No civil power backed it.[43]

Newtown's Presbyterians had settled down by 1723 and the other denominations followed shortly after. The Dutch Reformed in Newtown, although never a large enough congregation to support their own minister, did break from Kings County and form their own church. Meeting in 1731, "the members of the Reformed Low Dutch congregation of Newtown . . . and some others" decided to build a church on land donated by Peter Berrien. Abraham Remson, Isaac Burga, George Rapalje, Abraham Lent, Nicholas Berrien, and Isaac Brinkerhoff were appointed superintendents in charge of collecting private subscriptions from "members of said congregation and others who may be pleased to further this object." These "others" included Judge James Hazard, a member of the Church of England, his brother Captain Thomas Hazard, and both Samuel Fishes Sr. and Jr. These townsmen felt that religious observance outweighed denomination, as did townsmen in Norwalk, Stratford, New Milford, and other Connecticut towns.[44]

A 1785 floor plan of the Dutch church shows it to be different from the English structures surrounding it. Riker, who saw this building, noted:

> It was built of wood, and in shape an octagon, the favorite style for a church among the Dutch of that day, and a form confessedly suited for easy speaking. The roof ascended from all sides to a point in the centre, which was surmounted by a cupola. Inside, at the back end of the building stood the high narrow pulpit, with its sounding board projecting above it, while rows of seats or chairs extended across the main body of the church.

Once monies were raised and the church finished, the superintendents allocated the pew seats "in proportion to the subscriptions and payments towards building." The seats, segregated by sex, were the ultimate property of the church, and those owning them could only sell, give, or bequeath them to other members of the congregation. Those not subscribing to the building or unable to buy seats were still included in the congregation since single benches in the back were provided "for those who may hereafter be disposed to use them to hear the word of God preached."[45]

The Dutch Reformed version of the word of God was preached to Newtown as part of a circuit that included Jamaica, Hempstead, Oyster Bay, and Flushing. Church elders, first elected in 1736, called a Mr. Van Basten to be minister in 1739. Johannes Henricus Goetschius, a minister who became wrapped up in the ferment surrounding the Great Awakening and succeeded in splitting the Queens County Church, followed him.[46]

Johannes Goetschius, a native of Zurich, came to America with his clergyman father. Educated in both Switzerland and Pennsylvania, he was licensed and ordained in that colony. From there he went to eastern Long Island and then was called by the elders of the four united churches of Queens County. The Great Awakening, with its premium on emotion and individual spiritual rebirth, appealed to Goetschius, but not to some senior members of the Newtown congregation, who began to question the legitimacy of his ordination. This issue reflected a larger split in the Dutch Reformed church that centered around whether the Classis of Amsterdam had to ordain ministers or whether Reformed ministers in this country could do so. Would the church be controlled from Holland or in America?[47]

The question of ordination had personal implications for townsmen since only those who had been ordained could administer the sacraments. To sort out the problem, the Newtown church corresponded with the Amsterdam Classis and must have been both dismayed and unenlightened by their answer, which said baptisms performed by Dominie Goetschius were illegal, but that "on this account the scrupulous members of the congregation would do well to receive this seasonable advice . . . and hereafter arrange it to their own contentment and for the best interest of their children; although it is not of vital consequence whether the baptism be performed by a lawful or unlawful minister," as long as the children were accepted in God's covenant of Grace and incorporated into the Christian church. Disagreement flared into violence with the Jamaica church locking Goetschius out. In 1748 he left for the Hackensack Valley of New Jersey, a place much more torn by religious enthusiasm and dissension.[48]

From 1748 to 1754 the Dutch Reformed in Queens County had no minister. New York's orthodox dominie, Henricus Boel, duly ordained in Amsterdam, filled in and, more importantly, rebaptized the children of such "scrupulous members" as Jeromus Rapalje. In 1754 the Dutch Reformed congregation again found a minister, Reverend Thomas Romeyn. Romeyn was born in New Jersey, educated at Princeton, and ordained in Amsterdam. This was his first church, and he stayed for six years. In 1766 the Dutchman Hermanus Lancelot Boelen accepted Queens County's call. He stayed until 1772.[49]

During the ministry of Dominie Boelen New York's Dutch churches came of age. In 1771 the two competing factions joined and formed a separate American church, thereby bypassing the Classis of Amsterdam. The good dominie was opposed to this move and shortly resigned his pulpit. Apparently a powerful speaker, his Dutch was so pure that the native-born Queens County Dutch speakers had trouble understanding him. He eventually went back to Holland.[50]

By the 1770s language could separate the American Dutch from their European counterparts. Newtown's schools taught in English, and no recently arrived Dutchmen infused the existing population with fresh use of the language. Even by the 1740s Dutch was falling into disuse. Peter Kalm, travelling in 1748, observed that "the old people, speak their mother tongue . . . . Most of the young people now speak principally *English*." Indeed, according to Ronald Howard, language became the central issue for the Dutch Reformed church after 1754. In 1758 the Dutch town of Flatbush advertised in the *New-York Gazette and Weekly Post-Boy* for two schoolmasters, one to teach in Dutch and English and the other to teach only in English. Five years later members of the Dutch Reformed church of New York City petitioned the Amsterdam consistory for English-speaking ministers.[51]

Those whose religious needs went unmet because of language could choose to leave the Dutch Reformed church and join another. In New York City the Church of England provided at least one haven. Peter Kalm noted this trend and remarked that the younger people took it amiss if they were called Dutchmen and even joined the English church.[52]

Undoubtedly, assimilation proceeded faster in New York

City than in the countryside. Church records in Newtown show that neither Englishmen nor Dutchmen crossed religious barriers very often, and, more telling for ethnic assimilation, rarely crossed marriage barriers. The records of marriage show that the Dutch married the Dutch. At least 418 marriages took place between 1724 and 1775. Of these marriages only 42, or 10 percent, were ethnically mixed, and another 14, or 3 percent, could have been. Thus, a total of 13 percent of Newtown's marriages could have been exogamous. This figure is misleading, however. Of the 42 clearly mixed marriages, 16, or 38 percent, were somehow connected to the Berrien-Edsall connection of the previous century. The Alburtises contributed another 4 mixed marriages. Clearly, most families still kept their choices ethnically homogeneous, while a few families, once having married out, continued to choose from either group.[53]

Godparenthood shows ethnic retention even more strongly. The baptismal records state that godparents, who attended an infant's baptism, were also Dutch, or at least not English. Very few English names appeared among the Luysters, Rapeljes, Van Zandts, Berriens, Brinkerhoffs, Rikers, and Van Alsts of Newtown.[54]

Godparenthood, a form of ritual or fictive kinship, only appeared among the Dutch, even though it is popular in many other cultures and has attracted a fair amount of scholarly attention. Godparenthood helps the child. As Frederick C. Gamst notes, "Functions and benefits of ritual kinship are approximately those of 'real' kinship. Additionally, ritual kinship extends and/or reinforces a familial network of kinship, locally through unions with families in the home community, horizontally with families in neighboring . . . communities, and vertically to rural and urban superiors." Dutch godparents were usually family members already. Just as the Hallett marriages often made ties intensive by marrying into the same family, so Dutch parents often reinforced family ties by choosing relatives for godparents. In the year 1741 thirteen

258

children were baptized. Of the thirteen sets of godparents, eight had the surname of the child's father. The mother's name was omitted, but her family could have also served as coparents. In 1767–1768 eleven children were baptized, of whom seven had godparents. All mothers' names were listed. In all cases the godparents had the same surname as one of the parents. This pattern is consistent from 1736, when the records begin, through the 1790s. Parents chose to omit strangers from their networks and insisted on keeping family identity and resources within the family. Interestingly, this same pattern is found in Latin America, where societies are currently modernizing.[55]

The Church of England had no language barriers between its clergy and its congregants, but it did have ethnic ones. As the established church of the province set within a dissenter stronghold, it had the problem of attracting members and paying its clergy. Thomas Poyer, the Englishman who led the losing fight to make the church self-sufficient, wrote six months before his death in 1731 that he "has had great and almost continual contentions with the Independents in his Parish, has had several law suits with them for the salary settled by the country for the Minister of the Church of England, and also for some glebe lands, that by a late Trial at law he has lost them and the Church itself, which his congregation has had the possession of for 25 years."[56]

Poyer's successor to this unhappy situation was Thomas Colgan. Colgan was born in America and first held the position of catechist. In 1732 he was transferred to Jamaica Parish. The SPG paid his salary since the vestry refused to do so. He remained in Jamaica until his death in 1755.[57]

The demise of Thomas Colgan vacated a position which the governor appointed. Dissenters, who still composed the vestry, proposed a Presbyterian minister in one more attempt to overturn the Church of England's monopoly on parish churches. They lost when Governor Thomas Hardy appointed Samuel Seabury Jr. to that place. American-born,

Seabury later became the first Episcopal bishop in the United States. He remained at Jamaica until 1766, unsupported by his parishioners and dependent on the SPG for his salary.

In 1769, and only after the three congregations of Newtown, Flushing, and Jamaica had agreed to pay at least part of the minister's salary, the SPG appointed Joshua Bloomer minister. Graduated from Kings College, New York, he was first an officer in the provincial forces against Canada and then a New York City merchant. In 1765 he left for England to receive ordination. Like his predecessors, he made a circuit within his parish. He died in 1790.

Newtown shared its minister with other churches in the parish, but in 1733 local Anglicans decided to build their own church and asked the town for permission to use part of the town lot. Townsmen granted this request in true ecumenical spirit, "in consideration of said request and good intention being willing the worship of God should be promoted." This document was then signed by ninety persons, Dutch and English, dissenter and Episcopal, thereby reaffirming again the value of religion over denomination. In 1735 the Anglicans began building, and they finished in 1740 with the parcelling out of pew seats. Some of the wealthiest families in town belonged—Justice James Alsop, Justice Joseph Sackett, and a host of Halletts and Moores.[58]

In 1761 the Newtown church, possibly the fastest growing of the three in the parish, petitioned the provincial government for its own charter. In a letter signed by nine Halletts, seven Moores, and assorted Morrells, Hazards, Alsops, and others, the petitioners noted that they had a "decent church," cemetery, and the wherewithal to maintain a minister. The lieutenant governor agreed, and St. James received its patent. But nothing really changed, and no full-time minister took over St. James before the Revolution.[59]

Evidently, the appeal that the Church of England could make was limited. Around 1759 Seabury noted sadly to the SPG that "even among those who profess themselves members of the Church of England, a very great backwardness in attending her service prevails, and particularly with regard to the holy sacrament of the Lord's Supper; so great is their aversion to it, or neglect of it, I fear the number of communicants at present scarce exceeds twenty." Five years later, in the wake of a visit by the great orator and evangelist George Whitefield, Seabury observed that many of the dissenting ministers had adopted Whitefield's tenets and his oratorical style. Indeed, Jamaica was being overrun by itinerant preachers who not only stirred up the local population but also attacked the Church of England as popish.[60]

Dissenters and half-hearted Episcopalians made life difficult for the Anglican minister, but Seabury reserved his harshest words, as had those before him and those elsewhere in New York, for the Quakers. "Bred up in an entire neglect of all religious principles," he fumed, "in hatred to the clergy and in contempt of the sacraments, how hard is their conversion, especially as they disown the necessity of any redemption." And yet, the Quakers would probably have disagreed, as they saw the breakdown of their own discipline and the falling away of their brethren.[61]

The problems resulting from living in the Quaker brotherhood while simultaneously living in the world required strict oversight. Those who strayed were discussed in preparatory meetings and their cases referred to the regular monthly meeting. Every attempt was made to convince the wayward to see their errors and publicly condemn their ill behavior. Full reentry into the fellowship followed this confession. When, in 1759, "Abigail Field having committed the sin of inchastity and it obliged her to marry out of unity all which she has heartily condemn[ed] and desires to be in unity therefore Friends accepts her condemnation and receives her into unity again."[62]

"Upright carriage" marked the Quaker from the rest of the community. This distinction between Friends and others was crucial, and the Society went to great lengths to maintain it. Certificates of clearance remained necessary for those wishing to move or even to visit other Quaker meetings. Quakers visiting from England, Ireland, Pennsylvania, New Jersey, Rhode Island, and almost anyplace else where there were Quaker meetings established personal bonds that reinforced the institutional structure. And the monthly meeting itself examined its own health, quarterly asking such questions as: do Friends attend all meetings and are they "clear from drowsiness and sleep"; are Friends innocent of talebearing, backbiting, and meddling; are differences cleared up quickly; do they refrain from putting their children out to non-Quakers as apprentices; are they free from tippling and drinking to excess; do they stand faithful against paying of priests and bearing arms; do they make wills in time, pay their just debts, and bring in marriages, deaths, and sufferings to be recorded?[63]

Severe persecution of the Quakers ceased once the New York majority society accepted them as a legitimate religious body. Such toleration eased Friends' relationships with the outside, but it helped undermine discipline within. This trend shows clearly in the marriage records. The Quakers rightly feared marrying out of unity and spent much energy trying to prevent it. Forbidden marriages included those with close kin, with spouses too young, with those already promised to another, with those too recently widowed, with in-laws, and with non-Quakers. Marriage with non-Quakers was by far the most common disorderly marriage, and it became more frequent as time passed. Until 1691 none of the thirty marriages recorded were irregular. Between 1692 and 1723 only 6 percent, or 5 of 81 marriages, caused problems. But an increased number of irregular unions began in the 1740s and continued through the Revolution. From 1724 to 1743, out of 39 marriages 7, or 18 percent, were out of unity, but from 1744 to 1775 the number rose to 87 of 145, or 60 percent. Clearly, children were breaking away.[64]

The distressingly high incidence of Quaker outmarriage probably reflected the small size of the Queens County Quaker community. In 1756 only eight townsmen of arms-bearing age were Quakers. In the county there were another forty-five. Many of these fifty-three males were often closely related to one another, and therefore inappropriate potential spouses. Newtown's eight Quakers represented six families, but Hempstead's sixteen townsmen were from only nine families.[65]

Numbers aside, Quaker outmarriage was also a response to local land scarcity and some of the problems of dislocation in the larger society. It may be seen in the same way as the increasing incidence of premarital pregnancy that Daniel Scott Smith and Michael Hindus found for the late eighteenth century. The times were out of joint. Parents could no longer promise a secure future or delineate an appropriate model of behavior. Those who moved out might not go where other Friends lived. And some, especially younger males without prospect at home, might look to the wars as a way out. Elnathan Field Jr., for example, was cited for bearing arms in 1744. He declined to acknowledge his fault and two years later was read out of unity.[66]

Religious toleration, which helped undermine Quaker and other denominations' discipline, existed in many New England towns by mid-century. Moreover, religious organization was often similar. First, town and congregation rarely coincided. Either townsmen from a number of towns formed a congregation, or a town hosted two or more religious societies within its bounds. The choices that townspeople made undermined the authority of church and minister because they helped break down the parochialism of townsmen. Second, and related to growing heterogeneity, was a movement to standardize denominations. Presbyterian, Dutch Reformed, and Church of England ministers, as part of larger organizations with fixed rites and tenets, tried to make these churches distinct from one another but similar to Presbyterian, Dutch Reformed, and Anglican churches elsewhere. The denominations had recognizable forms wherever a congregant lived. The Quakers of different areas forged the same orthodoxy

through their self-consciously created hierarchy of meetings
and their constant self-examination and visitation. Third, the
religious hierarchy of those churches that ordained ministers
was incomplete. The Amsterdam classis, which appointed
Dutch Reformed dominies, and the bishops, who ordained
Church of England ministers, remained in Europe. Local autonomy based on necessity led to resentment of foreign interference. The churches, while still retaining Old World
sacraments, administered them by jealous locals. These men
resisted attempts to undermine their authority.

The larger decline of moral authority within all eighteenth-century churches was parallelled by the decline of
moral authority in the courts. Violence was still punished, but
violence was rare. Newtown remained a remarkably peaceful
place with few taking out their hostilities physically. William
Pettit was an exception. First indicted in 1723 for assault, he
confessed and threw himself upon the mercy of the court. It
fined him ten shillings. Two years later he beat Samuel Hallett, pleaded guilty, and was fined two pounds. Still at large in
1729, he was tried for assaulting Robert Coe. Only two other
townsmen appeared before the lower criminal court for assault, the blacksmith Bernardus Bloom and James Hunt.[67]
Elsewhere in New York assault might have increased.
Douglas Greenberg found it the most common type of crime
but also noted considerable regional variation. Throughout
New York, though, violence, or crime against persons, was
not prosecuted as effectively as theft, or crime against property. The same was true in Massachusetts. The sacrosanct nature of private property was more than an abstract notion. It
was a social more, known and accepted. At the same time that
property was protected morality became less of an issue.[68]
The growing lack of concern over sexual behavior by local colonial courts was noticed almost fifty years ago by Henry
Banford Parkes. He found that by 1704 Suffolk County, Massachusetts, had stopped punishing premarital sex and fornica-

tion. The rest of Massachusetts had done so by 1739, New Hampshire and Connecticut by the 1750s. More recent work supports Parkes and goes on to note that the issue came to be the economic cost of bastardy, not the morality of illicit sex. By the 1740s Massachusetts no longer prosecuted men for fornication—only single women with bastards. After 1768 fornication became the least seriously punished of all crimes. If the man and the woman worked out a financial arrangement adequate for support of the child, the law left them alone. Property, not abstract morality, required protection. And property, not person or belief, was what the British attacked in their various schemes to rationalize the empire.[69]

By 1775 Newtowners' social structure was more complex. The wealthier had more varied goods and even some luxuries. There were no truly rich townsmen, however. Increased social stratification was only one result of Newtown's integration into provincial society. Primary schools proliferated, and Newtown even hosted two academies. Both headmasters and merchants brought ideas and goods to townsmen. The churches also tied Newtowners to those beyond the town. All denominations but the Presbyterian worshipped with others outside.

Growing contact and sophistication broke down communal values. The Quakers felt this declension most as young adults sought marriage partners beyond the Society's boundaries. However, growing independence also undermined discipline elsewhere. Churches no longer could force conformity once individuals could choose to leave a congregation. The courts reinforced this personal choice becoming less eager to prosecute or publicly shame miscreants for purely moral offenses. Personal privacy and individual choice had begun to catch up with the sanctity of private property as desirable social goals. Once this process was complete Newtown would be "modern." It was well on its way by the mid-eighteenth century.

CONCLUSION

If the founding fathers of Newtown had returned in 1775 they would have seen much that seemed familiar but also much that was subtly different. A process was underway that had already broken down generalized political, economic, and social institutions into specialized constituent parts. This evolution from the simpler to the more complex pervaded all facets of town life.

Newtown's internal political life became routinized and pro forma, as townsmen filled more elected offices. Whereas the earliest magistrates had made law, enforced it, and judged those accused of disobeying it, by 1700 the very term "magistrate" had disappeared. The General Assembly had assumed responsibility for legislation, and the justices of the peace and the county courts tried cases once heard by an elected town bench. However, the town's administrative burdens had grown, and a greater number of people shared those tasks. Instead of a few officers performing many functions, now many officers conducted these same operations plus a host of other duties that the town and the province had added over the years.

Townsmen met less often to discuss town business and created fewer ad hoc committees to deal with specific problems. They increased the tenure of those holding most posts but seemed to give officeholders little increased responsibility. Newtowners held power in reserve. They never let implied authority reside with their own local elected town board.

County and provincial institutions became more complex at the same time that village political institutions did. County government replaced the older, larger shires in 1683. County responsibility differentiated between administration and justice. The Queens County Board of Supervisors, first constituted in 1686, taxed the towns for county-level needs, such as a jail, a court house, predator bounties, and the transportation of vagrants and vagabonds. It also served as the conduit through which the General Assembly levied provincial taxes. Townsmen yearly elected a representative to the county board. He tied town and county together in ways that were only necessary once the county became a viable unit of government.

New York's court system also evolved from the more general to the more specific. Appointed justices of the peace, who performed a variety of tasks, replaced elected town magistrates at the lowest level of petty law suits. Many of these justices also sat as judges on the county court bench, the next level of jurisprudence. These benches lost the earlier legislative powers held by the shire's Court of Assizes. The justices held more reserved power than did judges. Of all those in power they accrued the broadest set of functions, and if they had exercised their full complement of duties they would have been very powerful generalized officers. That they did not, in Newtown or elsewhere, confirms a drift toward narrow specialization and the careful doling out of authority. What justices did was to act as middlemen who linked town with town and lower units of justice with higher provincial levels.

New York's most radical political change was the creation of an elected general assembly. This body began meeting regularly in 1692 and gradually took control of provincial finances, as well as its law. Counties elected delegates, and the board of supervisors taxed county inhabitants for their salaries. No Newtowner ever sat in New York's General Assembly, however, individual townsmen and the town as a corporation petitioned the assembly and utilized its legislative capacities. The key person linking town to provincial assembly was the Queens County representative. He would presumably work on the town's behalf. Townsmen also lobbied provincial governors. They did not hesitate to use all levels of government to their advantage.

Newtowners apparently felt comfortable within an increasingly bureaucratized state. For most of their long history townsmen needed little of the real politicking that required connections within New York's and London's patronage networks. When outside demands finally required political identification and activity beyond Newtown's boundaries, town consensus fell apart. Unable to act as a town when New York's Committees of Correspondence required allegiance to the Continental Congress, townsmen made individual choices. London had made little immediate impact on Newtown; Philadelphia threatened to demand much more. Only some could think of themselves as townsmen, countymen, New Yorkers, *and* Continentals.

Newtown's political evolution from the simple to the more complex in some ways parallels the town's economy. From the beginning townsmen were farmers who often held other skills. They distributed town lands and begot sons who first moved on to unoccupied lands and then, when these were gone, carved up family farms, like their New England counterparts. With finite land resources gone, townsmen shifted their emphasis. Still both farmers and craftsmen, they began to identify themselves by mid-eighteenth century as artisans, not yeomen. Some left, seeking their way in newly settled areas of New York, New Jersey, or New York City.

Townsmen traded the goods they produced with each other and with outsiders. Even under Dutch rule they utilized New York City as a market. The English established both markets and fairs to which townspeople had access. During the early eighteenth century major road-building projects linked Newtown to Jamaica, the county seat, to eastern Long Island, and to New York City via the Brooklyn ferry. They traded with shopkeepers in Jamaica and New York City, and by the mid-eighteenth century had one or more merchants of their own.

Wills, inventories, and receipt books chronicle townsmen's increasing participation in a transatlantic economy. Black slaves were the most obvious of Newtowners' imported goods. They were well-established in Newtown by 1690.

Townsmen also owned guns, swords, Dutch Bibles, and English prayer books. After 1700 luxuries appeared among men's and women's possessions. They owned jewelry, silks, and forks. Some wished to have not only what was utilitarian but also what was fashionable. They learned about fashion through their access to New York City and through contact with cultural brokers, like merchants, academic headmasters, and eventually British and French army officers. Even on a daily basis townsmen consumed an international variety of commodities. They bought chocolate, sugar, cinnamon, and tea. None of these grew in the mainland colonies, much less New York or Newtown.

Not everyone could afford silks or fashionable bedding. Newtowners were more economically stratified and could choose more statuses and roles in 1775 than in 1642. The most obvious change was the distance between richer and poorer townsmen. Whereas, in the seventeenth century, the wealthier had more of the same sorts of possessions as their poorer neighbors, by the mid-eighteenth century the wealthy could acquire different kinds of goods. Everybody, however, had access to more, and the standard of living of the lowest 10 percent of the free population might well have equalled that of an earlier day's lower middle. Pauperism was apparently infrequent in Newtown.

Townsmen also identified with various religious groups. By 1710 all four of Newtown's denominations had a foothold in town. In 1715 the congregationalists became Presbyterian, thereby joining with other churches nearby and with one or another colonial presbytery into one discipline. The Church of England gained both proportionally and absolutely during the eighteenth century; the Quakers lost. The Dutch Reformed church underwent the greatest change by 1775, as it became an American institution by casting aside its dependence on the Amsterdam classis for either doctrine or ordained ministers.

Dutch religious forms survived in Newtown and so did

Dutch ethnicity, albeit in a creolized form. Dutch identification surfaced in choice of church and marriage partners. Few
Dutchmen strayed from the Dutch Reformed congregation.
And most married Dutch spouses, chose Dutch family members as godparents, and named their children Dutch names.
Before 1686 few Dutchmen participated in town affairs, as
most lived beyond the original purchase line which set Newtown's boundaries. After 1686 the outbounds were included
within Newtown's patent. Those living there became townsmen by fiat and increasingly held town office. Dutchmen
learned English, and many sent their children to English primary schools in Newtown. They became trustees of those
schools alongside their English neighbors.

Schools flourished after 1724 bringing both basic literacy
and arithmetic to the four corners of town and more sophisticated academies, with foreign-born headmasters, to those
wanting further training in Greek and Latin. That they found
encouragement is an indication of townsmen's identification
with a larger culture and its possibilities, since none of these
skills would have helped yeomen farmers in Newtown.

In another sense, education reflected the need to provide
the young with a means to face adulthood. Family responsibility for children, the old, and the disabled remained one of
townsmen's underlying assumptions. Some of the townsmen's
values changed less than the political, economic, and social life
that went on within their context. First, there was family.
The Dutch took great pains to bind the generations together
through godparenthood. Outsiders were seldom chosen. This
set of values resurfaced in choice of marriage partners. At least
some married kinfolk. Outmarriage was limited to a number
of families that were related by the second generation. Both
blood and matrimony, then, protected and delineated those
within from those without. Not only were members cared for
but they also had preferred access to scarce resources. Newtowners divesting themselves of large land holdings and farms
preferred not to put them on the open market. Instead, they

went to sons, grandsons, nephews, or in-laws, and often at reduced prices.

The careful devising of land underscored the importance of private property. The belief that possessions could not be taken except by the consent of the owner arrived as part of the first settlers' cultural baggage. They reminded their rulers of its importance, first in 1653, and several times thereafter. When the final challenge came in the 1770s no one would have denied the underlying premise of "no taxation without representation." The question was over whether or not this state of affairs actually existed.

The right to own property without molestation was closely tied to townsmen's conviction that sovereignty resided in the people. This theme also surfaced in the 1653 Remonstrance, when townsmen reminded the Dutch that they were not a conquered people and had full Dutch liberties. Closer to home, townsmen held most power in reserve, doling it out sparingly for specific tasks. They never elected all-purpose officials with broad responsibilities, like the Massachusetts selectmen.

Family, property, and sovereignty were powerful and stable foundations that allowed both toleration within limits and change. While heterogeneity for its own sake held little appeal, in fact, townsmen accepted different ethnic and religious groups right from the beginning. Newtowners' religious choices increased, as did support for them in the form of town land and ecumenical funding. These groups were all Protestant, however. Frenchmen, other Roman Catholics, Jews, and the more exotic might have strained local toleration. The colonial wars brought unwelcome strangers to town, and if townsmen could have kept them out they would have. Only toward the end of the colonial period did the foreign-born appear, and then they were possibly hired to fill town military quotas. They do not appear in later Newtown records.

Changes in values occurred along two fronts. The first was political. In 1653 townsmen might have agreed that their "betters" should hold political office, but few of the wellborn lived in any colonial town. While distinctions existed, they did not divide townsmen into qualitatively different strata. No aristocracy or gentry led the town's tax lists and the wretchedly destitute remained in England. By 1719, however, countyman Daniel Bull articulated the "country" ideal that only the independently wealthy should hold power. This notion, while never practicable in Newtown or Queens County, would remain to become part of the American ideological arsenal against Britain. More rhetoric than reality, it would help townsmen from all over colonial America talk to one another.

Newtown's second attitudinal change was economic. While profit was always permissible, it had come from land, crafts, or skills. After 1700 profit also came from money— from a commodity with no intrinsic value. Investment in bonds and mortgages proceeded initially at the local level, but the ethos that accepted the legitimacy of money-lending transcended Newtown. After mid–century, New York established a loan office whereby the provincial treasury reaped profits from mortgages. The General Assembly regulated interest rates on both private and public loans: capitalism was never unfettered. But gone was a medieval mentality that saw money-at-interest as un-Christian, hence unfit for decent folk. In the eighteenth century it was just part of the process that expanded economic opportunity.

Newtown was an old and well-established town by the eve of the Revolution but its evolution from a more generalized, simpler society to a more specialized, complex society continued far beyond 1775. In the 1800s, townsmen became more dependent on New York City, some establishing commercial apple orchards and truck farms. Late in the century parts of Newtown became cemetaries, since land on Manhattan was too valuable to house only the dead. Today, the center of Newtown is called Elmhurst, a name proposed by real estate developers who thought it more evocative of country serenity than Newtown. Only one colonial building still stands, forlorn behind a wrought-iron fence. Jonathan Fish's meadow is LaGuardia Airport. Its location on the water, yet close to the metropolis, appealed as much to the seventeenth-century townsmen as it does to us today. It also links us to them through our shared assumptions about access to the wider world.

NOTES

ABBREVIATIONS

AHR	*American Historical Review.*
Cal. Hist. Mss.	*Calendar of Historical Manuscripts in the Office of the Secretary of State*, ed. E. B. O'Callaghan, 2 vols. (Albany, N.Y., 1865–1866).
Colonial Laws	*The Colonial Laws of the State of New York from the Year 1664 to the Revolution*, 5 vols. (Albany, N.Y., 1894).
County Minute Book	Queens County Supervisor's Book (1709–1787), Museum of the City of New York, New York, N.Y.
DHNY	*The Documentary History of the State of New York*, ed. E. B. O'Callaghan, 4 vols. (Albany, N.Y., 1850–1851).
DRHNY	*Documents Relative to the Colonial History of the State of New York*, ed. E. B. O'Callaghan and Berthold Fernow, 15 vols. (Albany, N.Y., 1856–1887).
Eccles. Recs. of N.Y.	*Ecclesiastical Records of the State of New York*, ed. E. T. Corwin, 7 vols. (Albany, N.Y., 1901–1916).
HDC	Historical Documents Collection, Paul Klapper Library, Queens College, City University of New York, Flushing, N.Y.
HRR	Haviland Records Room of the New York Yearly Meeting, New York, N.Y.
Inventories of Albany	Unpublished inventories in the Historical Documents Collection, Paul Klapper Library, Queens College, City University of New York, Flushing, N.Y.
LIHS	Long Island Historical Society, Brooklyn, N.Y.
N.Y. Hist.	*New York History*.
NYHS	New York Historical Society, New York, N.Y.
NYHS, *Collections*	New York Historical Society, *Collections* (New York, 1811–).
Newtown Court Minutes	Historical Records Survey, Transcriptions of the Early Town Records of New York, *Minutes of the Town Courts of Newtown*, 1656–1690 (New York, 1940).

NYPL New York Public Library, New York, N.Y.
QBPL Queensboro Public Library, Jamaica, N.Y.
Q.C. Conveyances Queens County Conveyance Libers, Historical Documents Collection, Paul Klapper Library, Queens College, City University of New York, Flushing, N.Y., Reels QCV1–QCV3.
P.R.O., A.O. Public Record Office (London), Audit Office Series (Library of Congress, Manuscripts Division), 146 vols., microfilm.
Rec. of N. Amsterdam *Records of New Amsterdam from 1653 to 1674*, ed. Berthold Fernow, 7 vols. (New York, 1897, reprinted Baltimore, 1976).
Riker Collection Notes, scrapbooks, and original documents collected by James Riker Jr. and deposited in the Manuscripts Division, New York Public Library, New York, N.Y.
Town Book 287 Town of Newtown 287, Historical Documents Collection, Paul Klapper Library, Queens College, City University of New York, Flushing, N.Y. Also on HDC Reel TNT 10.
Town Book 288 Town Records, Queens County, New York, Newtown, Book 288, Dated 1710–1753, Historical Documents Collection, Paul Klapper Library, Queens College, City University of New York, Flushing, N.Y. Also on HDC Reel TNT 4.
Town Book 289 Town of Newtown 289, "June 16th, 1753, Jacob Reeder, Town Clerk, Book of Records," Historical Documents Collection, Paul Klapper Library, Queens College, City University of New York, Flushing, N.Y. Also on HDC Reel TNT 10.
Town Minutes Historical Records Survey, Transcripts of Early Town Records of New York, *Town Minutes*, 2 vols. (New York, 1940–1941).
WMQ *The William and Mary Quarterly.*

INTRODUCTION

1. Kenneth A. Lockridge, *A New England Town: The First Hundred Years: Dedham, Massachusetts, 1636–1736* (New York, 1970), p. xi.

2. Patricia U. Bonomi, *A Factious People: Politics and Society in Colonial New York* (New York, 1971); Milton Klein, "New York in the American Colonies: A New Look," in Jacob Judd and Irwin H. Polishook, *Aspects of Early New York Society and Politics* (Tarrytown, N.Y., 1974), pp. 23, 13.

3. Jack P. Greene, "Autonomy and Stability: New England and the British Colonial Experience in Early Modern America," *Journal of Social History* 7(1974): 188.

4. Patricia U. Bonomi, "Local Government in Colonial New York: A Base for Republicanism," in Jacob Judd and Irwin H. Polishook, *Aspects of Early New York Society and Politics* (Tarrytown, N.Y., 1974), pp. 29–50; Langdon G. Wright, "In Search of Peace and Harmony: New York Communities in the Seventeenth Century," *N. Y. Hist.* 61(1980): 5–21; Douglas Greenberg, "The Middle Colonies in Recent American Historiography," *WMQ*, 3rd ser. 36(1979): 396–427, 398, 410.

CHAPTER I

1. Richard Hakluyt, *Voyages to the New World*, ed. David Freeman Hawke (Indianapolis, 1972), pp. 30–31.

2. Bruce C. Daniels, *The Connecticut Town: Growth and Development, 1635–1790* (Middletown, Conn., 1979), p. 8.

3. Albert E. McKinley, "The English and Dutch Towns of New Netherland," *AHR* 6(1900): 6, n. 2, 12, n. 1, 10.

4. Bruce C. Daniels, "Economic Development in Colonial and Revolutionary Connecticut: An Overview," *WMQ*, 3rd ser. 37(1980): 430; E. L. Jones, "Creative Disruptions in American Agriculture, 1620–1820," *Agricultural History* 48(1974): 516; F. Grave Morris, "Some Aspects of the Rural Settlement of New England in Colonial Times," in Laurence Dudley Stamp and S. W. Woldridge, *London Essays in Geography* (London, 1951), p. 222; T. J. C. Brasser, "The Coastal Algonkians: People of the First Frontier," in Eleanor Burke Leacock and Nancy Oestreich Lurie, eds., *North American Indians in Historical Perspective* (New York, 1971), p. 64.

5. Morris, "Rural Settlement," p. 222; Jones, "Creative Disruptions," pp. 524–525. Smith's quote is found in Percy Wells Bidwell and John I. Falconer, *History of Agriculture in the Northern United States, 1620–1860* (Washington, D.C., 1925), p. 19.

6. Myron F. Fuller, *The Geology of Long Island, New York*, U. S. Department of the Interior, United States Geological Survey, Professional Paper 82 (Washington, D.C., 1914), p. 25; A. C. Veatch et al., *Underground Water Resources of Long Island, New York*, U. S. Department of the Interior, United States Geological Survey, Professional Paper 44 (Washington, D.C., 1906), p. 44; Daniels, *Connecticut Town*, p. 55 (Daniels suggests that modern soil maps can identify colonial soil types because soil compositions rarely change over short periods of time, even with modern agricultural techniques); Jay A. Bonsteel, "Soil Survey of the Long Island Area, New York," in U.S.

Bureau of Soils, *Field Operations of the Bureau of Soils, 1903* (Washington, D.C., 1903), pp. 102, 109, 126; Timothy Dwight, *Travels in New England and New York*, ed. Barbara Miller Solomon (Cambridge, Mass., 1969), III, 226.

7. Douglas B. Carter, "Climate," in John H. Thompson, ed., *Geography of New York State* (Syracuse, N.Y., 1966), pp. 64, 62, 72, 77.

8. David Peterson de Vries, "Voyages from Holland to America, A.D. 1632–1644," tr. Henry C. Murphy, in Cornell Jaray, ed., *Historic Chronicles of New Amsterdam, Colonial New York and Early Long Island*, 1st ser. (Port Washington, N.Y., n.d.), p. 75. For a criticism of New York see "Letter of Reverend Jonas Michaelius, 1628," in J. Franklin Jameson, ed., *Narratives of New Netherland, 1609–1664* (New York, 1909), p. 132; John Miller, *A Description of the Province and City of New York*, in Cornell Jaray, ed., *Historic Chronicles, of New Amsterdam, Colonial New York and Early Long Island*, 1st ser. (Port Washington, N.Y., n.d.), p. 31. If "ague" is really malaria, then the middle colonies must be considered malarial. Peter Kalm, without knowing the real causes and transmission of malaria, commented that swamps, especially tidal marshes, seemed more unhealthy than high, dry ground *(Travels Into North America*, tr. John Reinhold Foster [Barre, Mass., 1972], pp. 186–187). Mosquitoes are mentioned in a diary commencing in 1790, "Journal of John Baxter of Flatlands, Long Island, 1790–1828: Continued by his Son Garret Stouthoff Baxter 1826–1835," copied by Harriet Stryker-Rodda and Edna Huntington, 1954–1955, LIHS (typewritten), vol. I (1790–1804), p. 13.

9. Daniel Denton, *A Brief Description of New York, Formerly Called New Netherlands with the Places Thereunto Adjoining* (London, 1670; reprinted New York, 1845) in Cornell Jaray, ed., *Historic Chronicles of New Amsterdam, Colonial New York and Early Long Island*, 2nd. ser. (Port Washington, N.Y., 1968), p. 5; "Journal of New Netherland," in J. Franklin Jameson. ed. *Narratives of New Netherland, 1609–1664* (New York, 1909), p. 270; Peter Ross, *History of Long Island from Its Earliest Settlement to the Present* (New York, 1902), I, 5–6; "Letter of Isaack de Rasieres to Samuel Blommaert, 1628(?)," in J. Franklin Jameson, ed., *Narratives of New Netherland, 1609–1664* (New York, 1909), p. 114.

10. "Journal of John Baxter," I, 4; "Journal of New Netherland," p. 270; "Diary of Mary Cooper, October 3, 1768–October 8, 1773," NYPL, Mss. Div., Diaries Box, p. 44.

11. Adriaen Van der Donck, "Description of the New Netherlands," NYHS, *Collections*, 2nd ser. 1(1841): 186–187.

12. Denton, *Brief Description of New York*, p. 2.

13. Fuller, *The Geology of Long Island*, p. 25.

14. See Van Cleaf Bachman, *Peltries or Plantations: The Economic Policies of the Dutch West India Company in New Netherland, 1623–1639* (Baltimore,

1969); Thomas J. Condon, *New York Beginnings: The Commercial Origins of New Netherland* (New York, 1968); S. G. Nissenson, *The Patroon's Domain* (New York, 1937), and E. B. O'Callaghan, *History of New Netherland or New York under the Dutch*, 2 vols. (New York, 1848).

15. O'Callaghan, *History of New Netherland*, I, 168–170, 209, 210.

16. Sigmund Diamond, "From Organization to Society: Virginia in the Seventeenth Century," in *Colonial America: Essays in Politics and Social Development*, ed. Stanley N. Katz, 2nd ed. (Boston, 1976), p. 21.

17. Nissenson, *The Patroon's Domain*, pp. 22, 26.

18. Condon, *New York Beginnings*, pp. 150–152.

19. O'Callaghan, *History of New Netherland*, II, App. M.

20. Samuel Hopkins Emory, *History of Taunton, Massachusetts* (Syracuse, N.Y., 1893), p. 40; Thomas Lechford, *Plain Dealing or Newes from New-England* (London, 1642), pp. 40–42, 54; *Winthrop Papers, 1498–1649*, ed. Allyn B. Forbes (Boston, 1947), V, 298, 358.

21. In 1646 Director Kieft told the visiting Jesuit, Isaac Jogues, that eighteen different languages were heard on Manhattan ("Novum Belgium, by Father Isaac Jogues, 1646," in J. Franklin Jameson, ed., *Narratives of New Netherland, 1609–1664* [New York, 1909], p. 259); O'Callaghan, *History of New Netherland*, I, 257–258, 208. Some settlements did not survive the Indian wars. The number given here is taken from the patent list (O'Callaghan, *History of New Netherland*, II, 581–593).

22. "Journal of New Netherland," pp. 273–274; Allen W. Trelease, *Indian Affairs in Colonial New York: The Seventeenth Century* (Ithaca, N.Y., 1960), pp. 70–71.

23. "Journal of New Netherland," pp. 273–274; Trelease, *Indian Affairs*, pp. 71–80.

24. O'Callaghan, *History of New Netherland*, II, 17–18, 22–24; Condon, *New York Beginnings*, pp. 155–157, 165.

25. *DRHNY*, I, 550–552.

26. Ibid., pp. 551–552.

27. Edmund S. Morgan, *The Puritan Dilemma: The Story of John Winthrop* (Boston, 1958), p. 170; *DRHNY*, I, 551.

28. Arlin Ira Ginsburg, "Ipswich, Massachusetts During the American Revolution, 1763–1791," Ph.D. diss. (University of California, Riverside, 1972), pp. 15–16.

29. Harry H. Kessler and Eugene Rachlis, *Peter Stuyvesant and His New York* (New York, 1959), pp. 130–131. An analogy to calling upon Indian allies was calling in German mercenaries in the American Revolution. They also had a reputation for barbarity.

30. Ibid., p. 138

31. O'Callaghan, *History of New Netherland*, II, 242, 264, 266n.

32. Trelease, *Indian Affairs*, pp. 138–139; *DHNY*, III, 557.

33. *DRHNY*, I, 552.

34. David Konig, "English Legal Change and the Origins of Local Government in Northern Massachusetts," in Bruce C. Daniels, *Town and County: Essays on the Structure of Local Government in the American Colonies* (Middletown, Conn., 1978), p. 30.

35. *Town Minutes*, II, 218–219, I, 55.

36. Jerrold Seymann, *Colonial Charters Patents and Grants to the Communities Comprising the City of New York* (New York, 1939), pp. 553–554. Memoria, Riker Collection, Box 16, vol. 5, p. 62. These records are copies of materials in the State Archives at Albany. Riker was able to see the entire collection of colonial manuscripts before the Albany fire of 1911. James Riker Jr., *Annals of Newtown* (New York, 1852), p. 28.

37. David Konig says that town government was weak and limited, but David Grayson Allen asserts that it had wide latitude (Konig, "English Legal Change," p. 29; David Grayson Allen, *In English Ways: The Movement of Societies and the Transferal of English Local Law and Custom to Massachusetts Bay in the Seventeenth Century* [Chapel Hill, 1981], p. 39); Daniels, *Connecticut Town*, pp. 65, 75, 95–96, 74.

38. Allen, *In English Ways*, p. 43. The town minutes list town officials (*Town Minutes*, I, 49, 51). Riker also listed these in *Annals*, p. 418.

39. *Town Minutes*, I, 50, 52, 53; The Duke's Laws are printed in *The Colonial Laws*, I.

40. *Town Minutes*, I, 138, 41, 49; Memoria, Riker Collection, Box 16, vol. 5, p. 63.

41. Allen, *In English Ways*, p. 39; Thomas Walter Jodziewicz, "Dual Localism in Seventeenth-Century Connecticut: Relations Between the General Court and the Towns, 1636–1691," Ph.D. diss. (College of William and Mary, 1974), p. 34; Langdon Goddard Wright, "Local Government in Colonial New York, 1640–1710," Ph.D. diss. (Cornell University, 1974), p. 70.

42. Memoria, Riker Collection, Box 16, vol. 5, p. 76; *DRHNY*, XIV, 500. The New Amsterdam court records are published as *Rec. of N. Amsterdam*.

43. Memoria, Riker Collection, Box 16, vol. 5, pp. 117–118; *DRHNY*, XIV, 489–492.

44. *DRHNY*, XIV, 285, 286–287; *Town Minutes*, I, 123.

45. Memoria, Riker Collection, Box 16, vol. 5, p. 116; *Eccles. Recs. of N.Y.*, I, 410; *DRHNY*, XIV, 496.

46. Memoria, Riker Collection, Box 16, vol. 5, pp. 163–167.

47. *DRHNY*, XIV, 514, 517; *The Public Records of the Colony of Connecticut*, ed. J. Hammond Trumbull (Hartford, Conn., 1850), I, 425; Memoria,

Riker Collection, Box 16, vol.5, pp. 73−74; *Town Minutes*, I, 53, 52. A sche-
pel contains slightly more than three pecks.

CHAPTER II

1. Peter Clark, "Migration in England During the Late Seventeenth
and Early Eighteenth Centuries," *Past and Present* 83(1979): 59; James Horn,
"Servant Emigration to the Chesapeake in the Seventeenth Century," in
Thad W. Tate and David L. Ammerman, eds., *The Chesapeake in the Seventeenth Century: Essays on Anglo-American Society* (Chapel Hill, 1979), pp.
73−74; Peter Clark, "The Migrant in Kentish Towns, 1580−1640," in Peter
Clark and Paul Slack, eds., *Crisis and Order in English Towns, 1500−1700* (London, 1972), pp. 138, 134.

2. *Town Minutes*, I, 41, 79, 96−97; Benjamin F. Thompson, *History of
Long Island*, 3rd ed., 3 vols. (New York, 1918), II, 472, 595, III, 26.

3. *Town Minutes*, II, 218−219. The four excluded entries are Paya,
Brummes, Smith Island, and Trapsaus. The list has been annotated follow-
ing James Riker Jr. (Memoria, Riker Collection, Box 18, vol. 9, p. 63).
Other tax lists are the 1660 wolf rate, the December, 1666, rate, and the
January, 1667, rate. New England materials are from Douglas Lamar Jones,
"Geographic Mobility and Society in Eighteenth-Century Essex County,
Massachusetts," Ph.D. diss. (Brandeis University, 1975), p. 28. Crude per-
sistence rates are found by subtracting the persons on one list from the persons on a second list. A refined rate is calculated by tracing missing persons,
finding out who died, and counting the deceased as persisters.

4. David Grayson Allen, *In English Ways: The Movement of Societies and
the Transferal of English Local Law and Custom to Massachusetts Bay in the Seventeenth Century* (Chapel Hill, 1981), App. 1−5, p. 82; John J. Waters Jr., *The
Otis Family in Provincial and Revolutionary Massachusetts* (New York, 1968), pp.
6, 9, 16.

5. Genealogical materials come from James Riker Jr., *Annals of Newtown* (New York, 1852), and other standard sources, such as James Savage,
A Genealogical Dictionary of the First Settlers of New England, 4 vols. (Boston,
1860−1862; reprinted Baltimore, 1965). Jean Peyer has had little better luck
tracing her Jamaica founders. She was able to find eight of her twenty-four
patentees, all of whom came from the eastern counties. Her group and the
Newtown men are not mutually exclusive, and she and I disagree about the
origins of two settlers, Robert and Benjamin Coe (Jean Peyer, "Jamaica,
Long Island, 1656−1776: A Study of the Roots of American Urbanism,"
Ph.D. diss. [City University of New York, 1974], pp. 19−22).

6. *Town Minutes*, I, 79; Rev. E. B. Huntington, *History of Stamford, Connecticut, from Its Settlement in 1641 to the Present Time* (Stamford, 1868), p. 83; New York Colonial Manuscripts, XXVIII, 17b (State Library, Albany); *DHNY*, II, 298–299; Memoria, Riker Collection, Box 18, vol. 13, p. 122.

7. *Rec. of N. Amsterdam*, III, 282, 348, IV, 116.

8. Allen, *In English Ways*, p. 31; Linda Auwers Bissell, "Family, Friends, and Neighbors: Social Interaction in Seventeenth-Century Windsor, Connecticut," Ph.D. diss. (Brandeis University, 1973), p. 25.

9. *Town Minutes*, I, 47; Bissell, "Family, Friends, and Neighbors," p. 25, n. 2. Using a Gini coefficient, which measures increasing inequality on a scale from 0 to 1, the 1662 rate shows a low coefficient of .190. The Gini coefficient is discussed in Charles M. Dollar and Richard J. Jensen, *Historian's Guide to Statistics: Quantitative Analysis and Historical Research* (New York, 1971), p. 124. For a discussion of some of the benefits of this measure see G. B. Warden, "Inequality and Instability in Eighteenth-Century Boston: A Reappraisal," *Journal of Interdisciplinary History* 6(1976): 602–603. For a discussion of some of the problems involved in choosing the analysis groupings see James P. Whittenburg and Randall G. Penberton, "Measuring Inequality: A Fortran Program for the Gini Index, Schutz Coefficient, and Lorenz Curve," *Historical Methods Newsletter* 10(1977): 77–84.

10. *Town Minutes* I, 51. For a good discussion of open field farming in England and America see Sumner Chilton Powell, *Puritan Village: The Formation of a New England Town* (Middletown, Conn., 1963), chap. 1.

11. Allen, *In English Ways*, pp. 122, 131.

12. *Town Minutes*, I, 55. Even though the town passed a law requiring a vote on strangers, no such vote was ever entered in the minutes, nor were there any votes forcing people out of town (David Grayson Allen, "In English Ways: The Movement of Societies and the Transferal of English Local Law and Custom to Massachusetts Bay, 1600–1690," Ph.D. diss. [University of Wisconsin, 1974], p. 468).

13. Edna Scofield, "The Origin of Settlement Patterns in Rural New England," *Geographical Review* 28(1938): 653, 659; Carville V. Earle, "The First English Towns of North America," *Geographical Review* 67(1977): 36; David Konig, "English Legal Change and the Origins of Local Government in Colonial Connecticut," in Bruce C. Daniels, *Town and County: Essays on the Structure of Local Government in the American Colonies* (Middletown, Conn., 1978), p. 13; Kenneth A. Lockridge, *A New England Town: The First Hundred Years: Dedham, Massachusetts, 1636–1736* (New York, 1970).

14. T. H. Breen and Stephen Foster, "Moving to the New World: The Character of Early Massachusetts Immigration," *WMQ*, 3rd ser. 30(1973): 189–222; Powell, *Puritan Village*, chaps. 1, 2; Waters, *The Otis*

Family, p. 8; Memoria, Riker Collection, Box 18, vol. 9; *Town Minutes*, I, 41; Memoria, Riker Collection, Box 16, vol. 5, p. 115.

15. *Newtown Court Minutes*, p. 29. There must be an error in the value of cattle in the original inventory since there cattle are listed at £82 (Town Book 185 [Reel TNT 9, HDC]). This figure would make the total of the inventory £30 too high. I have reduced the value of the cattle by £30.

16. Seventy-two percent of Cornish's estate was personal property, 28 percent was real property (Jackson Turner Main, "The Distribution of Property in Colonial Connecticut," in James Kirby Martin, ed., *The Human Dimension of Nation Making: Essays in Colonial and Revolutionary America* [Madison, Wis., 1976], p. 77); Allen, "In English Ways," p. 116.

17. Gloria L. Main, "Probate Records as a Source for Early American History," *WMQ*, 3rd ser. 32(1975): 96; Savage, *Genealogical Dictionary*, I, 459; Riker, *Annals*, p. 378. My own work, as well as other studies on marriage ages, suggests that twenty-five is a good estimate of male first marriage age. See Robert V. Wells, "Quaker Marriage Patterns in a Colonial Perspective," *WMQ*, 3rd ser. 29(1972): 429. Jackson Turner Main notes that children under sixteen were economic liabilities ("Distribution of Property in Colonial Connecticut," in Martin, ed., *The Human Dimension of Nation Making*, p. 63).

18. Twelve was the mode of the 1660 rate; thirty acres was the mode of the 1662 tax list *(Town Minutes, I, 41, 47)*.

19. *Rec. of N. Amsterdam*, II, 169.

20. Ibid., p. 296.

21. *Records of the Towns of North and South Hempstead, Long Island, New York*, ed. Benjamin D. Hicks, 8 vols. (Jamaica, N.Y., 1896-1904), I, 24, 23.

22. *Rec. of N. Amsterdam*, II, 169, 338-339; IV, 96, 93; *Minutes of the Executive Council of the Province of New York: Administration of Francis Lovelace, 1668-1673*, 2 vols. (Albany, 1910), I, 89, n 2; *Newtown Court Minutes*, pp. 14, 15, 17.

23. Memoria, Riker Collection, Box 16, vol. 5, p. 89.

24. *Newtown Court Minutes*, p. 36; David E. Narrett, "Preparation for Death and Provision for the Living: Notes on New York Wills (1665-1760)," *N.Y. Hist.* 57(1976): 417-437. Thomas Cornish and Elizabeth Hallett both died in middle age. These deaths suggest that people died at an early age, but whether that was the norm can not be proved from the sparse evidence from this early period. However, New England materials suggest that townsmen north of the Chesapeake lived long lives. Balancing out Thomas Cornish were William Hallett, who lived to be ninety, and Captain Richard Betts, who died at the age of one hundred. (Riker, *Annals*, pp. 403 [402], 374). Philip Greven has dealt most extensively with early settler longevity, and he suggests that the founding generation lived long lives. Of his

first twenty-eight families, the average age of death for twenty-nine males was 71.8 years and for twenty females was 70.8 years *(Four Generations: Population, Land, and Family in Colonial Andover, Massachusetts* [Ithaca, N.Y., 1970], p. 26).

25. *Town Minutes*, I, 25, 33; *Newtown Court Minutes*, p. 263 ; *Minutes of the Executive Council*, I, 77.

26. There is at the moment a lively debate over the social standing of immigrants. Were they skilled or unskilled; middling or the common sort? See David W. Galenson, "'Middling People' or 'Common Sort'?: The Social Origins of Some Early Americans Reexamined," with a rebuttal by Mildred Campbell, *WMQ*, 3rd ser. 35(1978): 499–540. See also Breen and Foster, "Moving to the New World" (Breen and Foster conclude that the migrants were ordinary men and women neither at the top nor the bottom of society [p. 221]); Darrett B. Rutman, *American Puritanism: Faith and Practice* (Philadelphia, 1970), p. vi.

27. Rutman, *American Puritanism*, pp. vi, 9; George Selement, "Perry Miller: A Note on His Sources in *The New England Mind: The Seventeenth Century*," *WMQ*, 3rd ser. 31(1974): 459; Herbert Levy Osgood, *The American Colonies in the Seventeenth Century* (New York, 1904; reprinted, Gloucester, Mass., 1957), I, 70; Edmund S. Morgan, *American Slavery, American Freedom: The Ordeal of Colonial Virginia* (New York, 1975), pp. 151, 332.

28. Edmund S. Morgan, *Visible Saints: The History of a Puritan Idea* (Ithaca, N.Y., 1963); Allen, *In English Ways*, p. 92. For both the arguments and good bibliographic references to the plethora of literature on the Massachusetts franchise see B. Katherine Brown, "The Controversy over the Franchise in Puritan Massachusetts, 1954–1974," *WMQ*, 3rd ser. 33(1976): 212–241; Arlin I. Ginsburg, "The Franchise in Seventeenth-Century Massachusetts: Ipswich," *WMQ* 34(1977): 446–452; and Robert E. Wall, "The Franchise in Seventeenth-Century Massachusetts: Dedham and Cambridge," *WMQ* 34(1977): 453–458.

29. Powell, *Puritan Village*, p. 137.

30. *Rec. of N. Amsterdam*, I, 227; *Eccles. Recs. of N.Y.*, I, 410.

31. *Eccles Recs. of N.Y.*, I, 410, 397; Rev. John P. Knox, *Anniversary Discourse of a Twenty-five Years' Pastorate, Preached March 28, 1880, in the Presbyterian Church, Newtown, Long Island* (New York, 1880), p. 21.

32. Robert Hastings Nichols, *Presbyterianism in New York State: A History of the Synod and Its Predecessors* (Philadelphia, 1963), p. 11.

33. *Eccles. Recs. of N.Y.*, I, 396, 409–410.

34. *DRHNY*, XIV, 343, 369, 377.

35. *Newtown Court Minutes*, pp. 13, 14; *Rec. of N. Amsterdam*, I, 207.

36. Wright, "In Search of Peace and Harmony," *N.Y. Hist.* 61(1980): 7.

37. Thomas Walter Jodziewicz, "Dual Localism in Seventeenth-

Century Connecticut: Relations Between the General Court and the Towns," Ph.D. diss. (College of William and Mary, 1974), pp. 302–305.

38. *Newtown Court Minutes.*

39. Ibid., pp. 15, 17.

40. Ibid., pp. 15, 18. Although his information is from the eighteenth, rather than the seventeenth, century, Douglas Greenberg found that women were more likely to be prosecuted for selling liquor and the various nuisances that it created than for other kinds of anti-social or anti-authoritarian acts. While women numbered only 10 percent of prosecutions, they comprised 40 percent of those running disorderly inns and taverns and 32 percent of those selling liquor to slaves. Their other major crime was theft *(Crime and Law Enforcement in the Colony of New York, 1691–1776* [Ithaca, N.Y., 1976], pp. 49–51).

41. Burton Benedict, "Sociological Characteristics of Small Territories and Their Implications for Economic Development," in Michael Banton, ed., *The Social Anthropology of Complex Societies* (New York, 1966), pp. 23–35. See also Eric R. Wolf, "Kinship, Friendship and Patron-Client Relations in Complex Societies," in Michael Banton, ed., *The Social Anthropology of Complex Societies* (New York, 1966), pp. 1–22; *Newtown Court Minutes,* p. 27.

42. For a theoretical discussion on the way that such incidents reveal a culture's symbolic constructs, as well as structural complexity, see Clifford Geertz, "Thick Description: Toward an Interpretive Theory of Culture," in Clifford Geertz, *The Interpretation of Cultures: Selected Essays* (New York, 1973), pp. 3–30; *Newtown Court Minutes,* p. 16.

43. *Newtown Court Minutes,* p. 91; *Town Minutes,* I, 41.

44. David H. Flaherty, "Law and the Enforcement of Morals in Early America," *Perspectives in American History* 5(1971): 209–253.

CHAPTER III

1. *DRHNY,* XIV, 564; *Colonial Laws,* I; Robert C. Ritchie, *The Duke's Province: A Study of New York Politics and Society, 1664–1691* (Chapel Hill, N.C., 1971), p. 34; A. E. McKinley, "The Transition from Dutch to English Rule," *AHR* 6(1901): 693–724.

2. Vernon K. Dibble, "The Organization of Traditional Authority: English County Government, 1558 to 1640," in James G. March, ed., *The Handbook of Organizations* (Chicago, 1965), pp. 879–909; *Colonial Laws,* I, 43–44.

3. *Town Minutes,* II, 243. For a full description of New York's colonial judiciary see Julius Goebel Jr. and T. Raymond Naughton, *Law Enforce-*

ment in Colonial New York: A Study in Criminal Procedure (1664–1776) (New York, 1944); Patricia U. Bonomi, *A Factious People: Politics and Society in Colonial New York* (New York, 1971), p. 28.

4. Goebel and Naughton, *Law Enforcement in Colonial New York*, p. 21.

5. *DRHNY*, XIV, 585; Newtown paid the Indians £76 9s (Jerrold Seymann, *Colonial Charters, Patents and Grants to the Communities Comprising the City of New York* [New York, 1939], p. 554).

6. *Town Minutes*, II, 296; Seymann, *Colonial Charters*, pp. 559–567.

7. *DRHNY*, XIV, 592; *Cal. Hist. Mss.*, I, 223, 225; *Minutes of the Executive Council of the Province of New York*, ed. V. H. Paltsits, 2 vols. (Albany, 1910), I, 237, 238; *Town Minutes*, I, 115.

8. *Minutes of the Executive Council*, I, 238; James Riker Jr., *Annals of Newtown* (New York, 1852), pp. 82–83; *DRHNY*, XIV, 660, 669–670.

9. Jean Peyer, "Jamaica, Long Island, 1656–1776: A Study of the Roots of American Urbanism," Ph.D. diss. (City University of New York, 1974), pp. 165, 202; Kenneth A. Lockridge, *A New England Town: The First Hundred Years: Dedham, Massachusetts, 1636–1736* (New York, 1970), pp. 95, 14; Bruce C. Daniels, *The Connecticut Town: Growth and Development, 1635–1790* (Middletown, Conn., 1979), p. 14; Langdon G. Wright, "Local Government in Colonial New York 1640–1710," Ph.D. diss. (Cornell University, 1974), pp. 148–150 (In cases where information is given in square miles I have multiplied by 640 to find the acreage); Richard Dunn, *Puritans and Yankees: The Winthrop Dynasty of New England 1630–1717* (New York, 1962), pp. 250–251.

10. *Town Minutes*, I, 7, 111, 118; Peyer, "Jamaica, Long Island," p. 174; Thomas F. Gordon, *Gazateer of the State of New York* (Philadelphia, 1836), p. 512; David Grayson Allen, *In English Ways: The Movement of Societies and the Transferal of English Local Law and Custom to Massachusetts Bay in the Seventeenth Century* (Chapel Hill, N.C., 1981), p. 51.

11. *Town Minutes*, I, 141, 102; II, 356.

12. *Town Minutes*, I, 56, 100.

13. Sumner Chilton Powell, *Puritan Village: The Formation of a New England Town* (Middletown, Conn., 1963), p. 108; David Grayson Allen, "In English Ways: The Movement of Societies and the Transferal of English Local Law and Custom to Massachusetts Bay, 1600–1690," Ph.D. diss. (University of Wisconsin, 1974), p. 116; Philip J. Greven Jr., *Four Generations: Population, Land and Family in Colonial Andover, Massachusetts* (Ithaca, N.Y., 1970), p. 63; Nathaniel S. Prime, *A History of Long Island, from its first settlement by Europeans, to the year 1845* (New York, 1845), p. 72; *Records of the Towns of North and South Hempstead*, ed. Benjamin D. Hicks, 8 vols. (Jamaica, N.Y., 1896–1904), II, 119, 371; Wright, "Local Government," p. 331; Kenneth A. Lockridge and Alan Kreider, "The Evolution of Massachusetts Town Government, 1640 to 1740," *WMQ*, 3rd ser. 23(1966): 549–574.

14. *Town Minutes*, II, 216, I, 8, 70; Lockridge, *New England Town*, p. 12, Powell, *Puritan Village*, p. 107; Linda Auwers Bissell, "Family, Friends, and Neighbors: Social Interaction in Seventeenth-Century Windsor, Connecticut," Ph.D. diss. (Brandeis University, 1973), p. 22; Greven, *Four Generations*, p. 45.

15. *Town Minutes*, I, 111, 70, 100, II, 141. All of these meadows were sold to Newtowners.

16. *Town Minutes*, II, 252, 220–221.

17. Allen, "In English Ways," Ph.D. diss., p. 336; Kenneth A. Lockridge, "Dedham, 1636–1736: The Anatomy of a Puritan Utopia," Ph.D. diss. (Princeton, 1965), p. 25; Greven, *Four Generations*, pp. 46, 58.

18. Richard Bushman, *From Puritan to Yankee: Character and the Social Order in Connecticut, 1690–1765* (Cambridge, Mass., 1967); Dunn, *Puritans and Yankees*, passim; William Bradford is quoted in John Demos, *A Little Commonwealth: Family Life in Plymouth Colony* (New York, 1970), p. 11; Allen, "In English Ways," p. 176; Daniels, *Connecticut Town*, pp. 122–127.

19. *Town Minutes*, I, 7, 23, II, 356; *Records of the Town of Jamaica, Long Island, New York*, ed. Josephine C. Frost, 3 vol. (Brooklyn, N.Y., 1914), I, 11; Peyer, "Jamaica, Long Island," pp. 86, 87, 194.

20. *Town Minutes*, I, 55, II, 250, 252, 356.

21. Demos, *Little Commonwealth*, pp. 9–11; Greven, *Four Generations*, p. 55. The town was founded in 1646 (p. 21); Paul Boyer and Stephen Nissenbaum, *Salem Possessed: The Social Origins of Witchcraft* (Cambridge, Mass., 1974), pp. 37–39; David Grayson Allen, *In English Ways*, p. 94; Linda Auwers, "Fathers, Sons and Wealth in Colonial Windsor, Connecticut," *Journal of Family History* 3(1978): 140; Peyer, "Jamaica, Long Island," p. 189.

22. Greven, *Four Generations*, p. 43; Bushman, *From Puritan to Yankee*, chap. 4, passim; Boyer and Nissenbaum, *Salem Possessed*, p. 40; Powell, *Puritan Village*, p. 147.

23. In 32 years the court met 174 times, *Newtown Court Minutes*.

24. Highway Supervisors were court appointed in 1667–1670 *(Newtown Court Minutes*, p. 193).

25. Allen, *In English Ways*, pp. 43, 156; Lockridge and Kreider, "Evolution of Town Government," p. 574.

26. Wright, "Local Government," pp. 245, 244, 246; Peyer, "Jamaica, Long Island," p. 81.

27. Wright, "Local Government," pp. 244, 245; Peyer, "Jamaica, Long Island," p. 82.

28. Information on town meetings has been taken from the various town books. *Town Minutes*, I, 70, 118.

29. *Town Minutes*, II, 330–332.

30. Allen, *In English Ways*, p. 44; Allen, "In English Ways," Ph.D.

NOTES TO PAGES 72-78

diss., pp. 134, 141; Lockridge and Kreider, "Evolution of Town Government," p. 574.

31. There is insufficient data for supervisors and collectors. They were first chosen in 1685 and 1686, but neither was selected in 1688 or 1689. See Riker, *Annals*, App. F, for officeholders. Riker's lists were checked against the manuscripts and found to be accurate. Bruce C. Daniels found a similar pattern for town clerks in Connecticut. See "The Long-Lasting Men of Local Government: Town Clerks in Colonial Connecticut," The Connecticut Historical Society, *Bulletin* 41(1976): 90–96.

32. Allen, *In English Ways*, pp. 41, 40, 154, 120.

33. The 1666 rate is in the *Town Minutes*, I, 79. The 1683 rate is in *DHNY*, II, 298–299. Samuel Moore died in 1717. His first elected office was in 1677. John Lawrence died in 1729. Unless otherwise noted, genealogical information is from Riker, *Annals*, pp. 263–410. There is no evidence that townsmen absent from the rate lists differed economically from those who appeared on it.

34. The 1698 census is found in Memoria, Riker Collection, Box 16, vol. 5, pp. 147–150.

35. James Savage, *A Genealogical Dictionary of the First Settlers of New England*, 4 vols. (Boston, 1860–1862, reprinted Baltimore, 1965), IV, 405; *DHNY*, II, 266–267; *Rec. of N. Amsterdam*, IV, 255; "Calendar of the Proceedings of the Court of Assizes, 1665–1672," Manuscript Division, NYPL, p. 24; *Minutes of the Executive Council*, I, 208.

36. Riker, *Annals*, p. 341.

37. Edward M. Cook Jr., *The Fathers of the Towns: Leadership and Community Structure in Eighteenth-Century New England* (Baltimore, 1976), p. 178.

38. Riker, *Annals*, pp. 327–328; New York Genealogical and Biographical Society, *Collections* 8(1928), "Records of the Presbyterian Church, Newtown (now Elmhurst) Queens County, Long Island, New York," p. 29.

39. Land records are in the Town Minute Books; NYHS *Collections* 35(1902): 155; Inventories of Estates (Reel 2; NYHS); *DHNY*, II, 298–299.

40. Office holding is taken from the Town Minute Books. Trustees were elected before the office was institutionalized in 1717.

41. Ritchie, *The Duke's Province*, pp. 63, 64; *DRHNY*, XIV, 615.

42. *DRHNY*, XIV, 631.

43. *Jamaica Town Records*, I, 43; *Records of North and South Hempstead*, I, 260; *Town Minutes*, I, 161.

44. Joyce Diane Goodfriend, "Too Great a Mixture of Nations: The Development of New York City Society in the Seventeenth Century," Ph.D. diss. (UCLA, 1975), p. 63; *Newtown Court Minutes*, p. 224. This deposition suggests that not everybody was part of the town meeting. Perhaps these men lived on the outbounds, for there is no other evidence that

the town excluded townsmen from the meeting, nor is there any sense that this was a grievance.

45. There were 36 cases in 1682, 34 in 1670, and 27 in 1671 (Demos, *Little Commonwealth*, p. 49).

46. Ritchie, *The Duke's Province*, pp. 184–185.

47. Wright, "Local Government," pp. 172, 178, 182.

48. *Town Minutes*, II, 393.

49. Ibid., pp. 417c, 418.

50. Ibid.

51. *DRHNY*, III, 754–755; Memoria, Riker Collection, Box 16, vol. 5, pp. 95, 93; *Cal. Hist. Mss.*, II, 223.

52. *Rec. of N. Amsterdam*, V, 42; Memoria, Riker Collection, Box 16, vol. 5, p. 126. The 1686 Dongan patent has 113 inhabitants listed of which fourteen, or 12 percent, are non-English (Seymann, *Colonial Charters*, pp. 562–563).

53. Thomas F. Archdeacon, *New York City, 1664–1710: Conquest and Change* (Ithaca, N.Y., 1976), p. 109; Ritchie, *The Duke's Province*, pp. 215–216; John M. Murrin, "English Rights as Ethnic Aggression: The English Conquest, The Charter of Liberties of 1683 and Leisler's Rebellion in New York," (Paper delivered at the Annual Convention of the American Historical Association, San Francisco, December, 1973), pp. 19, 21 (The quote is on p. 18); Goodfriend, "Too Great a Mixture of Nations," pp. 257, 259.

CHAPTER IV

1. *DRHNY*, XIV, 569; James Riker Jr., *Annals of Newtown* (New York, 1852), p. 64; Q. C. Conveyances, Liber A (Reel QCV1), p. 114; Liber B1 (Reel QCV1), p. 147.

2. Land transactions were found mainly in the various town books and the Queens County Conveyance Libers.

3. Jean Peyer, "Jamaica, Long Island, 1656–1776: A Study of the Roots of American Urbanism," Ph.D. diss. (City University of New York, 1974), p. 91 (Peyer says that most land exchanges occurred between 1675 and 1720); David Grayson Allen, "In English Ways: The Movement of Societies and the Transferal of English Local Law and Custom to Massachusetts Bay, 1600–1690," Ph.D. diss. (University of Wisconsin, 1974), pp. 190–191, 263, 302; David Grayson Allen, *In English Ways: The Movement of Societies and the Transferal of English Local Law and Custom to Massachusetts Bay in the Seventeenth Century* (Chapel Hill, N.C., 1981), pp. 112–113, 129, 128.

4. *Town Minutes*, I, 81.

5. Sumner Chilton Powell, *Puritan Village: The Formation of a New Eng-*

land Town (Middletown, Conn., 1963), p. 122; Philip J. Greven Jr., *Four Generations: Population, Land, and Family in Colonial Andover, Massachusetts* (Ithaca, N.Y., 1970), p. 57.

6. Q. C. Conveyances, Liber A (Reel QCV1), p. 114; Liber B1 (Reel QCV1), p. 147. For a study of inheritance and land, see Greven, *Four Generations.* Townsmen gave land as gifts more often than did Jamaica's settlers (8% vs. 2.4%). It would be interesting to know when Jamaicans gave land as gifts, since the town had 53,000 acres to dispense; whereas Newtown had only 16,000 acres, including the outbounds (Peyer, "Jamaica, Long Island," pp. 193, 123).

7. Margaret Spufford, "Peasant Inheritance Customs and Land Distribution in Cambridgeshire from the Sixteenth to the Eighteenth Centuries," in Jack Goody et al., *Family and Inheritance: Rural Society in Western Europe, 1200–1800* (Cambridge, Eng., 1976), pp. 156–176; the quote is from Cicely Howell, "Peasant Inheritance Customs in the Midlands, 1280–1700," in Goody et al., *Family and Inheritance,* p. 146. The tax list is in *Town Minutes,* I, 19–20; Riker, *Annals,* pp. 316, 302. Greven found that in 22 of 23 first generation families, land was given to all sons where there were two or more sons *(Four Generations,* p. 83). Linda Bissell found that all sons inherited ("Family, Friends, and Neighbors: Social Interaction in Seventeenth-Century Windsor, Connecticut," Ph.D. diss. [Brandeis University, 1973], p. 90).

8. Greven's argument in *Four Generations* is that parents used land to control their children's behavior; Q. C. Conveyances, Liber A (Reel QCV1) p. 19; Bissell, "Family, Friends, and Neighbors," p. 87; Linda Auwers, "Fathers, Sons and Wealth in Colonial Windsor, Connecticut," *Journal of Family History* 3(1978): 141 and n. 7; Joyce Diane Goodfriend, "Too Great a Mixture of Nations: The Development of New York City Society in the Seventeenth Century," Ph.D. diss. (UCLA, 1975), pp. 75, 72.

9. NYHS, *Collections* 25(1892): 55. This is just one volume of a set of will abstracts published by the New York Historical Society as their *Collections* 25–41(1892–1908). The abstracts were checked against the original wills, which are located in the Historical Documents Collection, Paul Klapper Library, Queens College, Jamaica, N.Y.

10. Q. C. Conveyances, Liber A (Reel QCV1), pp. 48, 89; David E. Narrett, "Preparations for Death and Provisions for the Living: Notes on New York Wills (1665–1760)," *N. Y. Hist.* 57(1976): 417–437.

11. Robert C. Ritchie, *The Duke's Province: A Study of New York Politics and Society, 1664–1691* (Chapel Hill, 1977), p. 131; the 1675 and 1683 tax lists are in *DHNY,* II, 266–267, 298–299. The 1678 tax list has not been published and is found in the New York State Library (Albany), New York Colonial Manuscripts 28:17b. *Minutes of the Executive Council,* I, 331–340.

12. *Newtown Court Minutes*, 220, 216, 148; Q. C. Conveyances, Liber A, (Reel QCV 1), p. 19; Memoria, Riker Collection, Box 16, vol. 5, pp. 147–150.

13. William Hallett died in 1706, eighteen years later *(Town Minutes, II, 378)*; Q. C. Conveyances, Liber A (Reel QCV 1), pp. 44, 38–39.

14. Q. C. Conveyances, Liber A (Reel QCV 1), p. 68.

15. Edmund S. Morgan, *American Slavery, American Freedom: The Ordeal of Colonial Virginia* (New York, 1975), p. 299.

16. Q. C. Conveyances, Liber A (Reel QCV 1), pp. 19, 2, 48–49, 45–46, 19–20; Inventories of Albany, I, 17, I, 67 (HDC).

17. *DHNY*, II, 266–267, 298–299; Inventories of Albany, I, 17.

18. Q. C. Conveyances, Liber A (Reel QCV 1), pp. 19–20; *Town Minutes*, II, 431; Allen, "In English Ways," p. 44.

19. Occupations were taken from land records in the town books. *Newtown Court Minutes*, pp. 181, 74, 77, 265, 234, 135; New York Colonial Manuscripts 29:164 (Reel COM4, HDC); *Records of the Towns of North and South Hempstead, Long Island, New York*, ed. Benjamin D. Hicks, 8 vols. (Jamaica, N.Y., 1896–1904), I, 431, 433.

20. *Colonial Laws*, I, 99, 92. Both Peyer's work on Jamaica and Dennis Ryan's study of six towns in East New Jersey stress townsmen's participation in the provincial economy (Dennis Patrick Ryan, "Six Towns: Continuity and Change in Revolutionary New Jersey, 1770–1792," Ph.D. diss. [New York University, 1974]).

21. *Newtown Court Minutes*, pp. 214, 215.

22. Ibid., p. 144. Wright argues much the same case and cites other examples of the complexity of local economic life (Langdon G. Wright, "Local Government in Colonial New York 1640–1710," Ph.D. diss. [Cornell University, 1974]), p. 288.

23. Langdon G. Wright, "In Search of Peace and Harmony: New York Communities in the Seventeenth Century," *N. Y. Hist.* 61(1980): 18.

24. A Gini score of .700 is considered high and shows inequality. A score of about .300 is low and suggests more equality. G. B. Warden, "Inequality and Instability in Eighteenth-Century Boston: A Reappraisal," *Journal of Interdisciplinary History* 6(1976): 602, 603.

25. These figures were calculated from genealogies and probate records. Two men and one woman were omitted from these figures since they probably lived elsewhere. At least one, Robert Coe, resided in Jamaica. One inventory gave no values. All of colonial New York has inadequate probate data. Gary Nash found, for New York City, too few inventories exist to be statistically significant (Gary B. Nash, *The Urban Crucible: Social Change, Political Consciousness, and the Origins of the American Revolution* [Cambridge, Mass., 1979], p. 18).

26. Q. C. Conveyances, Liber A (Reel QCV1), pp. 2, 48–49, 45–46, 68, 25, 36, 18; Inventories of Albany, I, 17; Record of Wills, Book 1 (Reel SAD3), p. 426.

27. *Newtown Court Minutes*, p. 196.

28. *Cal. Hist. Mss.*, II, 116. Unfortunately, the original petition containing names no longer exists.

29. David M. Schneider, *The History of Public Welfare in New York State 1609–1866* (Chicago, 1938), p. 71; *Newtown Court Minutes*, p. 264*.

30. Schneider, *Public Welfare in New York*, pp. 10, 11, 38, 36, 43; John Demos, *A Little Commonwealth: Family Life in Plymouth Colony* (New York, 1970), pp. 79–81.

31. *Town Minutes*, II, 278, 457; Flushing Monthly Meeting, vol. 15-A, 1001, (HRR), pp. 47, 49; William Wade Hinshaw, *Encyclopedia of American Quaker Genealogy* (Ann Arbor, Mich., 1940), p. 278.

32. Greven, *Four Generations*, pp. 192, 195; Demos, *Little Commonwealth*, p. 193.

33. The pattern of shifting two and three generational households is called a stem family. See Lutz K. Berkner, "The Stem Family and the Developmental Cycle of the Peasant Household: An Eighteenth-Century Austrian Example," *AHR* 77(1972): 398–418.

34. On the 1675 list 11 of 82, or 13.4 percent, of the households held more than one male *(DHNY, II, 266, 267)*. The figures for 1678 are 16 of 102, or 15.6 percent, and for 1683 are 11 of 90, or 12.2 percent (New York Colonial Manuscripts, 28:17b).

35. Lawrence Stone, *The Family, Sex and Marriage in England 1500–1800* (New York, 1977), p. 7. (He was describing upper and middle class families.); Demos, *Little Commonwealth*, p. 63; Bissell, "Family, Friends, and Neighbors," p. 58.

36. Bissell, "Family, Friends, and Neighbors," p. 55, n. 1; Greven, *Four Generations*, pp. 29, 111; Demos, *Little Commonwealth*, p. 194.

37. *Colonial Laws*, I, 45–46.

38. Ibid., p. 9; Q. C. Conveyances, Liber B1 (Reel QCV1), p. 156; Liber A (Reel QCV1), p. 19. Wills and Administrations, No. 1, From 1665 to 1683 (Reel SAD2, HDC), p. 113.

39. I lumped all non-English together as Dutch. One wife was one-half English, but she is excluded from the sample. There are many more cases of marriage where the wife's maiden name is unknown than cases where her name is known. Judging from first names, and sometimes from evidence that marriage took place in Europe, it is clear that almost all marriages were endogamous.

40. Goodfriend, "Too Great a Mixture of Nations," pp. 36, 203, 204.

41. Flushing Monthly Meeting Marriages 1663–1766, Births 1640–179. [sic], Deaths 1669–1796, no. 213 (HRR), p. 15a.

42. New York Genealogical and Biographical Society, *Collections*, 8(1928), 49; NYHS, *Collections* 27(1894): 174; *Colonial Laws*, I, 46, 47, 78; *Minutes of the Executive Council*, I, 333, 331, 334, 335, 336, 72.

43. *Minutes of the Executive Council*, I, 336.

44. Ibid., p. 148, n. 1.

45. Nancy F. Cott, "Divorce and the Changing Status of Women in Eighteenth-Century Massachusetts," *WMQ*, 3rd ser. 33(1976): 601.

46. Matteo Spalletta, "Divorce in Colonial New York," *N.Y. Hist.* 39(1955): 434, 435, n. 21; Henry Banford Parkes, "Morals and Law Enforcement in Colonial New England," *New England Quarterly* 5(1932): 447; Nancy F. Cott, "Eighteenth-Century Family and Social Life Revealed in Massachusetts Divorce Records," *Journal of Social History* 5(1976): 21.

47. Memoria, Riker Collection, Box 16, vol. 5, p. 140; *Cal. Hist. Mss.*, II, 26; New York Colonial Manuscripts 14:30(3).

48. *Newtown Court Minutes*, p. 198; *Cal. Hist. Mss.*, II, 17. There is some evidence to suggest that premarital pregnancy was widespread, at least in the eighteenth century. Stephanie Grauman Wolf found that 25 percent of the babies she found in Germantown were born less than nine months after their parents' marriage (Stephanie Grauman Wolf, *Urban Village: Population, Community, and Family Structure in Germantown, Pennsylvania 1683–1800* [Princeton, 1976], p. 259). For a discussion of the trends and meaning of premarital pregnancy, see Daniel Scott Smith and Michael S. Hindus, "Premarital Pregnancy in America 1640–1971: An Overview," *Journal of Interdisciplinary History* 5(1975): 537–570.

49. New York Colonial Manuscripts 25:57 (Reel COM2, HDC).

50. The 1698 census lists 153 households containing 883 free persons and 93 slaves (Memoria, Riker Collection, Box 16, vol. 5, p. 150).

51. Demos, *Little Commonwealth*, p. 64; Kenneth A. Lockridge, "Dedham, 1636–1736: The Anatomy of a Puritan Utopia," Ph.D. diss. (Princeton, 1965), p. 139; Robert V. Wells, "Household Size and Composition in the British Colonies in America, 1675–1775," *Journal of Interdisciplinary History* 4(1974): 547.

52. Deriving population figures without reliable census materials is a refined form of guesswork. The 1656 population estimate was calculated by taking the 54 heads of households from the Indian rate and multiplying that number by 5.7 for a total of 308. There probably were no slaves in 1656. The 1686 estimate is based on the 113 names in the Dongan patent multiplied by 6.4 for a total of 723. These figures are slightly different from those that appeared in Jessica Kross Ehrlich, "A Town Study in Colonial New York: Newtown, Queens County (1642–1790)," Ph.D. diss. (The University of Michigan, 1974). The discrepancy is caused by omitting two names from the 1656 list as not being heads of households and correcting an arithmetic error.

53. Surnames are a crude measure, and the tax lists are imperfect surrogates for censuses, since people can live in town but slip through the meshes of a tax list. The Halletts did.

54. Peyer, "Jamaica, Long Island," p. 87.

55. Ira Berlin, "Time, Space and the Evolution of Afro-American Society on British Mainland North America *AHR* 85(1980): 44–78; See also Sidney W. Mintz and Richard Price, *An Anthropological Approach to the Afro-American Past: A Caribbean Perspective, ISHI Occasional Papers in Social Change*, vol. II (1976).

56. John M. Murrin, "English Rights as Ethnic Aggression: The English Conquest, The Charter of Liberties of 1683, and Leisler's Rebellion in New York," paper delivered at the annual AHA convention (San Francisco, 1973), p. 6; Goodfriend, "Too Great a Mixture of Nations," pp. 181, 182.

57. *Town Minutes*, I, 116.

58. *Town Minutes*, II, 173, 328; *Cal. Hist. Mss.*, II, 121.

59. Riker, *Annals*, p. 236.

60. See Flushing Monthly Meeting, vol. 15-A, 1001 (HRR), pp. 47, 49.

61. Riker, *Annals*, p. 98; *Newtown Court Minutes*, pp. 88–89.

62. Memoria, Riker Collection, Box 16, vol. 5, p. 155.

63. *Cal. Hist. Mss.*, II, 40; Memoria, Riker Collection, Box 16, vol. 5, pp. 157, 156, 158, 160.

64. Q. C. Conveyances, Liber A (Reel QCV1), p. 77.

65. All materials on the town court are from the *Newtown Court Minutes*, which is indexed. For more detail see Jessica Kross Ehrlich, "'To Hear and Try All Causes Betwixt Man and Man': The Town Court of Newtown, 1659–1690," *N. Y. Hist.* 59(1978): 277–305. Langdon Wright also notes the broad range of litigiousness found within towns ("Local Government," pp. 283–318).

66. *Newtown Court Minutes*, pp. 186, 234.

67. Memoria, Riker Collection, Box 18, vol. 10, pp. 88–90, 91–93, 101–102. These documents are entitled "Extracts from Court of Sessions Minutes for West Riding of Yorkshire in the County Clerks Office, Brooklyn, Long Island. Made June 22, 1846"; *Cal. Hist. Mss.*, II, 110; *Calendar of Council Minutes,1668–1783*, New York Library, *Library Bulletin* 6 (Albany, 1902), p. 39.

68. *Town Minutes*, II, 161, I, 11.

69. Memoria, Riker Collection, Box 18, vol. 10, p. 92; *Cal. Hist. Mss.*, II, 150; NYHS, *Collections* 25(1892): 75–76.

70. Memoria, Riker Collection, Box 16, Vol. 5, pp. 81, 82, 106; *DRHNY*, XIV, 685, 686.

71. *Newtown Court Minutes*, pp. 211, 206, 134.

72. Bissell, "Family, Friends, and Neighbors," p. 187; Wright, "In Search of Peace and Harmony," *N. Y. Hist.* 61(1980): 18; Demos, *Little Commonwealth*, p. 49.

73. *Newtown Court Minutes*, p. 207.

74. Eli Faber, "Puritan Criminals: The Economic, Social, and Intellectual Background to Crime in Seventeenth-Century Massachusetts," *Perspectives in American History* 11(1977-78): 138; Bissell, "Family, Friends, and Neighbors," pp. 110-112, 113-118, 123-128.

CHAPTER V

1. *Colonial Laws*, I, 328-329; *DHNY*, III, 150. The Society for the Propagation of the Gospel in Foreign Parts (SPG) was the missionary arm of the Church of England. It would oversee the Anglican Church in America.

2. *Town Minutes*, II, 501; *DRHNY*, IV, 719; *DHNY* III, 76.

3. Secret instructions to establish the Anglican Church can be found in *Eccl. Rec. N. Y.*, II, 1033, III, 1487; *DHNY*, III, 126; E. B. O'Callaghan, "Lists of Officials" Queens County (NYHS); *Calendar of Council Minutes 1668-1783*, New York Library, *Library Bulletin* 6(Albany, 1902), p. 179.

4. *DHNY*, III, 128-129; *Colonial Laws*, I, 576.

5. The use of the term "lawyer" substantiates Michael Kammen's comments on the professionalization of the law *(Colonial New York: A History* [New York, 1975], p. 131); *Town Minutes*, II, 450, 451; Town of Newtown 287, (Reel TNT 10, HDC), p. 374.

6. Memoria, Riker Collection, Box 16, vol. 5, p. 99. Langdon Wright notes how unwilling the provincial authorities were to impose solutions upon towns. They preferred that local disputants work things out and continually referred cases back to them for arbitration ("Local Government in Colonial New York 1640-1710," Ph.D. diss. [Cornell University, 1974], pp. 148-150).

7. The interpretation of Cornbury's motives was given by an obvious partisan (Mr. Cockerill to the Earl of Stamford, read November 14, 1709, *DRHNY*, V, 111); James Riker Jr., *Annals of Newtown* (New York, 1852), pp. 140-141, 145; *Calendar of New York Colonial Manuscripts Indorsed Land Papers in the Office of the Secretary of State of New York, 1643-1836* (Albany, 1864), p. 86.

8. Riker, *Annals*, pp. 131-132.

9. Town Book 287, p. 366; *Calendar of New York Land Papers*, p. 66; One minor dispute over patent right was arbitrated out of court in 1686 *(Town Minutes*, II, 356-357).

10. David Konig, "Community Custom and the Common Law: So-

cial Change and the Development of Land Law in Seventeenth-Century Massachusetts," *American Journal of Legal History*, 18(1974): 157; Patricia J. Tracy, *Jonathan Edwards, Pastor: Religion and Society in Eighteenth-Century Northampton* (New York, 1979), p. 45; Town Book 287, p. 87.

11. *Town Minutes*, II, 564, 536; Town Book 287, p. 361; Town Book 288, p. 566.

12. *Colonial Laws*, I, 44; *Town Minutes*, II, 330, 356; Town Book 287, p. 362. Quitrents were not paid during Leisler's administration, but the three years 1689–1691 were made up in 1692. Arrears were due and paid in 1702 and 1706 (Town Book 287, p. 370; Record of Strays Etc: Quit Rents from 1706, Long Island Room, QBPL). The 1706 payment of £38 17s. 6d. brought the town up to date. It is probably more than coincidence that 1702 and 1706 were also years in which Newtown was fighting for town rights and boundaries. After 1717 Newtown was never more than two years in arrears until the Revolution, but during and after the War the town did not keep up with the rents. When the quitrents were finally commuted in 1815 the town owed $348.81, which it paid to the State of New York. Provincial officials and subsequent historians, such as Beverly W. Bond argued that New York's quitrents could have paid for the costs of provincial government, but they were never paid. Newtown fulfilled its obligation, but the amount of the quitrent was trifling. Quite possibly the unimportance of the town, together with its constant visibility due to the boundary disputes, made it seek the prudent course of paying its quitrent.

13. *Colonial Laws*, I, 654, 730, 352.

14. It is hard to calculate a range since expenditures came in bunches. Between 1691 and 1696 taxes were £716; in 1708 and 1709 £544 (*Colonial Laws*, I, 308, 550, 682).

15. Ronald Kingman Snell, "The County Magistracy in Eighteenth-Century Massachusetts: 1692–1750," Ph.D. diss. (Princeton University, 1971), pp. 15, 185, 201, 53. Queens County assessments are from the Queens County Supervisors Book (1709–1787), Museum of the City of New York.

16. Averages can be misleading because they smooth out the highs and the lows. For example, from 1691 to 1696 Newtown's provincial taxes averaged £119 per year because of King William's War, but from 1710 to 1724 taxes averaged £43 per year.

17. *Colonial Laws*, I, 286; Memoria, Riker Collection, Box 18, vol. 10, p. 123; Beverly McAnear, "Politics in Provincial New York, 1689–1761," Ph.D. diss. (Stanford University, 1935), p. 207; Notebook of Joseph Burroughs, containing records of his administration of his Brother, Jeremiah Burroughs, 1697–1735 with additional entries in another hand until 1735," Riker Collection, Box 21.

18. *DHNY*, III, 175–176, 173, 174–175.

19. Ibid., p. 176. See Bernard Bailyn, *The Ideological Origins of the American Revolution* (Cambridge, Mass., 1967), chap. 2, and Edward M. Cook Jr., *The Fathers of the Towns: Leadership and Community Structure in Eighteenth-Century New England* (Baltimore, 1976), p. 86.

20. *DHNY*, III, 177–179.

21. Materials were gathered on Newtown's 106 men who held office between 1692 and 1723. One hundred appear in the land records. Eight of these were justices who were removed from the sample before the mean number of land transactions was calculated. Richard Betts' will is in NYHS, *Collections* 26(1893): 83; New York County, Will Liber 8 (Reel WL2, HDC), p. 79.

22. *DHNY*, III, 183.

23. Ibid., p. 178.

24. *Colonial Laws*, I, 226, 258, 328, 576, 456, 832, II, 62, 67, 64. Wright also notes the mediating role that justices played between the towns and the provincial government ("Local Government," p. 135).

25. Snell, "County Magistracy," pp. 89–90, 185, 186.

26. *Colonial Laws*, I, 308–309; New York Colonial Manucripts 39:53a (New York State Library, Albany); *Town Minutes*, II, 472, 501; Memoria, Riker Collection, Box 16, vol. 5, p. 154.

27. *Calendar of Council Minutes*, p. 180; *Cal. Hist. Mss.*, II, 308; Town Book 287, p. 372.

28. *Colonial Laws*, I, 225, 532, II, 68; Snell, "County Magistracy," p. 211; Town Book 287, p. 372.

29. Town Book 287, pp. 184, 365, 755; Town Book 288, p. 567; *Colonial Laws*, I, 427; *Town Minutes*, II, 424.

30. Jean Peyer, "Jamaica, Long Island, 1656–1776: A Study of the Roots of American Urbanism," Ph.D. diss. (City University of New York, 1974), p. 81; Bruce C. Daniels, *The Connecticut Town: Growth and Development, 1635–1790* (Middletown, Conn., 1979), p. 80; Kenneth A. Lockridge and Alan Kreider, "The Evolution of Massachusetts Town Government, 1640–1740," *WMQ*, 3rd ser. 23(1966): 574.

31. *Town Minutes*, II, 7, 562; *Colonial Laws*, I, 832; Town Book 287, p. 377.

32. Town Book 288, pp. 563, 564.

33. Town Book 287, p. 376. The increased number of town offices over time was also common outside New York. The same thing happened in Connecticut, although there this increase apparently gave the selectmen more authority. See Bruce C. Daniels, "Connecticut's Villages Become Mature Towns: The Complexity of Local Institutions 1676–1776," *WMQ*, 3rd ser. 34(1977): 83–103.

34. Town Book 288, p. 566.

35. Bruce C. Daniels, "The Long-Lasting Men of Local Government: Town Clerks in Colonial Connecticut," The Connecticut Historical Society, *Bulletin*, 41(1976): 90–96.

36. New York State Historian, *Second Annual Report* (Albany, 1897), pp. 499–500, 504–505. These 106 men include some of the 37 from the 1665–1691 period.

37. In the absence of tax lists, slave-holding was calculated from wills. Memoria, Riker Collection, Box 16, vol. 5, pp. 147–150.

38. Justices were removed from the sample before the average number of years was calculated.

39. Riker, *Annals*.

40. Land records are in the town minute books; NYHS, *Collections* 26(1893): 204–206.

41. Office-holding is taken from the town minute books. Townsmen elected trustees before they institutionalized the office in 1717.

CHAPTER VI

1. Q. C. Conveyances, Liber B2 (Reel QCV1), pp. 191, 178; Liber B2 (Reel QCV2), p. 387; Town Book 288, p. 93.

2. Q. C. Conveyances, Liber B2, p. 386; Memoria, Riker Collection, Box 17, vol. 8, pp. 196–197. This manuscript is a copy of "Entrees by William Hallett, Esq."

3. Town Book 288, p. 146.

4. Q. C. Conveyances, Liber B2, pp. 178, 192; Town Book 288, p. 146.

5. Linda Auwers, "Fathers, Sons and Wealth in Colonial Windsor, Connecticut," *Journal of Family History* 3(1978): 136–149; Philip J. Greven Jr., *Four Generations: Population, Land, and Family in Colonial Andover, Massachusetts* (Ithaca, N.Y., 1970); NYHS, *Collections* 35(1902): 157.

6. The other 1 percent of transactions are either rents or too ambiguous to classify.

7. Lots declined from 16 of 351 transactions in the earlier period to 3 of 694 transactions at this time.

8. Of the 694 transactions, 479 give acreage. Jean Peyer's figures for Jamaica are computed differently, but she says that after 1700 80.5 percent of the population owned fifty acres or less ("Jamaica, Long Island, 1656–1776: A Study of the Roots of American Urbanism," Ph.D. diss. [The City University of New York, 1974], p. 177).

9. Peyer, "Jamaica, Long Island," pp. 191, 192; Greven, *Four Genera-*

tions, p. 128; Patricia J. Tracy, *Jonathan Edwards, Pastor: Religion and Society in Eighteenth-Century Northampton* (New York, 1979), p. 16.

10. Town Book 288, p. 37; Town Book 287, p. 210; James A. Henretta, "Families and Farms: *Mentalité* in Pre-Industrial America," *WMQ*, 3rd ser. 35(1978): 3–32.

11. Town Book 288, p. 174; Q. C. Conveyances, Liber B2 (Reel QCV2), pp. 501, 503. Jamaica also had few absentee owners. Peyer notes that only 2 percent of Jamaica's lands were owned by outsiders ("Jamaica, Long Island," p. 174).

12. Town Book 288, pp. 28, 36; Town Book 287, p. 126.

13. Q. C. Conveyances, Liber C (Reel QCV2), pp. 63–64; NYHS, *Collections* 26(1893), 204, 181–182. More Newtowners held land in Jamaica than any other outside group (Peyer, "Jamaica, Long Island," p. 174). Lands farthest away from Newtown might have been bought for speculative purposes.

14. These percentages are based on a total of only thirty-nine wills and should be used cautiously.

15. Town Book 287, p. 93; Town Book 288, p. 33; Town Book 287, p. 171; Memoria, Riker Collection, Box 17, vol. 8, pp. 197, 196, 195; Note Book of Joseph Burroughs, Riker Collection, Box 21.

16. Memoria, Riker Collection, Box 18, vol. 10, pp. 123–125.

17. Memoria, Riker Collection, Box 18, vol. 10, p. 125; Accounts 1693–1703. Woolsey General Store Account Book, Woolsey Family Papers, ms. no. 562, Hillhouse Family Collection, Yale University Library.

18. NYHS, *Collections* 26(1893): 206; Memoria, Riker Collection, Box 16, vol. 5, pp. 147–150; vol. 14, p. 28.

19. New York County, Surrogate Court Wills, 503; Q. C. Conveyances, Liber C (Reel QCV2), 71; Liber A (Reel QCV 1), 179; Inventories of Albany, II, 125. All are in the Historical Documents Collection.

20. Printed in *Flushing Daily Times*, No. 3114.

21. Q. C. Conveyances, Liber A (Reel QCV1), p. 161; Inventories of Albany, II, 295.

22. Inventories of Albany, II, 143.

23. Inventories of Albany, II, 126.

24. Inventories of Albany, II, 125.

25. Note Book of Joseph Burroughs, Riker Collection, Box 21.

26. Memoria, Riker Collection, Box 17, vol. 8, p. 17; Inventories of Albany, II, 143; II, 108; Town Book 287, pp. 139, 288, 114.

27. Q. C. Conveyances, Liber A (Reel QCV1), p. 161; Inventories of Albany, II, 295, 143; William Applebie Eardeley, "Records in the Office of the County Clerk of Jamaica, Long Island, New York, 1680–1781. Wills and Administrations. Guardians and Inventories," typewritten (LIHS),

p. 67; New York County Surrogate Court Wills, p. 503; NYHS, *Collections* 35(1902): 15.

28. Harry S. Stout, "Remigration and Revival: Two Case Studies in the Social and Intellectual History of New England, 1636–1745," Ph.D. diss. (Kent State University, 1974), p. 28; Ronald Kingman Snell, "The County Magistracy in Eighteenth-Century Massachusetts: 1692–1750," Ph.D. diss. (Princeton University, 1971), p. 329.

29. At least eighty-four people died in these years, seventy-three men and eleven women. The number of land transactions which men engaged in tell nothing. They do not include legacies, and there seems to be little correlation between the number of transactions and the goods which appear in the surviving inventories.

30. John McCusker, *Money and Exchange in Europe and America 1600–1775: A Handbook* (Chapel Hill, N.C., 1978), pp. 162–163; Memoria, Riker Collection, Box 18, vol. 10, p. 123; Town Book 287, pp. 239–241; Inventories of Albany, I, 163, II, 126, 295, 22, 143, 145; Q. C. Conveyances, Liber A (QCV1), pp. 163, 167.

31. Tracy, *Jonathan Edwards*, p. 92; Lois Green Carr and Lorena S. Walsh, "Inventories and the Analysis of Wealth and Consumption Patterns in St. Mary's County, Maryland, 1658–1777," *Historical Methods Newsletter*, 13(1980): 85, 87; James W. Deen Jr., "Patterns of Testation: Four Tidewater Counties in Colonial Virginia," *American Journal of Legal History* 16(1972): 163.

32. *Town Minutes*, II, 375.

33. *Colonial Laws*, I, 296–297.

34. Q. C. Conveyances, Liber C (Reel QCV2), pp. 1–2, 4–5, 35–36, 48; Liber D (Reel QCV3), p. 3; Newtown Records edited for *The Newtown Register* by William O'Gorman, Town Clerk, 1934 (QBPL), p. 172; *Cal. Hist. Mss.*, II, 253.

35. Bruce C. Daniels, *The Connecticut Town: Growth and Development, 1635–1790* (Middletown, Conn., 1979), pp. 140–141.

36. *Colonial Laws*, I, 237; *Town Minutes*, II, 430b; Town Book 287, p. 564.

37. Presbyterian and Episcopal Churches, Burroughs Family 1711–1788, Riker Collection, Box 21; Minutes of Flushing Monthly Meeting (later called New York Monthly Meeting), vols. 2, 3, nos. 1002, 1003 (HRR), p. 9. Brishey did not live in Newtown.

38. Q. C. Conveyances, Liber A (Reel QCV1), p. 163; Eardeley, "Records in the Office of the County Clerk of Jamaica," p. 43.

39. Town Book 288, pp. 563, 143; Note Book of Joseph Burroughs, Riker Collection, Box 21; Entries by William Hallett, Esq., Memoria, Riker Collection, Box 17, vol. 8, p. 197. Jamaica's educational efforts paralleled Newtown's (Peyer, "Jamaica, Long Island," p. 94).

40. Ronald William Howard, "Education and Ethnicity in Colonial New York, 1664–1763: A Study in the Transmission of Culture in Early America," Ph.D. diss. (University of Tennessee, 1978), pp. 50, vi.

41. Town Book 288, pp. 24, 102, 26; Robert Francis Seybolt, *Apprenticeship and Apprenticeship Education in Colonial New England and New York*, Teachers College Contribution to Education, no. 85 (New York, 1917), p. 93, n. 8.

42. NYHS, *Collections* 26(1893): 181–182, 43–44.

43. New York Colonial Manuscripts 49:18a; NYHS, *Collections* 25(1892): 382 (William Lawrence did not live in Newtown).

44. Greven, *Four Generations*, p. 110. Of his men 84 percent reached forty, and 72 percent reached sixty; of his women, 82 percent reached forty, and 60 percent reached sixty.

45. Flushing Monthly Meeting, Marriages 1663–1766, Births 1640–179. [sic], Deaths 1669–1796, no. 213 (HRR). We know very little about attitudes toward death. David E. Stannard found that in seventeenth-century New England people feared death and made no effort to make death more palatable. As Puritan tensions and self-doubt eased in the eighteenth century, so did the terror associated with meeting one's God and being found wanting (Stannard, "Death and Dying in Puritan New England," *AHR* 78[1973]: 1305–1330).

46. Note Book of Joseph Burroughs, Riker Collection, Box 21; Q. C. Conveyances, Liber A (Reel QCV1), p. 145; Flushing Monthly Meeting, Marriages, Births, and Deaths, no. 213.

47. Henry Onderdonk Jr., *Antiquities of the Parish Church, Jamaica (including Newtown and Flushing)* (Jamaica, N.Y., 1880), p. 23.

48. Peter Dobkin Hall, "Family Structure and Economic Organization: Massachusetts Merchants, 1700–1850," in Tamara K. Hareven, ed., *Family and Kin in Urban Communities, 1700–1930* (New York, 1977), pp. 38–61.

49. Memoria, Riker Collection, Box 16, vol. 5, pp. 147–150; New York State Historian, *Second Annual Report*, (Albany, 1897), pp. 499–500, 504–505. The old names on the 1698 census would be those there in the 1686 Dongan patent. The militia list is selective and fails to include some men in their fifties (Douglas Lamar Jones, "Geographic Mobility and Society in Eighteenth-Century Essex County, Massachusetts," Ph.D. diss. [Brandeis University, 1975] pp. 28, 18).

50. Greven assumes that those who disappeared from the record moved *(Four Generations*, pp. 211–212).

51. A total of 118 sons from the 24 families moved. The residence of 112 has been found. Most information on mobility comes from the genealogies in James Riker Jr., *Annals of Newtown* (New York, 1852).

52. *Town Minutes*, II, 506, 547, 533, 301; Rev. William H. Hendrick-

son, "A Brief History of the First Presbyterian Church, Newtown, Long Island," (unpub., 1902), p. 23.

53. *Colonial Laws*, I, 427; Town Book 287, p. 376.

54. Hendrickson, Brief History of the First Presbyterian Church, p. 24; Rev. John B. Knox, *Anniversary Discourse of a Twenty-Five Years Pastorate; Preached March 28, 1880 in the Presbyterian Church, Newtown, Long Island* (New York, 1880), p. 9.

55. Hendrickson, "Brief History of the First Presbyterian Church," pp. 27, 28.

56. Tracy, *Jonathan Edwards*, pp. 24–25, 28, 30; Stout, "Remigration and Revival," pp. 293–298.

57. See Robert F. Scholz, "Clerical Consociation in Massachusetts Bay: Reassessing the New England Way and Its Origins," *WMQ*, 3rd ser. 29(1972): 391–414; Perry Miller, *The New England Mind: From Colony to Province* (Boston, 1953), pp. 216–217, 266; Tracy, *Jonathan Edwards*, p. 48.

58. Riker, *Annals*, p. 147.

59. "Transcript of an Old Book of Records belonging to the Presbyterian Church of Newtown, Long Island, finished June 6th, 1846," Riker Collection, Box 16, pp. 2, 5; Town Book 288, p. 294; Hendrickson, Brief History of the First Presbyterian Church, p. 28.

60. Riker, *Annals*, p. 236; Memoria, Riker Collection, Box 15, vol. 2, p. 17.

61. Ethnicity was judged by surnames. Genealogical data came from my family reconstitution files.

62. *Colonial Laws*, I, 328, 576.

63. Onderdonk, *Antiquities of the Parish Church*, pp. 20, 32.

64. Ibid., p. 20.

65. Ibid., p. 33.

66. Horatio Oliver Ladd, *The Origin and History of Grace Church Jamaica, New York* (New York, 1914), pp. 269, 270, 282.

67. Onderdonk, *Antiquities of the Parish Church*, pp. 32, 33; *Classified Digest of the Records of the Society for the Propagation of the Gospel in Foreign Parts 1701–1892*, comp. Charles Frederick Pascoe (London, 1893), p. 61.

68. Minutes 15-A, no. 1001 (HRR), pp. 23, 32, 42.

69. Minutes Flushing Monthly Meeting . . . , vols. 2, 3, nos. 1002, 1003, pp. 78, 6, 2 (HRR).

70. Flushing Monthly Meeting Marriages . . . , no. 213, pp. 55–56 (HRR).

71. Minutes Flushing Monthly Meeting . . . , vol. 15-A, no. 1001, pp. 125, 128, 129, 130. "Suffering" is a stock term derived from seventeenth-century English Quakerism.

72. Memoria, Riker Collection, Box 16, vol. 5, p. 127; *Colonial Laws*, I, 617–618.

73. Edgar McManus, *A History of Slavery in Colonial New York (Syracuse*, 1966), p. 95; Memoria, Riker Collection, Box 16, vol. 5, p. 127.

74. Town Book 288, p. 129.

CHAPTER VII

1. Town Book 288, pp. 575, 576; Town Book 289, p. 210; *Colonial Laws*, IV, 982; James Riker Jr., *Annals of Newtown* (New York, 1852), pp. 170−171.

2. Robert Gross, *The Minutemen and Their World* (New York, 1976), Chap. 3, passim.

3. Town Book 288, p. 582; *Colonial Laws*, III, 1.

4. *Colonial Laws*, III, 1068−1069; County Minute Book, 1775; *DHNY*, III, 623−624.

5. Lord Loudoun to Pitt, New York, 25th April, 1757, in *Correspondence of William Pitt*, ed. Gertrude Selwyn Kimball, vol. I (New York, 1906), p. 44. All taxes are found in the colonial laws. Bills of credit were paper monies floated against future tax revenues.

6. County Minute Book.

7. The estimate of £15 per year for town taxes is probably too high. The price of wheat is taken from the inventories; the price of labor is the standard estimate (Samuel McKee Jr., *Labor in Colonial New York 1664−1776*, Studies in History, Economics and Public Law, 410 [New York, 1935], p. 25). The estimate of 210 taxpayers was calculated by assuming that the population remained at its 1711 figure of 839 and that one-fourth of the population were taxpayers (Evarts B. Greene and Virginia D. Harrington, *American Population before the Federal Census of 1790* [Gloucester, Mass., 1966], p. xxiii). There is little evidence that taxes were paid in gold or silver, but after 1709 they could have been paid in the paper money called bills of credit. *Colonial Laws*, I, 695.

8. County Minute Book, 1744 (All levies and county quotas are in the *Colonial Laws*. Newtown's share is in the County Minute Book).

9. The number of taxpayers used in these calculations is 256. This figure was derived by first calculating the number of taxpayers in 1756, the mid-year for wartime taxes. Using the formula $\bar{P} = P_1(1 + r)^n$ where $P_1 = 839$ (the 1711 population), r = .0045 (derived through the formula $\log P_2 \div P_1 = n\log (1 + r)$ where $P_2 = 1096$, the calculated white population in 1771, and n = 60) and n = 45. In 1756 there should have been 1025 whites in Newtown which divided by four gives 256 taxpayers. All of these calculations assume a linear growth rate which might not be true. Indeed, there is some evidence for a population decline in the 1749 Queens County

census (Greene and Harrington, *American Population*, p. 100). However, these numbers are so small that the real figures should be fairly close to those given here.

10. Arthur H. Cole, *Wholesale Commodity Prices in the United States 1700–1861* (Cambridge, Mass., 1938), pp. 120–121. Sterling rates are from John McCusker, *Money and Exchange in Europe and America 1600–1775: A Handbook* (Chapel Hill, N.C., 1978), pp. 164–165.

11. Queens County posted lookouts from 1757 to 1761. They cost £104. Barracks and the hospital cost another £105 (County Minute Book). The 5 shillings estimate for wheat is based on the commodity index. Privates in the army ended up with three shillings per day if bounties are included with their wages (*Colonial Laws*, IV, 64, 66).

12. Gary B. Nash, *The Urban Crucible: Social Change, Political Consciousness, and the Origins of the American Revolution* (Cambridge, Mass., 1979), pp. 60, 173, 252.

13. David Grayson Allen, "The Zuckerman Thesis and the Process of Legal Rationalization in Provincial Massachusetts," *WMQ*, 3rd ser. 29(1972): 448.

14. *Journal of the Votes and Proceedings of the General Assembly of the Colony of New York (1691–1765)*, 2 vols. (New York, 1764, 1766), II, 770, 776; Gordon S. Wood, "Rhetoric and Reality in the American Revolution," *WMQ*, 3rd ser. 23(1966): 3–32.

15. *Journal of the General Assembly*, II, 770. See, for instance, Virginia's petition of December 18, 1764, reprinted in Edmund Morgan, *Prologue to Revolution: Sources and Documents on the Stamp Act Crisis, 1764–1766* (Chapel Hill, N.C., 1959), p. 14.

16. Town Book 289, pp. 70, 104; *Calendar of Council Minutes*, p. 427; Richard G. Lowe, "Massachusetts and the Acadians," *WMQ*, 3rd ser. 25(1968): 228.

17. Henry Onderdonk Jr., *Long Island in Olden Times* (Jamaica, N.Y., 1870), p. 18; Town Book 289, p. 70; *Journal of the General Assembly*, II, 574; *Colonial Laws* IV, 314.

18. Town Book 288, pp. 579, 580; Town Book 289, p. 223. (There are no town minutes for 1761.)

19. Jean Peyer, "Jamaica, Long Island 1656–1776: A Study of the Roots of American Urbanism," Ph.D. diss. (City University of New York, 1974), p. 81; Bruce C. Daniels, *The Connecticut Town: Growth and Development, 1635–1790* (Middletown, Conn., 1979), pp. 81, 82, 83; Ronald Kingman Snell, "The County Magistracy in Eighteenth-Century Massachusetts: 1692–1750," Ph.D. diss. (Princeton University, 1971), p. 187.

20. Town Book 288, p. 576; *Colonial Laws*, III, 55.

21. Hendrick Hartog, "Public Law of a County Court: Judicial Gov-

ernment in Eighteenth-Century Massachusetts," *American Journal of Legal History* 20(1976): 284; Edward M. Cook Jr., "Social Behavior and Changing Values in Dedham, Massachusetts, 1700–1775," *WMQ*, 3rd ser. 27(1970): 578; Daniels, *Connecticut Town*, pp. 7, 93.

22. Town Book 289, p. 210.

23. Bruce Daniels has analyzed the increasing opportunities for the average citizen to participate in politics. See "Democracy and Oligarchy in Connecticut Towns: General Assembly Office-holding, 1701–1790," *Social Science Quarterly* (1975): 460–475; and "Large Town Office-Holding in Eighteenth-Century Connecticut," *Journal of American Studies*, 9(1975): 1–12.

24. See Riker *Annals* for genealogical information; NYHS, *Collections* 31(1898): 116–119.

25. Land records are in the town minute books; NYHS, *Collections* 26(1893): 281.

26. NYHS, *Collections* 31(1898): 116–119.

27. Town office data are in the town minute books.

28. The Dutch Reformed and Quakers made such a good showing partly because they are so easy to identify. Unknowns were probably Presbyterian.

29. Bruce E. Steiner, "Anglican Office-Holding in Pre-Revolutionary Connecticut: The Parameters of New England Community," *WMQ*, 3rd ser. 31(1974): 370, 380, 390, 378; Edward M. Cook Jr., *The Fathers of the Towns: Leadership and Community Structure in Eighteenth-Century New England* (Baltimore, 1976), pp. 136–137, 141.

30. In 1755 eighty households owned slaves. The closest census, of 1771, lists 189 households. *If* population remained stable the eighty slave-owners would be 42% of the households. NYHS, *Collections* 30(1897): 186.

31. Cook, *Fathers of the Towns*, p. 80.

32. The Pearson product-moment correlation between justices and ad hoc offices is .52 at the .001 level. The correlation between justices and appraisers of intestate estates is .34 at the .001 level. The sample size of eighteen is very small, however.

33. Michael Kammen, *Colonial New York: A History* (New York, 1975), p. 330.

34. Peter Force, *American Archives*, 4th ser., 6 vols. (Washington, D.C., 1837–1853), I, 819. Joseph S. Tiedemann, who studied the Revolution in Queens County, notes that county Sons of Liberty sent a petition protesting the Stamp Act to their fellow sympathizers in New York City, but could not mobilize again until 1774 ("Response to Revolution: Queens County, New York, During the Era of the American Revolution," Ph.D. diss. [City University of New York, 1977], pp. 14–15).

35. Force, *American Archives*, I, 1035; Riker, *Annals*, p. 178.

36. Henry Onderdonk Jr., *Documents and Letters Intended to Illustrate the Revolutionary Incidents of Queens County, New York* (New York, 1846), pp. 18–19.

37. Ibid.

38. Ibid., p. 19.

39. Ibid.

40. Richard L. Bushman, "Massachusetts Farmers and the Revolution," in Richard M. Jellison, ed., *Society, Freedom, and Conscience: The American Revolution in Virginia, Massachusetts, and New York* (New York, 1976), p. 78; Arlin Ira Ginsburg, "Ipswich, Massachusetts During the American Revolution, 1763–1791," Ph.D. diss. (University of California, Riverside, 1972), pp. 18, 21.

41. Bushman, "Massachusetts Farmers and the Revolution," p. 86.

42. Ibid., pp. 77–78; Robert E. Brown, *Middle-Class Democracy and the Revolution in Massachusetts, 1691–1789* (Ithaca, 1955), p. 351.

43. Onderdonk, *Documents and Letters*, p. 20.

44. Riker, *Annals*, pp. 179, 180–181; New York Commissioners of Forfeitures, Southern District, Abstracts of Sales, New York City and Vicinity, 1784–1787 (NYHS), p. 8.

45. Force, *American Archives*, II, 1828; IV, 858, 372–375; P.R.O., A.O. 12, vol. 23, p. 395.

46. Hallett Family Folder II, 1727–1791, Riker Collection, Box 21.

CHAPTER VIII

1. Darrett Rutman, "People in Process: The New Hampshire Towns of the Eighteenth Century," *Journal of Urban History* 1(1975): 268–292.

2. Nathaniel's will is in NYHS, *Collections* 28(1895): 398.

3. No will survives for Joseph Hallett. The Hallett land transactions are in the various town books and the Queens County Conveyances. Loyalist Samuel Hallett's property of 160 acres is confirmed in P.R.O., A.O. 12, vol. 23, p. 399.

4. Richard's will is in NYHS, *Collections* 31(1898): 266.

5. The sharp decline in conveyances might reflect missing records rather than fewer conveyances. However, Jean Peyer found the same pattern in Jamaica ("Jamaica, Long Island 1656–1776: A Study of the Roots of American Urbanism," Ph.D. diss. [City University of New York, 1974], pp. 193–194). Her sources were Jamaica's town records and the Queens County Conveyances while mine were Newtown's town records and the Queens County Conveyances. The two towns are compared in the following table which shows the total number of transactions and their frequency per annum.

YEARS (JAMAICA)	JAMAICA NO.	NEWTOWN NO.	JAMAICA P.A.	NEWTOWN P.A.	YEARS (NEWTOWN)
1656−1690	627	351	18.1	13	1665−1691
1691−1720	960	694	32.0	21.7	1692−1723
1721−1750	288	414	9.6	11.8	1724−1759
1751−1780	149	68	4.9	4.3	1760−1775

The wills list some land not accounted for in the conveyances but they do this for all periods. There are too few wills with sufficient detail on land to use them as a statistical control. The tax list is labelled Queens County, New York (Return of the Tax List of the Township of Newtown [NYHS]).

6. Town Book 289, p. 79.

7. Town Book 288, pp. 194, 196, 492; NYHS, *Collections* 30(1897): 288.

8. Town Book 289, p. 191.

9. Patricia J. Tracy, *Jonathan Edwards, Pastor: Religion and Society in Eighteenth-Century Northampton* (New York, 1979), pp. 97−100; Philip J. Greven Jr., *Four Generations: Population, Land, and Family in Colonial Andover, Massachusetts* (Ithaca, N.Y., 1970), p. 127; Kenneth A. Lockridge, *A New England Town: The First Hundred Years: Dedham, Massachusetts, 1636−1736* (New York, 1970), pp. 148−149; Arlin Ira Ginsburg, "Ipswich, Massachusetts During the American Revolution, 1763−1791," Ph.D. diss. (University of California, Riverside, 1972), pp. 40−41; Bruce C. Daniels, "Economic Development in Colonial and Revolutionary Connecticut: An Overview," *WMQ*, 3rd ser. 37(1980): 432; Dennis Patrick Ryan, "Six Towns: Continuity and Change in Revolutionary New Jersey, 1770−1792," Ph.D. diss. (New York University, 1974), p. 111. See also Kenneth A. Lockridge, "Land, Population and the Evolution of New England Society, 1630−1790," *Past and Present*, no. 39 (April 1968): 62−80. Philip Greven says that after 1750 land prices fell to 17th-century levels (*Four Generations*, p. 226).

10. Town Book 289, pp. 217, 222; James Henretta, "Families and Farms: *Mentalité* in Pre-Industrial America," *WMQ*, 3rd ser. 35(1978): 25.

11. Hallett occupations are in the Q. C. Conveyances, Liber E (Reel QCV3), pp. 106−107; Town Book 289, p. 77; P.R.O., A.O. 12, vol. 23, p. 392.

12. Town Book 289, pp. 3, 1, 7; Town Book 288, p. 555. Occupations of other townsmen are in Town Book 288, pp. 305, 231, 301, 444, 299; Memoria, Riker Collection, Box 18, vol. 9, p. 242.

13. Ginsburg, "Ipswich, Massachusetts," pp. 41, 43; Greven, *Four Generations*, p. 154; Daniels, "Economic Development in Colonial and Revolutionary Connecticut," p. 439; Ryan, "Six Towns," pp. 32, 34; Ronald William Howard, "Education and Ethnicity in Colonial New York, 1664−

1763: A Study in the Transmission of Culture in Early America," Ph.D. diss. (University of Tennessee, 1978), pp. 345–347.

14. Quoted in Samuel McKee Jr., *Labor in Colonial New York 1664–1776*, Studies in History, Economics, and Public Law, 410 (New York, 1935), p. 24.

15. *Town Minutes*, II, 157; Queens County Conveyances, Liber C (Reel QCV2), pp. 97, 99; Town Book 288, pp. 140, 262; Town Book 289, pp. 125, 232, 128; NYHS, *Collections* 30(1897): 186; James Riker Jr., *Annals of Newtown* (New York, 1852), p. 404; Hallett Family Folder 1, 1703–1783, Riker Collection, Box 21.

16. David Grayson Allen, "The Zuckerman Thesis and the Process of Legal Rationalization in Provincial Massachusetts," *WMQ.*, 3rd ser. 29(1972): 457; Henretta, "Families and Farms," p. 24; Bruce C. Daniels, *The Connecticut Town: Growth and Development, 1635–1790* (Middletown, Conn., 1979), p. 148; Robert E. Mutch, "Yeoman and Merchant in Pre-industrial America: Eighteenth-century Massachusetts as a Case Study," *Societas—A Review of Social History* 7(1977): 292.

17. The Delaplain papers contain a subscription for Queens Friend William Palmer which lists Quaker names. These names match those in the ledger (NYHS).

18. Hallett Family Folder 1, Riker Collection, Box 21

19. Presbyterian and Episcopal Churches Burroughs Family, Riker Collection, Box 21; New York County Surrogate Court Wills, no. 850; NYHS, *Collections* 30(1897): 215; New York County Will Liber 23 (Reel WL6, HDC), p. 586.

20. *Town Minutes*, II, 186, 205; *Town Minutes*, I, 122, Q. C. Conveyances, Liber B1 (Reel QCV1), p. 131.

21. It is always possible that other mortgages failed to survive. Town Book 287, p. 171.

22. *Colonial Laws*, III, 957. The mortgages are found in the City Registers Office of Queens County, Jamaica, Mortgages Reels QM1, QM2; Peyer, "Jamaica, Long Island," p. 294; Ginsburg, "Ipswich, Massachusetts," p. 46.

23. Riker Collection, Hallett Family Folder 1, Box 21; Burton Benedict, "Sociological Characteristics of Small Territories and Their Implications for Economic Development," in Michael Banton, ed., *Social Anthropology of Complex Societies* (New York, 1966), pp. 29–30.

24. Mortgage Liber B46–7, no. 234, Liber B68, no. 262, Liber B68, no. 263, Liber, B123, no. 339 (all in Reel QM2); *Colonial Laws*, IV, 530.

25. NYHS, *Collections* 31(1898): 116; Mortgage Liber B11, no. 323 (Reel QM2).

26. Mortgage Liber B147, no. 382, Liber B132, no. 357, Liber B117–8, no. 332, Liber B185–6, n.p., Liber D5, D6–7 (all in Reel QM2).

27. *Colonial Laws*, II, 1015; County Minute Book, 1737/1738.

28. County Minute Book, 1738.

29. The county clerk noted the popularity of the loan office, when, in 1770, as the judges and county supervisors met to choose loan officers, they were told the act was repealed. "Thus ended this meeting to the great disappointment of the raised expectation of many people" (County Minute Book, 1770).

30. Queens County Loan Office, Liber D, Long Island Division, QBPL.

31. Peyer, "Jamaica, Long Island," p. 328.

32. P.R.O., A.O. 12, vol. 23, pp. 396–397; NYHS, *Collections* 35(1902): 95–96, 43; 28(1895): 328; 29(1896): 44, 80; 31(1898): 242; New York County Surrogate Court Wills, 866, 863.

33. Peyer, "Jamaica, Long Island," pp. 199–200; Edward M. Cook Jr., "Social Behavior and Changing Values in Dedham, Massachusetts, 1700–1775," *WMQ*, 3rd ser. 27(1970): 572.

34. New York Surrogate Court Wills, 863; NYHS, *Collections* 27(1894): 179; 28(1895): 190–191; Douglas Lamar Jones, "Geographic Mobility and Society in Eighteenth-Century Essex County, Massachusetts," Ph.D. diss. (Brandeis University, 1975), p. 205.

35. Queens County, New York, Return of the Tax List of the Township of Newtown (NYHS).

36. Genealogical information is from Riker, *Annals*, supplemented by wills and land transactions. I have not counted daughters.

37. John J. Waters, "Family, Inheritance, and Migration in Colonial New England" (Paper delivered at the Annual Convention of the American Historical Association, New York, December 1979), pp. 23, 25; Daniel Scott Smith, "A Perspective on Demographic Methods and Effects in Social History," The Newberry Papers in Family and Community History, Paper 77–4K (1977), p. 22.

38. Tracy, *Jonathan Edwards*, p. 103; Greven, *Four Generations*, p. 228.

39. There are 120 wills, 109 for men and 11 for women. Two additional women's wills never went through probate (New York County Will Liber 14 [Reel WL3, HDC], pp. 318–319, Will Liber 26, 89–90, Will Liber 25 [Reel WL7], pp. 108–109). Anna probably had received part of her share already. New Jersey towns underwent a similar increase in the sales of estates (Ryan, "Six Towns," p. 85).

40. NYHS, *Collections* 26(1893): 301; 27(1894): 56; Town Book 288, p. 309.

41. NYHS, *Collections* 31(1898): 224; 28(1895): 436, 427–428, 459; 27(1894), 36; 35(1902): 176; Town Book 287, p. 277.

42. *DHNY*, III, 517; Evarts B. Greene and Virginia D. Harrington,

American Population before the Federal Census of 1790 (Gloucester, Mass., 1966), pp. 96–102.

43. New York County Surrogate Court Wills, 866; Will Liber 11 (Reel WL2), pp. 157–158.

44. "Records of the Presbyterian Church of Newtown [now Elmhurst] Queens County Long Island, New York," New York Genealogical and Biographical Society, *Collections* 8(1928): 6, 31; Howard, "Education and Ethnicity," p. 428; NYHS, *Collections* 27(1894): 175; 28(1895): 436; 30(1897): 1.

45. New York Surrogate Court Wills, 866; William Parcell's inventory is in Inventories of Estates, New York City and Vicinity 1717–1844 (Reel 1), NYHS; Howard, "Education and Ethnicity," pp. 327, 342.

46. The inventories of Joseph Hallett and William Lawrence are in Inventories of Estates, New York City and Vicinity (Reel 1). Content Titus' estate is in Reel 2; NYHS, *Collections* 35(1902): 155.

47. Inventory of Estates, New York and Vicinity (Reel 1); Inventories of Albany, II, 125.

CHAPTER IX

1. New York Surrogate Court Wills, 669 (HDC); NYHS, *Collections* 35(1902): 133–134, 156–158; 29(1896): 135–136; 30(1897): 186; 31(1898): 116.

2. NYHS, *Collections* 27(1894): 174, 414; 28(1895): 61; 31(1898): 176–177.

3. James T. Lemon and Gary B. Nash, "The Distribution of Wealth in Eighteenth-Century America: A Century of Change in Chester County, Pennsylvania, 1693–1802," *Journal of Social History* 2(1968): 1–24; Edward M. Cook Jr., *The Fathers of the Towns: Leadership and Community Structure in Eighteenth-Century New England* (Baltimore, 1976), p. 71; Bruce C. Daniels, "Long Range Trends of Wealth Distribution in Eighteenth Century New England," *Explorations in Economic History* 11(1973–74): 123–135.

4. *Journal of the Votes and Proceedings of the General Assembly of the Colony of New York* (1691–1765), 2 vols. (New York, 1764, 1766), II, 764, 765, 769; County Minute Book.

5. Gary Nash, *The Urban Crucible: Social Change, Political Consciousness, and the American Revolution* (Cambridge, Mass., 1979), p. 117; "Urban Wealth and Poverty in Pre-Revolutionary America," *Journal of Interdisciplinary History* 6(1976): 562, 533; Douglas Lamar Jones, "Geographic Mobility and Society in Eighteenth-Century Essex County, Massachusetts," Ph.D. diss. (Brandeis University, 1975), p. 58.

6. Douglas Lamar Jones, "The Strolling Poor: Transiency in Eigh-

teenth-Century Massachusetts," *Journal of Social History* 8(1975): 46–48; Hallett Family Folder 1, 1703–1783, Riker Collection, Box 21. The sons mentioned were probably Joseph's by his first marriage and so would be Mary's stepsons.

7. Will Liber 16 (Reel WL4, HDC), pp. 331–332; Will Liber 26 (Reel WL7, HDC), pp. 437–439.

8. NYHS, *Collections* 27(1894): 179; 31(1898): 257–259, 266; Will Liber 16 (Reel WL4), pp. 411–412.

9. Minutes of the Court of General Sessions of the Peace and also of Common Pleas, 1722, Queens County, Manuscripts Records Room, Queens County Court House, Jamaica, N.Y., May 15, 1739; Ronald Kingman Snell, "The County Magistracy in Eighteenth-Century Massachusetts: 1692–1750," Ph.D diss. (Princeton University, 1971), pp. 201–202.

10. Fourth Book Monthly Meeting 6 mo 1756 to 1 mo 1771 (no. 239, HRR). The Tileys did not live in Newtown.

11. Presbyterian and Episcopal Churches, Burroughs Family, Riker Collection, Box 21; *Cal. Hist. Mss.*, II, 494; Minutes of the Court of General Sessions; Town Book 289, pp. 269, 279; Hendrick Hartog, "The Public Law of a County Court: Judicial Government in Eighteenth-Century Massachusetts," *American Journal of Legal History* 20(1976): 294, 298.

12. NYHS, *Collections* 27(1894): 48–49; 28(1895): 302–303, 365–366; 29(1896): 197; 31(1898): 242. Corrections to Lawrence's will are in Will Liber 11 (Reel WL2, HDC), pp. 219–220, and to Langdon's are in Will Liber 20 (Reel WL5, HDC), pp. 381–382.

13. Woodward Family, 1750–1784, Riker Collection, Box 21; James Riker Jr., *Annals of Newtown* (New York, 1852), pp. 158–159; Town Book 288, p. 200; Town Book 289, pp. 68, 245; Memoria, Riker Collection, Box 18, vol. 9, p. 309; NYHS, *Collections* 28(1895): 459, 389.

14. Bruce C. Daniels, *The Connecticut Town: Growth and Development, 1635–1790* (Middletown, Conn., 1979), pp. 108–109; Robert Francis Seybolt, *Apprenticeship and Apprenticeship Education in Colonial New England and New York*, Teachers College Contributions to Education, no. 85 (New York, 1917), p. 47; Snell, "County Magistracy," 190.

15. *New York Mercury*, April 26, 1762. These men also offered to board students.

16. *New York Weekly Mercury*, April 15, 1765.

17. Ronald William Howard, "Education and Ethnicity in Colonial New York, 1664–1763: A Study in the Transmission of Culture in Early America," Ph.D. diss. (University of Tennessee, 1978), p. 358; Daniels, *Connecticut Town*, p. 150.

18. NYHS, *Collections* 31(1898): 240; Q. C. Conveyances, Liber C (Reel QCV2), p. 352, Liber D (Reel QCV3), p. 390.

19. "Records of the Chancery Court Province and State of New York.

Guardianships, 1691–1815," abstracted by Kenneth Scott (New York, 1971), p. 11; County Minute Book, 1760. The committee of inquiry which looked into John Renne's sanity included his relatives James and William Hazard and Samuel Renne. The violently insane might have been locked up in the Queens County jail, even though the jail was usually in notoriously bad repair. For a general discussion of the disabled see David J. Rothman, *The Discovery of the Asylum: Social Order and Disorder in the New Republic* (Boston, 1971), chaps. 1–2.

20. Riker, *Annals*, p. 160; Woodward Family, Riker Collection, Box 21.

21. *Cal. Hist. Mss*, II, 583. For information on epidemics in New York see John Duffy, *A History of Public Health in New York City 1625–1866* (New York, 1968). For more on the dangers of inoculation see Dennis Don Melchert, "Experimenting on the Neighbors: Inoculation of Smallpox in Boston in the Context of Eighteenth Century Medicine," Ph.D. diss. (University of Iowa, 1973).

22. Henry Onderdonk Jr., "An Historical Sketch of Ancient Agriculture, Currency, Stock-Breeding and Manufactures in Hempstead, 1867," Mss. File 112 (LIHS), p. 23; Woodward Family, Riker Collection, Box 21.

23. The age of four Halletts born between 1700 and 1729 has been calculated by using their marriage dates and assuming that they married at age twenty-five. There is almost no information on Hallett women.

24. Philip J. Greven Jr., *Four Generations: Population, Land, and Family in Colonial Andover, Massachusetts* (Ithaca, N.Y., 1970), p. 192; Rose Lockwood, "Birth, Illness, and Death in 18th-Century New England," *Journal of Social History* 12(Fall, 1978): 111–128; Daniel Scott Smith, "The Demographic History of Colonial New England," *Journal of Economic History* 32(1972): 180.

25. No new clerk or other outside agent seems responsible for the sudden inflation of recorded deaths in the Presbyterian record. They are, therefore, treated as equally valid as the earlier deaths. These mortality rates are based upon a number of other assumptions (see following table). The raw number of deaths which included non-Presbyterians were found in the Presbyterian church records and are called AD (Actual Deaths). Unfortunately, church records underrecorded deaths. Kenneth Lockridge calculated that Dedham recorded deaths were 43 percent of real deaths if migration were zero. In Newtown emigration was not zero, but, judging from the twenty-four most persistent families, at least 20 percent over the course of the eighteenth century. Therefore, 20 percent of Lockridge's remaining 57 percent were not deaths but emigration, and underrecorded deaths would be 54 percent of that total. Computed deaths are calculated according to the formula $CD = AD \div .54$ where AD is the average number of Actual Deaths. The population of Newtown (P) was calculated according to the formulas given

(chap. 7, n. 9) for the midyear of the ten-year period except for 1771, when census material is available. These population figures are probably a little high for the 1752 and 1762 decades because they assume an even growth rate, which would not be the case due to the higher death rates. Assuming a linear rate of growth depresses the death rates, they are probably a bit higher. The errors introduced by this assumption are to a large degree offset by the small size of the population. The death rates are calculated on the formula CD/P x k (k = 1000).

YEARS	AD	CD	P	MORTALITY RATE
1728–1737	99/10			
	eq 9.9	18.3	922 (1732)	19.8
1738–1747	74/10= 7.4	13.7	964 (1742)	14.2
1748–1757	188/10=18.8	34.8	1009 (1752)	34.4
1758–1757	224/10=22.4	41.5	1055 (1762)	39.3
1768–1773	100/6 =16.7	30.9	1096 (1771)	28.2

Modern rates are much lower. In 1970 the death rate for the United States was 9.5 per thousand. This figure is lower than even the best year in Newtown (U.S. Bureau of the Census, *Historical Statistics of the United States* I, 58).

James Riker made his copy of the original Presbyterian record which has since disappeared. In it he listed cause of death. His copy has been used as the more authoritative source (Riker Collection, Box 16). The Presbyterian church supposedly recorded all deaths, not just Presbyterian deaths. Lockridge's calculations are found in "The Population of Dedham, Massachusetts, 1636–1736," *Economic History Review*, 2nd ser. 19(1966): 318–344.

26. "Transcript of the Presbyterian Record," Riker Collection, Box 16, p. 104; Memoria, Riker Collection, Box 17, vol. 8, p. 181. The Presbyterian records list 684 deaths, of which 173 listed some cause. Three deaths were attributed to childbirth, and by now most colonialists agree that few women died in childbirth (see Daniel Scott Smith, "A Perspective on Demographic Methods and Effects in Social History," The Newberry Papers in Family and Community History, Paper 77–4K [1977], p. 24 and n. 45). All percentages are rounded to the nearest whole percent.

27. Queens County census materials are in Evarts B. Greene and Virginia D. Harrington, *American Population before the Federal Census of 1790* (Gloucester, Mass., 1966), pp. 95–102. These two censuses sometimes use age 10. Greven, *Four Generations*, p. 188; Harry S. Stout, "Remigration and Revival: Two Case Studies in the Social and Intellectual History of New England, 1636–1745," Ph.D. diss. (Kent State University, 1974), p. 357.

28. Long Island Hallett Family Folder II, 1729–1791, Riker Collection, Box 21; Information on funeral practices is from a later period (Ac-

count Book of Aaron Van Nostrand [chair-maker, 1767] Sexton for grave digging, bellringing, pall, and attendings at the Grace Episcopal Church of Jamaica, Long Island New York 1773-1820, copied by Josephine C. Frost, Long Island Division, QBPL).

29. There are 34 families in the 1670-1699 sample, 41 in the 1700-1729 sample, and 61 in the 1730-1759 sample. The pattern of smaller familes is widespread, occurring also in Andover and among the Quakers (Greven, *Four Generations*, p. 203; Robert V. Wells, "Family Size and Fertility Control in Eighteenth-Century America: A Study of Quaker Families" *Population Studies* 25 [1971]: 75).

30. Population growth is most easily compared using a rate of growth rather than raw figures. Between 1656 and 1698 the white population grew at the rate of 2.2 percent per year. Between 1698 and 1711 the rate declined, and if the censuses are accurate, Newtown actually lost people. After 1711 the population rose at the lower rate of .45 percent per year. This rate increased after 1771 to .98 percent per year, but it never recovered its seventeeth-century momentum.

Newtown's black population grew much faster than the town's white population. Between 1698 and 1711 the slave community grew at the amazing rate of 4.5 percent per year. At this rate it almost doubled in just thirteen years. After 1711 the growth rate declined, but never to the low rate of the white population. Between 1711 and 1790 the black slave's rate of increase was 1.5 percent per year.

The percentage of children in the population was taken from Greene and Harrington's census figures *(American Population before the Federal Census,* pp. 95-102); In 1703 children comprised 46 percent of the black population, in 1746 those under age sixteen were 46 percent, and in 1756 50 percent. There is some evidence that blacks were more resistant to malaria and yellow fever than were whites (see Darrett B. Rutman and Anita H. Rutman, "Of Agues and Fevers: Malaria in the Early Chesapeake," *WMQ*, 3rd ser. 33[1976]: 35, and Kenneth F. Kiple and Virginia H. Kiple, "Black Yellow Fever Immunities, Innate and Acquired, As Revealed in the American South," *Social Science History* 1[1977]: 419-436).

31. Town Book, 289, pp. 216, 256. The 1784 tax list is in the New York Historical Society.

32. NYHS, *Collections* 28(1895): 61, 436.

33. Memoria, Riker Collection, Box 16, vol. 5, p. 52; The 1771 census based on heads of households contains nineteen names which might be new. Seven of these are in the land records; at last four married into existing families. Eight of these names still exist in Newtown in 1790.

34. "Transcript of the Presbyterian Record," Riker Collection, Box 16, p. 10.

35. Daniels, *Connecticut Town*, pp. 96–97, 105; Edward M. Cook Jr., "Social Behavior and Changing Values in Dedham, Massachusetts, 1700–1775," *WMQ*, 3rd ser. 27(1970): 559–560, 563.

36. Riker, *Annals*, p. 229. According to Riker, Horton was accused of being too "dull."

37. Ibid., p. 230. Riker quotes from the ballot but omits his sources.

38. "Transcript of the Presbyterian Record," Riker Collection, Box 16, pp. 36, 48.

39. Ibid., p. 7.

40. Ibid., p. 13.

41. Page Smith, *As a City Upon a Hill: The Town in American History* (New York, 1966), p. 132.

42. Patricia J. Tracy, *Jonathan Edwards, Pastor: Religion and Society in Eighteenth-Century Northampton* (New York, 1979), pp. 56–57.

43. "Transcript of the Presbyterian Record," Riker Collection, Box 16, p. 12.

44. "Minutes of the Board of Elders of the Reformed Dutch Church," ed. Richard G. Debevoise, 1936, Long Island Collection, Long Island Division, QBPL, p. 16; Bruce E. Steiner, "Anglican Office-holding in Pre-Revolutionary Connecticut: The Parameters of New England Community," *WMQ*, 3rd ser. 31(1974): 399–400.

45. Riker, *Annals*, p. 237; Minutes of the Board of Elders of the Reformed Dutch Church, pp. 16, 17, 18.

46. Riker, *Annals*, p. 238.

47. "A Curious Call from the Elders of New-Town Jamaica Hempstead and Oyster Bay to the Revd. Hendricus Goetens—1740," Queens County New York (NYHS). These contending groups were called the "coetus" and the "conferentie" parties.

48. "Newtown in Queens County on Long or Nassau Island the 27th September 1748," Miscellaneous Records and Clippings III (First Reformed Church of Jamaica, Jamaica, N.Y.). For more on the disorder in the Hackensack Valley see Adrian C. Leiby, *The Revolutionary War in the Hackensack Valley* (New Brunswick, N.J., 1962).

49. Baptismal Record of the Reformed Dutch Church at Newtown, Long Island New York, 1736–1846, copied by Josephine C. Frost (typewritten, QBPL), p. 3; Riker, *Annals*, pp. 240–241.

50. Riker, *Annals*, pp. 240–241.

51. Peter Kalm, *Travels Into North America*, tr. John Reinhold Foster (Barre, Mass., 1972), p. 140; Howard, "Education and Ethnicity," p. 461; William Heard Kilpatrick, *The Dutch Schools of New Netherland and Colonial New York*, U.S. Bureau of Education Bulletin, no. 12 (Washington, D.C., 1912), p. 183.

52. Howard, "Education and Ethnicity," pp. 438, 495; Kalm, *Travels*, p. 140.

53. Ethnicity was determined by last name. A marriage was counted if there was a record of it having taken place in these years, or if through birth records it was obvious that the marriage took place between 1724 and 1775.

54. Baptismal Record of the Reformed Dutch Church at Newtown, Long Island, N.Y., 1736–1846, typewritten (QBPL).

55. Frederick C. Gamst, *Peasants in Complex Society* (New York, 1974), p. 60; Baptismal Record of the Reformed Dutch Church, pp. 2, 6–7.

56. Thomas Poyer to the SPG, *Classified Digest of the Records of the Society for the Propagation of the Gospel in Foreign Parts, 1701–1892*, comp. Charles Frederick Pascoe (London, 1893), p. 61.

57. See Riker, *Annals*, pp. 245–252, for information on the Protestant Episcopal church.

58. Town Book 288, pp. 332–334.

59. The letter requesting a minister is in Newtown, Queens County, N.Y. (NYHS).

60. E. Edwards Beardsley, *Life and Correspondence of the Right Reverend Samuel Seabury, D.D.* (Boston, 1882), pp. 10, 16.

61. Ibid., p. 9.

62. "Fourth Book Monthly Meeting 6 mo 1756 to 1 mo 1771" (no. 239, HRR).

63. "The Minutes of Flushing Monthly Meeting (later called New York Monthly Meeting)," vols. 4, 5, nos. 1004, 1005 (HRR), p. 14.

64. "Marriage Intentions and Dealings Relating to Marriage, from the Men's and Women's Minutes of Flushing (now New York) Monthly Meeting 1676 to 1800," compiled by John Cox Jr., 1903–1913 (HRR); "Flushing Monthly Meeting Marriages 1663–1766, Births 1640–179. [sic], Deaths 1669–1796" (no. 213, HRR).

65. *DHNY*, III, 623–624.

66. "Minutes of Flushing Monthly Meeting," vols. 4, 5, pp. 22, 34; Daniel Scott Smith and Michael S. Hindus, "Premarital Pregnancy in America: 1640–1971: An Overview," *Journal of Interdisciplinary History* 5(1975): 537–570.

67. Minutes of the Court of General Sessions.

68. Douglas Greenberg, "The Effectiveness of Law Enforcement in Eighteenth-Century New York," *American Journal of Legal History* 19(1975): 197, 199, 195; Hartog, "Public Law of a County Court," pp. 318, 321.

69. Henry Banford Parkes, "Morals and Law Enforcement in Colonial New England," *New England Quarterly* 5(1932): 442; Hartog, "Public Law of a County Court," pp. 300, 301, 305.

INDEX

Burd, Thomas, 154
Burga, Burgoon. *See* Burgaw, Burgoon
Burga, Isaac. *See* Burgaw, Isaac
Burgaw, Burgoon, 229
Burgaw, Hillietie, 163
Burgaw, Isaac (d. 1757), 229
Burgaw, Isaac (d. 1760), 163, 254
Burroughs, Elizabeth, 88
Burroughs, Jeremiah, 157, 163, 166
Burroughs, John (d.·?), 241
Burroughs, John (d. 1678), 70, 90, 93, 118–119
Burroughs, John (d. 1699), 90, 155
Burroughs, John (d. 1700s), 163
Burroughs, John (d. 1750), 218, 224
Burroughs, John (d. 1755), 224
Burroughs, Joseph (?), 243
Burroughs, Joseph (d. 1738?), 162
Burroughs, Joseph (son of Jeremiah), 163
Burroughs, Margaret, 236
Bushman, Richard, 67, 202
Bushwick, 4, 21, 65, 127, 128, 129, 153, 182

Caesar (Negro), 232
Cambridge Association, 170
Carr, Lois Green, 160
Cary, Joseph, 215
Case, Mary Meacock, 114, 174
Case, Thomas, 114–115, 117
Case, William, 224
Case, William Jr., 115, 158

Census (1698), 167
Charitable bequests, 236
Charles (Negro), 156
Charter: Dutch, 21, 22; English, 22
Chesapeake, 13, 31
Chester County, Pennsylvania, 96
Children, responsibility for, 40–41, 240
Chock, Peter, 161
Church of England, 125–127, 144, 168, 172–174, 257, 259–261, 263, 279; establishment of, 125–127, 134, 140; size of, 174
Clark, Peter, 31
Classis of Amsterdam, 112, 256–257, 279
Clerk, James, 243
Climate, 6, 8
Clock, Elizabeth, 230, 249
Clock, Martin, 230, 249
Cloth, 93
Cocherin, John, 24, 41
Cochran, John, 100, 108
Coe, Abigail, 238
Coe, Benjamin, 281n
Coe, Capt. John, 20, 29, 37, 49, 54, 70
Coe, John (d. 1748), 224, 238
Coe, John (Judge), 224, 239
Coe, Jonathan, 240
Coe, Robert (d. 1672), 21, 32, 62, 281n
Coe, Robert (d. 1777), 264
Coe, Samuel, 250, 254
Colden, Cadwallader, 199
Colgan, Rev. Thomas, 259

Domestic Price Index, 187
Dominion of New England, 56, 60
Dongan, Gov. Thomas, 79
Dongan patent of 1686, 66, 130
Dorcas (Negro), 232
Dorchester, 60
"Double safety valve," 224
Doughty, Francis, 70
Doughty, Rev. Francis, 3, 13, 20, 33, 44, 112, 119
Dover, New Hampshire, 225
Doxey, Ralph, 218
Doxey, William, 108
Drisius, Dominie, 45
"Dual localism," 25, 53, 138
Duke's Laws, 25, 53–54, 101, 103
Dutch, hostility toward, 11, 19
Dutch land grants, 13
Dutch Reformed Church, 44–45, 101, 112–113, 172, 254, 263, 270–271; Americanization of, 257; elders of, 255
Dutch West India Company, 11, 12
Duxbury, 225
Dwight, Dr. Timothy, 6

Earhart, John, 163
Earhart, John Coonroes, 163
Earle, Carville, 36
Eastchester, 112
Easthampton, 69
Eaton, Gov., 19
Economy: diversification of, 158, 269; local, xiv, 38–39, 92, 94–95, 154–155, 156–157, 218, 222, 269; mechan-

ics of, 39, 155; provincial, xiv, 39–40, 92, 94, 154–155, 162, 218, 269, 291n; stratification of, 38, 96, 228, 236–237, 273, 279, 300n; structure of, xiv, 225
Ecumenicism, 171, 254–255, 260; New England, 255
Eddes, Nicholas, 97, 99
Edsall, Philip (justice), 240, 243
Edsall, Samuel, 75, 81, 157, 194
Education, 162–163, 240–242, 257, 271; New England, 241
Edwards, Jonathan, 253, 254
Edwards, Rev. Timothy, 253–254
Elderly, responsibility for, 100–102
Ellen Wall v. *John Lorison*, 47
Elmhurst, 273
Emigration, 224, 228; of sons, 225–227
English conquest, 50, 53
English Kills, 4
Entail, 149
Essex County, 237
Etben, Seres, 190
Etherington, Thomas, 218
Ethnic: assimilation, 145; background, xv, 111, 219, 279n; identity, 57, 182–183, 198, 200, 269, 271; pluralism, 58, 111, 143–144, 163, 196; relations, 82–83, 190–191

Faber, Eli, 121
Fairs, 95, 161

Hallett, Mary Lawrence Green-oak, 238, 247
Hallett, Mary Way, 246
Hallett, Moses, 156, 157, 230, 233
Hallett, Phoebe, 225
Hallett, Richard Jr., 245, 246
Hallett, Richard (cordwainer), 203, 215, 225
Hallett, Richard (d. 1769), 155, 163, 174, 175, 217, 239, 246
Hallett, Robert, 208, 210, 238
Hallett, Samuel Jr. (?), 252
Hallett, Samuel Jr. (boatman), 215
Hallett, Samuel (d. 1724), 87, 91, 148
Hallett, Maj. Samuel (d. 1756), 148, 163, 167, 264
Hallett, Capt. Samuel (d. 1798), 204–205, 221, 225, 246, 247
Hallett, Samuel (son of Maj. Samuel), 264
Hallett, Stephen, 225
Hallett, Susannah, 108
Hallett, Lt. Thomas, 218, 225, 238
Hallett, Thomas (carpenter), 215
Hallett, Thomas (son of Capt. Samuel), 204
Hallett, William (cordwainer), 215
Hallett, William (d. 1706), 6, 10, 13, 20, 33, 40, 45, 85, 87, 91, 108, 147, 154, 160, 218
Hallett, William Jr. (d. 1708), 127, 148, 160, 161, 176, 246;

family of, 156; inventory of, 156–157; murder of, 156, 176
Hallett, Capt. William (d. 1729), 87, 121, 147, 156, 208, 210, 223, 246
Hallett, William (tailor), 215
Hallett, William Jr. (1784), 225
Hallett, William Moses, 243, 245, 246
Hallett, William Sr.(1784), 225
Hallett family, 147–149, 207–211; debts of, 220; emigration of sons, 225; genealogy of, 149, 209; land holdings of, 147–149, 207–211; mortality of, 245; occupations of, 215; wealth of, 225
Halletts Cove, 148
Hampshire Association, 170
Hampshire County (Massachusetts), 159, 192, 238
Harck, William, 46
Hardy, Gov. Thomas, 259
Hare, Ludlum, 208
Hare, Patrick, 104
Harper, James, 241
Harry (Negro), 156
Hartford, 34
Hartog, Hendrik, 192
Hastings (later Newtown), 29
Hazard, Abigail, 220
Hazard, Gershom, 78
Hazard, James (justice), 167, 177, 254
Hazard, Jonathan, 168
Hazard, Morris, 221
Hazard, Nathaniel, 216, 218
Hazard, Capt. Thomas, 254

Kalm, Peter, 8, 257
Ketcham, Lt. John, 70, 78, 93
Kidd, Capt. William, 161
Kieft, Gov. William, 3, 15
Kieft's War, 14–15
King Charles II, 55
King George III, 200; petition
  to, 189–190
King George's War, 183–186
King James II, 55, 56
Kings College, 260
Kings County, 13, 110, 161,
  224, 254
King William and Queen Mary,
  56
King William's War, 132
Kinship: advantages of, 147–
  148, 151–152, 208, 211–
  213, 214; limits of, 219
Kip, Jesse, 158
Kirsted, Hare, 218
Klein, Milton, xi
Konig, David, 21, 36

Labor (free), 91, 154, 155, 216,
  233
Labor (slave). See Slaves
LaGuardia Airport, 274
Land: attitudes toward, 38; division of, 63–64; exchanged
  for services, 35, 62; grants of,
  Newtown, 35; holding patterns of, 34–36, 131, 153,
  212–213; house lots, 150,
  212, 298n; Jamaica, 210–211;
  meadow, 60, 150, 212; New
  England, 34–36, 62, 63,
  213–214, 229; New Jersey,
  214; price of, 151–152; reg-

ulation of, 60; scarcities of,
  xiv, 130, 188, 208–213, 214–
  216, 229–230, 271; specula-
  tion in, 65, 153, 223–224;
  timber, 60–61, 213; transactions (1665–1691), 85–88,
  151, 306–307n; transactions
  (1692–1723), 136–137, 149–
  150; transactions (1724–
  1775), 210–211; upland, 150,
  212
Landlessness, 90–91, 153, 210–
  211
Langdon, Richard, 240
Lawrence, Daniel, 139, 152,
  155
Lawrence, Elizabeth Hallett,
  208
Lawrence, John (d. 1729), 73,
  152
Lawrence, John (d. 1765), 241;
  will of, 230
Lawrence, Jonathan, 152
Lawrence, Joseph, 197
Lawrence, Mary, 152, 164–165
Lawrence, Nathaniel, 216
Lawrence, Thomas, 24, 49, 70,
  119, 140
Lawrence, Maj. Thomas, 24,
  70, 85, 119, 129, 140, 164
Lawrence, William (Council-
  man), 164
Lawrence, William (d. 1700s),
  208
Lawrence, William (d. 1731),
  233, 240
Lawrence, William (patentee),
  32, 45–46
Lechford, Thomas, 13

Leisler, Jacob, 75, 81
Leisler's Rebellion, 56, 80–83
Lemon, James T., 236
Lent, Abraham, 254
Leverich, Daniel, 155
Leverich, Eleazer, 90, 106, 225
Leverich, Martha, 212
Leverich, Rebecca Wright, 106
Leverich, Widow, 141
Leverich, Rev. William, 44,
    112, 208, 212, 225
Leverich family, 225–228
Leverich family genealogy, 226
Lexington, 204
Linter, Mary, 164
Literacy, 139
Litigiousness, 116, 119;
    Plymouth, 79, 120; Windsor,
    Connecticut, 110
Livestock, 37, 156, 233; prices
    of, 133–134
Lockridge, Kenneth A., xi, 36
Lodt, Hendrick, 224
Long Island, 13
Loockermans, Govert, 34
Lorison, James, 37, 62
Lorison, John, 47–49, 78, 98,
    109
Lorison, Mary, 48, 119
Loudoun, Lord, 183
Lovelace, Gov. Francis, 59, 74,
    77, 82
Lutherans, 101
Luxuries, 99, 157, 160, 230,
    235–236, 279
Luyster, Cornelius, 168
Lyme, 65
Lynch, Gabriel, 120–121
Lynch, Mary, 108

McAnear, Beverly, 133
McCarrell, James, 242
McCarty, Hugh, 155
McDonnaugh John, 242
MacKemie, Francis, 169
MacNish, Rev. George, 251
Magistrates, 23, 24, 67
Main, Gloria L., 38
Main, Jackson Turner, 37
Manhattan Island, 13
Marriage, 103–105; age at, 283n;
    function of, 106–107; pat-
    terns of, 167, 246–247, 271;
    problems with, 106–108; ra-
    cial endogamy, 104; religious
    endogamy, 104–105, 172,
    248, 258, 262, 292n
Martha's Vineyard, 224
Martin, Mary, 239
Maspeth (later Newtown), 15, 20
Mayflower Compact, 17
Medfield, 60
Medicine, 243–244
Megapolensus, Dominie, 45
Mental illness, 243, 312n
Mercenaries, 279n
Merchants, 216–218
Middleburgh (later Newtown),
    20–28
Milbourne, Jacob, 75, 81
Miller, John, 8
Miller, Perry, 42, 170
Mills, William, 220
Minisink, 224
Ministers, 112, 169; authority
    of, 42–43; property of, 44;
    salary of, 171
Ministry Act of 1693, 126, 140,
    172; opposition to, 126–127

Semisse, Elizabeth, 240
Sension, Nicholas, 121
Settlement patterns, 36; Jamaica, 66; New England, 66; Newtown, 4, 65–66
Settlers, origins of, 31–33
Seven Years' War, 182, 186–187, 198, 236
Severence, Widow, 250
Seybolt, Robert, 164
Sharp, Charles, 154
Shopkeepers, 216
Shotwell family, 246
Skillman, Thomas, 163
Slander, 48, 116, 119, 177
Slavery, 73, 91–92
Slaves, xiv–xv, 91, 109, 136, 144, 155–156, 176, 195, 230–232, 239, 248; attitudes toward, 177; Indian, 91, 92, 99, 156, 176, 232; lives of, 232–233; number of, 231; punishment of, 177; value of, 92, 156
Sloan, Hannah, 220
Sloughter, Gov. Henry, 56
Smallpox, 244, 245
Smit, Anneken, 34
Smit, Dirk, 34
Smith, Daniel Scott, 229, 263
Smith, Edward, 241
Smith, Capt. John, 4
Smith, John (justice), 135
Smith, John (1600s), 93, 141, 228, 252
Smith, John (1700s), 141, 252
Smith, Page, 253
Smith, William, 114
Smits, Claes, 15

Snell, Ronald, 159
Social structure, 41–42, 48–50, 63, 99, 119, 136–137, 138, 160, 190, 218, 222, 284n
Societies, small-scale, 48, 119, 122, 127, 138, 182, 210, 217
Society for the Propagation of the Gospel (SPG), 126, 173, 259–260, 295n
Soil types, 277n
Sons of Liberty, 305n
South Hills, 10
Spalletta, Matteo, 107
Springsteen, Casparus, 213
Springsteen, Casper, 171
Springsteen, David, 213
Springsteen, Jacob, 241
Spufford, Margaret, 88
Stadum, Elizabeth, 92, 98, 99
Stamford, 33
Stamp Act Congress, 199
Staten Island, 13, 20
Steiner, Bruce F., 197
Stevenson, Edward, 61, 94, 109
Stevenson, John, 152
Stevenson, Thomas Jr., 176
Stevenson, Thomas (d. 1668?), 28
Stevenson, Thomas (d. 1725), 55, 61, 94, 176, 218, 223
Stevenson, Thomas (1600s), 64
Stoddard, Solomon, 170–171, 254
Stone, Lawrence, 103
Stout, Harry S., 159, 245
Strangers, attitudes toward, 65
Strickland, Hannah, 177
Strickland, Jonathan, 92, 97, 99, 164